Praise For *Shattered Stars, Healing Hearts*

"I just finished reading "Shattered Stars, Healing Hearts" and I am writing these words with tears in my eyes. I felt like I was inside Irene Stern Frielich's story as each part of her father's journey was uncovered. Throughout, I felt Irene's father's presence, long after he had died, guiding her, encouraging her, and pushing her in her search, not only of the tragedies and horrors, but also of the incredible righteousness of those who helped. Irene's ability to imagine her father within the facts she was learning was poignant and powerful and her perseverance was breathtaking."

— Jane Taubenfeld Cohen, Jewish Day School
educator and child of a survivor

"A thoroughly readable, bitter-sweet exploration of one family's story of survival. Irene has successfully used her father's testimony, family treasures, and her own imagination to weave a compelling narrative highlighting emotional, personal, and physical connections to the not-too-distant past, while at the same time leaving the reader wondering whether enough lessons have been learned for the future."

— Jessica Feinstein, Managing Editor, *JewishGen Press*

"Irene Stern Frielich has taken us all on her journey to connect us to her personal pursuit of healing and our collective need for understanding, remembrance, and reconciliation. It is as important as ever for those who carry the generational trauma of Holocaust survivors to tell the stories so they may heal and we can protect ourselves from future atrocities. Thank you, Irene, for your courage."

— Mara Safer, Program Facilitator, Anti-Defamation League

"Irene is a remarkable, courageous woman with a story of reconciliation to tell. Her journey to retrace her father's steps and heal from the horrors he faced is a powerful one that gripped me every step of the way."
—Virginia Swain, Reconciliation Leader, Institute for Global Leadership

"Irene's beautifully written memoir will resonate with anyone who has grappled with the inherited trauma of a family's persecution."
—Donna Swarthout, Editor and Co-Author of *A Place They Called Home. Reclaiming Citizenship. Stories of a New Jewish Return to Germany*

"It is estimated that six million European Jews were killed during the Holocaust. The brutal killings started during Kristallnacht in Nov 1938 and continued with systematic mass murders in concentration camps finally ending in May 1945 with the allied defeat of the Nazis during World War II. This devastating loss represented two-thirds of the Jewish population in Europe at that time. However, it's important to note that there were an estimated three million survivors as well. Each survivor's harrowing story was different. Irene's compelling story of her father's survival and liberation captures the very personal trauma of one Jewish Holocaust survivor's unique challenges and hardships living through this most devastating period in Jewish history and the impact it had on his daughter."
—Irv Kempner, Chairman, New England Friends of the March of the Living

SHATTERED STARS

HEALING HEARTS

Unraveling My Father's Holocaust Survival Story

IRENE STERN FRIELICH

Shattered Stars, Healing Hearts: Unraveling My Father's Holocaust Survival Story
Published by Prince Dome Press, LLC Boston, MA

ISBN: 979-8-218-24944-1
BIOGRAPHY & AUTOBIOGRAPHY / Personal Memoirs
HISTORY / Modern / 20th Century / Holocaust

Publisher's Cataloging-in-Publication data

Names: Frielich, Irene Stern, author.
Title:Shattered stars, healing hearts : unraveling my father's Holocaust survival story / Irene Stern Frielich. Description: Boston, MA : Prince Dome Press, LLC, [2023]
Identifiers: ISBN: 979-8-218-24944-1. Subjects: LCSH: Stern, Walter. | Holocaust survivors--Biography. | Children of Holocaust survivors-- Massachusetts--Biography. | Holocaust, Jewish (1939-1945)--Personal narratives. | Escapes --Germany--Biography. | Europe--Description and travel. | LCGFT: Biographies. | BISAC: BIOGRAPHY & AUTOBIOGRAPHY / Personal Memoirs. | HISTORY / Modern / 20th Century / Holocaust.
Classification: LCC: D804.196.S74 F75 2023 | DDC: 940.53/18092--dc23

PRINCE
DOME
PRESS

BROOCH

Blue image on the book cover is a photo of the brooch Walter Stern painted while he was in hiding. On the dark blue brooch is a white Magen David, shield of David, inside of which is an orange-yellow rising sun, and above which is orange-red Hebrew lettering "Tikvat Yisrael," hope of Israel.

This book is dedicated to those who, throughout time, show courage in standing up against tyranny; to those who demonstrate compassion to care for people in the crosshairs of hatred and devastating public policy; and to those who pour out kindness that saves a life or simply brings a smile to a lost soul.

This book would not be possible without:

my Oma, Hilde Stern May, whose strength I knew

my grandfather, Moritz Stern, who always had a plan yet didn't survive to see the fruits of his planning

my father, Walter Stern, whose love and dedication to his family gave us the ability and strength to honor his memory

my sons, Josh and Jonah, who bring their own courage, compassion, and kindness into this world

"Conceal the exiles, reveal not the wanderer."
—Isaiah 16:3

CONTENTS

AUTHOR'S NOTE

THIS IS A WORK OF NONFICTION. The narrative in my timeline relies on my personal experiences and memories, and on research that I conducted between 2017 and 2023. At times, I've compacted multiple scenes into one to create a tighter narrative while staying true to my experience. In places, I've tried to recreate dialogue that I cannot recall accurately. I have added nothing to my own story that did not happen. I've changed names and identifying details of certain individuals, including in documents and direct quotes, to protect their privacy. Some of the translated segments have been edited for clarity, length, and literary cohesion.

As I share throughout the narrative, I felt driven to imagine my father's life as a way of filling in the missing pieces of my family's story and as an attempt to touch his life as closely as I can. Some of the information in these imagined scenes, told in the present tense, are drawn from my father's video recordings and documents, my memories of him, and my own extensive research.

Memories are not fixed. They are inexact and changeable. My aim in this memoir was to document, to the best of my ability, the facts and emotions of my own experiences and to convey the essence of the journey. The story is my personal "Truth."

My research continues. The information I share in this memoir, including in my father's timeline, is based on the research I have completed to date. Any missing or incorrect information is unintentional. Follow https://www.facebook.com/ShatteredStarsHealingHearts to join the ongoing journey as I uncover new information.

MY GREAT-GRANDPARENTS

SOLLY STERN
1872–1902

SELMA STERNBERG
1873–1945

EDUARD HERZFELD
1872–1938

MY GRANDPARENTS

MORITZ STERN
1891–1942

HILDE STERN (MY OMA)
1902–1987

KURT HERZFELD
1913–1942

MY GREAT
UNCLE

MY
FATHER

WALTER STERN
1926–1994

I invite you to follow along at **www.shatteredstars.org/book-notes**
for chapter-by-chapter images, notes, and source information
that add depth to the book.

PART I:
HOME

Geburtsstrasse #35, Bocholt, Germany

Walter Stern: Recollection of November 10, 1938

THE SOUND WAS SO SHRILL AND LOUD: *"Jude" and whatever they said there. It was, the hatred, you could hear the hatred and feel the hatred. It was a vibration in the air. There were numerous men in brown uniforms on the street, holding a steel I-beam.*

They just demolished [our store and house windows and doors] so you could walk all the way through. It was so bad that the glass particles were in the clothing that were hanging in the store way in the rear. Nothing of it was usable anymore. It was loaded with glass. And then we heard also gunshots in the street.

And now we knew they meant business, they really wanted to get rid of us.

"The November Pogrom struck like lightning, suddenly shattering everything it touched, shocking those who suffered it … no one expected the widespread violence … The public manifestations of Jewish life in Germany stood covered with broken glass."

—Marion A. Kaplan, *Between Dignity and Despair: Jewish Life in Nazi Germany*

CHAPTER 1
MAYBE ONE DAY

FOR YEARS, DECADES REALLY, whenever Holocaust stories and related discussions arose, whether in my life or in the media, memories of my father's secretive nature tugged at me, and I'd think, *Maybe one day.* Maybe one day when I had more time I would rewatch his testimony video, this time with the clarity and focus I would need in order to uncover who he really was, once. And to uncover who I am, though I wouldn't realize that for some time.

My father had made the testimony video in 1993, describing his childhood in Nazi Germany and his survival in Holland during the Holocaust. I would never learn where in the United States this testimony video was recorded. Within months, he passed away of a blood disease, an illness his cousin would blame on the Nazis. He was only sixty-seven years old. My mother had died ten years earlier. In my memory, a close friend of my father's had sent me the testimony video a few months after my father died, when it would no longer be possible to ask my parents any questions.

The first time I watched my father's testimony video, I'd had a hard time following it. The names of the people and the places my father mentioned were mysteries to me. The chronology was difficult to keep track of.

What I hadn't yet comprehended was that, to understand his story, I would need to inhabit it. Back then, I worked, and my precious days and evenings were overfilled with managing the busy schedules of my two school-aged sons, building and running my training consulting company, taking classes to further my own spirituality, playing flute in a local band, volunteering, and daring to have a social life. Overachievement was the expectation I'd always felt my parents demanded of me as a child. I'd grown up and complied. *Maybe one day I'll get back to the testimony video,* I thought, as I tucked it away.

In 2016, *one day* suddenly got closer. I sat on our comfortable red couch in the family room, joining my twenty-three-year-old younger son, Jonah, and his friends to play our game of bingo. The game had become a tradition to help us get through the many 2016 presidential debates we'd viewed together. It was a way to lighten up the long evenings as we awaited a mention of "fake news" or a nose scratch or other things to match what we wrote on our individual cards. It was Tuesday, November 8, and we settled in to watch the results come in from each state, waiting to hear the official pronouncement that Hillary Rodham Clinton would be our first woman president.

Soon it became clear that the country was going down a different path. I felt shock, anger, and betrayal, as well as fear for the unrest that might follow the election of *this* president. I shot up from my seat and hurled my bingo card into the trash can. "I shouldn't have made watching the returns into a game," I said, disappointed in myself and my country for our overconfidence that our better natures would prevail.

Later, Jonah told me, "It didn't seem real. It felt like a dream, like a weird mistake. This wasn't how the election was supposed to turn out."

While Jonah was disappointed, maybe even subconsciously worried, it hit much closer to home for me. As much as I kept hoping the United States presidential election results would turn the other direction by morning, I sensed this was a defining moment in American history.

After the election, my alertness heightened. I began to sense faint and distant echoes of another time. A time deeply connected to my family legacy. Media polarization and suppression, alignment with foreign dictators, surprise raids, subhuman detention camps, blaming of the "other" even with no evidence of wrongdoing. I'd always experienced triggers that reminded me of a time I'd never lived through. But this was different. These weren't faraway synagogue attacks. This was happening in my own country. Confederate flags. Swastikas. Hate rallies. And these events weren't isolated.

I couldn't help thinking about my father's childhood years and how Germany, his Heimat, homeland, became so changed. *But that couldn't happen here,* I told myself. *That wouldn't happen here.*

Yet, isn't that what people said when they meant to rationalize the way something was? Terrible things happened because we allowed them to. So, I began to take action. I participated in a women's march, made monetary contributions to select organizations, and learned what our community does to support refugees in my area. I sought to understand others' opinions, especially the ones I didn't agree with, and more actively engage in conversations about a breadth of issues.

My *one day* had finally arrived. I now felt compelled to discover for myself as much of my father's story as possible. I dug through the boxful of VHS tapes we kept in the basement, relegated to being forgotten. I was looking for a tape with the words "Walter Stern testimony" on it. This tape would not be forgotten. There it was. My father's 1993 testimony video. Now I wanted, no, I *needed*, to rewatch it.

With the week off from work and no travel plans, I sat at the oversized teak Ikea desk in my home office and inserted into my computer the DVD I'd had converted from its original VHS version.

Before starting the testimony video, I took a deep breath. I reached for the decorative brown cloth box that I still kept close by, still dear to my heart even after all these years. I opened it and gently removed a wooden Tikvat Yisrael brooch, the sole physical item of my father's that he had personally given to me. It was a round, wooden brooch about an inch and a half in diameter, painted a bright, Israeli-flag blue. Prominent and centered was a white-painted Magen David, Shield of David, the triangles of the six-pointed star linked together with painstaking care. In the middle was a rising yellow-orange half-sun, and along the top was Hebrew lettering that read: Tikvat Yisrael, hope of Israel. *Hope, always hope.* The brooch rested in my bare hands, one hand slightly overlapping the other in what would have appeared as an image of supplication if left empty. I held it one last time before slipping it into an archival sleeve, or plastic protector, slightly annoyed with myself for not having safeguarded it more carefully decades earlier.

I finally clicked play, ready, after all these years, to give my father's memories, his story, their due.

My father appeared before me, back from the dead, on my computer screen. My spine involuntarily straightened. There he was, in his signature plaid, short-sleeved, button-down shirt and oversized 1980s-style glasses. His body was nestled in the flower-print wingback chair whose arms supported his arms; an ottoman similarly supported his legs, which were crossed at the ankles. It looked to me as if he were telling himself to relax, but I didn't feel he was relaxed. He spoke. I tilted my head, my ears straining for the sound. For the first time in decades, my father spoke to me.

And then, much more quickly than I'd expected, the testimony video was over. But, this time, it meant so much more to me than the first time I'd viewed it. There was so much I needed to hear again, so many questions I would have asked my father had he still been alive, had he been there with me. Watching his testimony video, this time, invigorated me with purpose in a way I'd never expected. I felt driven, but full of questions, wanting to share his story, and wanting to understand it fully, completely. I knew I needed to make something of this story for myself, and then for my children, for all my father's descendants. But how? My father was gone. What I had now were his words. And so I began with those words. I set to my task, transcribing his words, spending hours alone with my video father, listening, typing, listening again, learning his story by heart.

My father spoke English in the testimony video, his third language after German and Dutch, and the only language he'd ever spoken to my brother and me. As I watched, I remembered that sometimes my father and his mother, my Oma, spoke German with each other. That way, they could talk about us kids. Or adult things. Or the canasta game they played together some evenings at the table in our home's wood-paneled dining room, their cards laid out on the clear plastic sheet protecting my mother's white tablecloth, the one with the red embroidered flowers I loved so much. Or perhaps, I realized later, they discussed the reparations payments or their lost property.

I felt compelled to capture my father's exact words and the incomplete sentences and names of people and towns and foreign words I didn't—yet—know. These were my mysteries, my puzzles to disentangle. My father spoke in a quirky manner. He used the gerund, or *ing* tense I prefer to say, for almost all his verbs. *My father was smuggling. And we were hiding in a ditch. And I was churning the butter.* He also started a lot of sentences with *and*. I felt that's how he kept himself going through it all. "And then ... and then ... " My heart clenched as I wondered if it was painful for him to tell his story, or a relief to get it out, like the loosening of the throat when we finally let ourselves cry.

My father frequently used the word *would*. *Nobody would know about it. I would ride the other bicycle with my mother on the luggage rack.* To me it sounded tentative, as though he were separating the experience from the fact that it happened to him. I'd been told that his speech pattern was typical of a German person speaking English and trying hard not to sound German. All these things I had never noticed about him when we were alive together because, back then, his only identity was as my father. He had no role, no life, that preceded his becoming my parent. Now he was changing. He was becoming Walter, a person separate from his role as my father. It was a bookend to my life, in a way, as my children were also becoming people beyond their roles and existence as my children. My eyes were opening, as was my heart. As for my father, he was opening too, at last. His story opened as well, and like all good storytellers, he began with an introduction of sorts.

> *It's a long story and there are a lot of things to be told. A lot of episodes in a lifetime of discrimination. I may start in the early years of 1933, 1934 when Hitler came into power. At the time I was six to eight years of age.*

I listened to the same passages over and over and over again, striving to get it all just right, pausing frequently to clear the tears from my eyes, to catch my breath, or to sob aloud. At times, with my head in hands, I'd ponder how any human being could have endured this pain. And how any human being could inflict it.

And I would think about my own childhood.

CHAPTER 2

SECRETS

I GREW UP IN SUBURBAN Long Island in the 1960s and '70s sensing something was off. Though I didn't hear my father's heavy German accent as my friends did, even at the ages of six, seven, and eight, I had a sense there was something deeply troubling from his younger life hidden within that accent. The secrets weren't discussed. I didn't ask why our family wouldn't join the town pool or send me to the summer camp I so badly wanted to go to with my friends. I didn't ask anything about my father's childhood. Perhaps I was too timid. Perhaps I was concerned that my questions would upset him, would cause him to share something he didn't want to share.

From as young as I can recall, I worked hard to gain acceptance. I felt like an outsider with my friends, who heard my father's accent when their own parents had none. I also felt like an outsider within my extended family, who, as it turns out, had secrets of their own.

I recall that my father also seemed secretive about his egg and chicken delivery business. Even so, I was proud that my father, with his eighth-grade education, could, along with my mother's bookkeeping income, support our family—my younger brother, David, and me.

Each week, my father followed the same routine. On Mondays, he drove to a farm and picked up eight cases of eggs. He cleverly transported each of the fifty-pound cases from the car to the basement, a place our friends were never permitted, through a small window onto a wooden slide he had built. After storing each case, he candled the eggs, holding each one up to a special lamp, one by one, in the dank basement—conveniently cool in the summer and thick with its cold dampness in the winter—to cull out eggs with cracks or blood spots. Next, he sent the unblemished eggs down a conveyor that sorted them by weight so he could place them into the appropriate carton. Sometimes my mother helped or, when she had her own job, my brother or I might help after school. Often, though, we did not, leaving my father to his solitary work in the basement.

He interspersed the candling with customer phone calls. When he answered the heavy black phone, whose short cord tethered him to the wall, he would always say, "Dee … hallo?"

I wondered about the utterance *dee*, even more than my father's accent, the one I hadn't heard. It sounded like a kind of stutter. Or was it a fear of receiving some bad news from the person on the other end of the call? Like so many other things about him, I would never find out.

Tuesdays and Wednesdays were reserved for delivering the eggs to homes and to restaurants. My father drove his route, getting in and out of the car dozens of times, all day long. His outfit was always the same: khakis, white T-shirt, and work boots lined with metal orthotics. In the winter, a faux fur–trimmed leather jacket was added.

He grabbed a dozen or two of the eggs from the back of the car and walked to each customer's front door. "Eggman here," he called as he handed over the eggs and collected a few cents here, a dollar there.

He sometimes had time for a short conversation, perhaps even a friendship. Elsie was the baker at one of my father's restaurant customers. Each autumn she baked him a Zwetschgenkuchen and handed it to him on a large pizza tin. At home, he would place this plum tart, a variation of a German specialty, onto our aqua-colored kitchen counter. I don't know how we—more likely how he—managed to eat the whole thing. In retrospect, I wonder about the memories the tart must have brought back to my father.

On Thursdays, my father picked up the butchered chickens and sorted the livers, hearts, kidneys, and necks, sometimes halving or quartering the chickens before the late Thursday and Friday deliveries to yet more customers. It was the smell of these chickens and their parts that permeated the dankness, hanging in the air as though it belonged there, another accepted aspect of the way things were in my house. It added to the discomfort I could not name.

At the end of the week, my father sat at his desk to review his books. His desk was nestled in a nook he had created within our den, where we also kept an old piano and an uncomfortable convertible love seat. There, he managed his accounting ledgers and counted out the money he'd earned from his deliveries. He piled up the quarters, dimes, nickels, and pennies, until there were enough to put in a roll to be deposited in the bank.

For my father, the painting above his desk was possibly the most important item in the den. It depicted three rabbis, with their long white beards and fur-brimmed hats, arguing over a piece of Jewish text or law. It seemed as if they were watching over him.

On cooler nights, my father loaded up his car with the eggs he'd be delivering to homes and restaurants the next day. While this saved him time the following morning, on these nights, he moved the car from the driveway into the garage and closed the rickety sliding door. Eventually, I learned how to move the door on its rollers to avoid one roller coming off and the door getting stuck. It was a good challenge and left me somehow satisfied that I could support my father's need for secrecy, to prevent anyone from seeing the car filled with cases of eggs.

This need to close the garage door seemed odd to me at the time. It did not seem likely that someone would walk all the way up our long driveway to peek inside the car windows.

Even my father's passenger bench seat held secrets. He'd removed it from the back of the red-and-white, ambulance-like station wagon to make room for the egg cases and set it down in the storage side of our two-car garage, propped up against a makeshift divider wall. My brother David and I, and our friends, were not permitted to play near the car bench seat.

Another memory has stayed with me. One evening in the late 1960s, when I was around seven or eight years old, I was sitting on my bed, perhaps supposed to be asleep, when I heard a sound from the living room that caught my attention. My parents were watching the new sketch comedy called *Laugh-In*. It was a sound I hadn't heard before. I tiptoed to my bedroom door and listened. It was my father. Laughing a short laugh.

This is a visceral childhood memory. I cannot recall hearing him laugh before that night. Even then, I knew there was something monumental about this moment, but I couldn't explain why.

My father was unconventional. He seemed to take a little too much joy on April 1, focusing on that holiday as though it were Halloween or New Year's Eve. "Irene, go look. There's a big box for you on the front steps." I ran to look. And there it was, a box to open. There was only a single slip of paper inside. "April Fools," the note read.

And there was the brooch my father gave me when I was around nine years old. It was an acknowledgment that, for the first time, I had fasted on Yom Kippur, the holiest and most austere of Jewish holidays.

A few days after I received the brooch, I wore it to Hebrew school. We were seated in the slightly musty sanctuary, a place typically reserved for prayer, a sacred space. My teacher singled me out for taking on the Jewish adult requirement of fasting on Yom Kippur, even though I had not yet reached the age of twelve, Jewish adulthood for a girl. "Irene, stand up," Mr. Bloom said.

I rose in front of my entire class with the trepidation of a shy child, not wishing to be singled out. Then, unexpectedly, he looked at my brooch and asked, "What are you wearing there?"

I told my class what I knew, though I can't now recall when I had first learned this. "My father painted this when he was underground during the war."

Back then, I pictured a dark, dank basement, without understanding more than a few words he had shared with me. Still, when he presented it to me, I knew the brooch was very important, a meaningful object to him.

Furtive work. Infrequent laughter. A treasured gift.

Throughout my childhood, my father would say things without explanation. No seeming logic. I remember he once said out of the blue, "Those new state police cars mean trouble. Stay away from them."

As a young adult, when I understood a bit more about my father's wartime experience, I didn't want to upset him by asking him what happened during the war, so I didn't.

Decades later, as I yearned to understand the details of my father's life before I knew him, the pain and the sadness, I also felt gratitude that he'd created that brooch and saw fit to give it to me.

My most treasured possession, lovingly stored in a special box, only to be touched for special reasons, remains always close to me.

CHAPTER 3

HOME

I BEGAN TO ABSORB my father's testimony of surviving the Holocaust. I craved to know more about what I could not truly know. I had so many questions. Was he nervous about attending a new school? What were his friends like? What did he love most about each of his family members?

Yet, my father's secrets were not all buried. Among the documents he had saved, I found letters he wrote in Dutch to his protectors' family, including one about his close friend who had survived Auschwitz. He *had* needed someone with whom he could share these stories. Though my father was lost to me by the time my *one day* came, I also wanted to be one of those people.

As I watched and rewatched the testimony video over the course of several months, I tried to recall what my father had told me about his childhood home and family. He was born in Bocholt, Germany, in 1926, and was the only child of Moritz and Hilde, my Oma, grandmother. Hilde's mother, Selma, lived with them. There was "Opa," Selma's second husband, whose last name was different from Oma's birth name. And there was Uncle Kurt,

Oma's half-brother, whose name I don't remember being mentioned. Yet, somehow, I knew it.

I also knew that Aunt Mathilde, Moritz's sister, had visited them from Frankfurt on the eve of my father's twelfth birthday.

In his testimony video, my father readjusted himself in the living room chair. He moved one foot from the ottoman onto the floor, as though needing to feel grounded or to protect himself from what was yet to come. He intertwined his fingers and talked about Aunt Mathilde.

She had her papers to go to America. She had a number. We also had a number, but our number was higher, so we had to wait.

As I watched and listened to the testimony video and began seeking details of my family's life, I felt two stories begin to intertwine—my father's and mine—both on a physical level and on another, unseen spiritual plane. How else to explain the many signs that would point my way, the conversations and experiences I would have that were never sought or planned? The way one experience would lead to the next, revealing the truth that we are all interconnected, if only we would open our hearts?

From the safety of my desk in Massachusetts, an ocean and eighty years distanced, I began to imagine how specific scenes of my father's early life might have unfolded.

ELEVEN-YEAR-OLD WALTER finishes up supper with his family. It's November 9, 1938, and he sits in the dining room on the floor above their men's clothing and textiles store. Walter is excited that Aunt Mathilde is visiting overnight. She has come from Frankfurt to celebrate Walter's birthday the next day. She has big news to share.

The family enjoys Kaffee und Kuchen, coffee and cake, in the dining room overlooking Geburtsstrasse. Then they move to the living room to discuss plans of leaving Germany and of reuniting in America one day. Aunt Mathilde wants to hug, to hold close, the family one last time until—with the greatest of hope—they would all meet again in America. Mathilde's husband hadn't known initially that she had gotten them onto the immigration list. He didn't want to leave Germany, but he followed along after Mathilde told him she was leaving, with or without him. Mathilde and her husband and their girls would make the move to Riverside Drive in New York City, in 1939, just in time.

A sound catches their attention, pauses their conversation. The plinking sound of a pebble hitting their living room window, the only street-facing room in the living quarters that has a light on. The family members look at one another, brows furrowed. When no other plinks come, they resume their conversation. They don't recognize the plink as a signal from a friend or a neighbor tossing a pebble up to their window as a warning of the violence to come later that night.

Walter goes to bed before the others. "Gute Nacht. Schlaf gut," his mother says to him with a smile and a hug. "Träume süss." Good night, sleep well, pleasant dreams. Walter crawls into bed, under the covers, and reaches for his drawing pad and colored pencils. Sketching is one of the things that helps to calm him, along with the medication prescribed by his doctor years earlier to help manage his long periods of shaking out of fear. He soon tires, puts aside the pad and pencils, and falls asleep.

Sleep brings Walter sweet dreams about the day to come, knowing that his family has something special planned for him. He will skip school and thereby avoid encounters with hateful people, he will play a game of chess with his Uncle Kurt, and he will have more of his mother's delicious plum cake.

The rest of the family members are in their pajamas, snug under the covers in their beds, sated from a celebratory birthday meal, safe and unaware of what is to come in the next hour.

Moritz and Hilde are trying to fall asleep in their bedroom. Moritz runs through the plans he has made, seeking hidden problems that can be solved, his indigestion kicking in. Their immigration number is high. He is concerned that something terrible, even more terrible than having to rent out their store to a neighbor, could happen. His son, Walter, comes home from school each day shaking because the other children taunt him in the streets. His mother-in-law, Selma, in her sixties, has recently lost her second husband, the man who started the business Moritz has been running for over ten years. Mathilde and her family will leave soon for the safety of another country far away, thank goodness.

Hilde, a strong, calm, and confident German mother, wife, and daughter, keeps her anxiety, her feelings, to herself as she questions how this town where she was born and had lived the entire thirty-six years of her life, could turn against them. Wasn't it enough that her own father had died when she was a baby? She doesn't remember him, never would be able to tell stories of his life. And wasn't it enough that Eduard Herzfeld, Hilde's de facto father, had died not even three months earlier, leaving her own mother in deep grief? She is pleased that her husband had planned so thoroughly. She hopes the planning was unnecessary. Perhaps it is better to be prepared, to have that peace of mind knowing that, if they needed to, they could find safety. Perhaps it is better instead to dream about the day she has planned for her only child's twelfth birthday and to think about better days in the town. Hopefully Walter will be able to attend Gymnasium with the other children in a couple of years.

Selma, Hilde's mother, tries to find rest in her own room. She is lonely now that Eduard is gone and makes plans to visit both husbands' graves again before winter sets in, in the small Jewish cemetery under the Wasserturm, the water tower. Now, at her age, she isn't likely to find another husband. At least she has her family. And her dear, beloved son Kurt is back home.

Kurt, Uncle Kurt to Walter, is awake in his room, struggling with his own challenges. At twenty-five years old, he is still working out how to navigate the current family dynamic given that his father has died. He and his half-sister, Hilde, had inherited the business that Moritz manages.

I DON'T KNOW HOW THEY SLEPT that night or what they were thinking about before dozing off. I don't know if my father regularly sketched as a child, though I had one page he drew in September 1938, a Rosh Hashanah card. As an adult, my father often sketched drawings of furniture—bookshelves and cabinets—that he would then build from wood.

Yet, I was curious about these and other details. I had bits and fragments, and so I imagined the scenes. Something I would find myself doing frequently as I watched my father tell his survival story. The imagined narrative that unfolded beside my research seemed the only way I could get a close-to-full understanding of my father's life.

Perhaps a little more than I should have, I fixated on those images of my father and his family tucked in their beds. I was aware that it began to consume me, but I needed to do it. I needed to stay awhile in their temporary tranquility. My family, who were sated from a lovely meal, warm and cozy in their pajamas under the covers. Me, knowing what would happen next. They, having no idea that they would soon be awakened from their sleep, their home and lives shattered.

I restarted the testimony video to listen to more of my father's story.

So. Alright. During, when we grew up, we had Kristallnacht, which was November 10, 1938. My birthday, by the way, when I turned to be from eleven to twelve years of age. It happened to be my birthday.

In that moment, I understood. I wanted to linger in my reverie about the birthday celebration that should have come in the morning. To delay hearing the details of Kristallnacht, the Night of Broken Glass that occurred throughout Germany, the night that would come to signify the beginning of the Holocaust.

There would be no cause for celebration on my father's twelfth birthday, or on any other.

Once, as a young girl, I said, "Happy birthday, Daddy!" I was proud of myself for remembering to acknowledge his special day, independent of prompts. I remembered my father sitting on the edge of his bed, applying his foul-smelling ointment to the psoriasis on his knees and elbows, these rough discolorations marking him as "different" and marred.

He looked up at me for a moment. "Don't you know? I don't celebrate my birthday. It wasn't something to celebrate, with the things that happened back then."

As a child, I hadn't understood why he couldn't let the past go, in favor of living in the present, enjoying the anniversary of his birth.

Instead, for him, this birthday marked the beginning of the shattering of the stars—*the shattering of the Sterne*—the Stern family.

Over the next few years, I would need to face the pervasive pain that was left unspoken yet palpable. Like the layers of earth that accumulate from generation to generation, the layers of a family's story, constantly impacted by the effects of erosion and destruction, build, break down, and build up again. Eventually all the layers intermingle. Some cannot exist without the foundation of those that came before or even those that might come after.

As I listened to my video father, I decided to dig through the layers of my father's story, at once the foundation and the future of my own, to follow the physical path of his life from escaping Germany on Kristallnacht to the Netherlands, and his survival in hiding there. I was not yet aware how my father's story and my own would intertwine. The fluidity of time encapsulated us inescapably together, and the *one day* of discovering in what ways our layers connected had arrived.

CHAPTER 4

SHATTERED STARS

SITTING AT THE SAME DESK for hours and hours, I tried different methods of transcription. I'm a fast typist, but it was hard for me to type my father's words because the syntax wasn't easy to decipher. I tried using voice to text, but it didn't understand his accented speech. I finally found success in listening to my father while repeating his words aloud in real time into my phone, which typed it for me. Essentially, I "gave" my father's testimony, word for word.

Overwhelmed with repeating the story aloud, I needed to pause the testimony video frequently. Listening to my father was hard enough. Then I'd go back over it again, listening to him, editing-fixing-trying-to-discern-the-exact-words, his fumbles and all. Speaking my father's exact words brought me into his story in a more direct way, and I unexpectedly became more a part of his story.

Discerning his timeline also proved difficult. He didn't tell the story chronologically, and it took a bit of heavy thinking to put his stories in the right order so I could follow the sequence of events that he was describing.

There's a place early in my father's testimony video, at time stamp seven minutes and fifty-eight seconds, where he was talking about the early-morning hours of November 10, 1938. His voice pitched up and he called out on the word *YOOdeh*—Jude—the German word for Jew, attempting to recreate the shrill quality he'd heard in the street below. He moved both hands upward, as though beseeching, then rested them on his thighs in tight fists.

The sound was so shrill and loud: "Jude" and whatever they said there. It was, the hatred, you could hear the hatred and feel the hatred. It was a vibration in the air. There were numerous men in brown uniforms on the street, holding a steel I-beam.

They just demolished [our store and house windows and doors] so you could walk all the way through. It was so bad that the glass particles were in the clothing that were hanging in the store way in the rear. Nothing of it was usable anymore. It was loaded with glass. And then we heard also gunshots in the street.

And now we knew they meant business, they really wanted to get rid of us.

And, in order to avoid confrontation with these drunken people, whatever they were, animals, they sounded like animals, my father directed us all to escape to the roof. He had always planned an escape route in many different ways.

WALTER AND HIS FAMILY run to the top floor of their home. They gather around the stepladder that awaits its final use by this family of soon-to-be escapees. Each family member climbs the stepladder, then squeezes through a little square window, like a porthole, that takes them onto the roof. Heavyset Aunt Mathilde has a challenge fitting through the window. The others coax her to position herself diagonally so that she can fit through the largest area of the window, then they give her a push on her tuchus to help her get through the window and onto the roof.

They all slide down on the slanted roof shingles to an area that is flat, where they can stand facing the street side where the brownshirts are demolishing the building.

Walter stands, hugging himself in a vain attempt to quell the shivers, as the sounds of breaking glass travel upward to his place on the roof. He hears his mother whispering worriedly to his grandmother, "Wo ist Moritz?" Had Moritz gone back into the house while the brownshirts were at work demolishing the building?

"Ja," Selma nods her head. "I don't know what he wants, I saw him go back inside."

Moritz hadn't thought about the cold air before bringing the family to the roof, and he heads to the ground-level store to retrieve everyone's coats. As he enters the rear of the store, a man runs over to him, wielding a pistol. Moritz quickly grabs the coats, pulling them through the door that leads back into the private quarters. He locks the door behind him. His heart beats hard as his feet propel him back up the flights of stairs.

"What did you do?" Hilde scolds her husband when she sees the panicked look on his face as he rejoins his family. He hands them their coats, then puts on his own and reaches into the pocket.

"Look at this," he says, diverting his wife's anger as he pulls out twenty Marks from his pocket. "At least we have some money."

Walter's coat atop his pajamas doesn't quell the shivers. The shivers from the cold. And the shivers of anxiety, which have become so familiar. What will become of their home? Of their lives?

After about two hours, the horde of people, the brownshirts, finally move on. Throughout the night, the family hears gunshots in the distance.

Uncle Kurt points beyond the Rathaus, town hall, that is nearby. "Look, there, a fire."

"I wonder what is burning?" Selma's voice is steeped in sadness, as it had been in the weeks after burying her husband.

IN MY EXPERIENCE with my father, I recall him taking sick time off from work only once, to recover from a hernia operation. He worked even when he was sick, whether it was the flu or a painful back or bouts of anxiety that he kept hidden from us children. Perhaps his childhood, Kristallnacht and all that transpired after, planted the seed of this way of being for my father. He did not have time to quell the shivers back then, neither from cold nor anxiety, because he and the rest of the family were thrust into survival mode. He had learned to keep moving and never slow down, because that is what he had always had to do.

In my research into that night, I would learn that the Stern-Herzfeld store in Bocholt, Germany, was one of at least a dozen Jewish-owned shops and homes destroyed in the town, and one of 7,500 Jewish-owned shops destroyed and looted throughout the Reich on the night of Kristallnacht.

CHAPTER 5

HEIMAT

IN BETWEEN WATCHING and transcribing the testimony video, I dug into other artifacts. I waded through some of the old photos and documents that I had saved when my brother and I cleaned out our father's condo after his death in 1994. I didn't know then that these treasures I'd saved would help me paint the picture of the story my father never told me.

I scanned the items and placed them into archival sleeves. Most documents were written in German, which I don't understand. But some included English words.

One photo was captioned "our house," in Oma's handwriting. This photo was in an album Oma had made for my father's fiftieth birthday, so the caption was in English. In the photo, HERZFELD was spelled out in capital letters atop the store's display windows.

Geburtsstrasse #35. The place of my father's birth, in his Heimat, homeland, a word whose meaning is deep in a way the English word doesn't quite convey. Germany had been the documented Heimat of my father's ancestors for generations, over hundreds of years.

We had a beautiful home, a house. It was a business, a storefront in the bottom, and two stories on top, a three-story house and forty-three rooms. My parents were pretty well off. They had a very nice business there.

The building plan from the town archives showed that the Stern-Herzfeld family's living quarters were on the second and third floors of Geburtsstrasse #35. The family also had boarders. I could not confirm that there were forty-three rooms in their building. However, according to the building plans, there were at least twenty rooms. Based on my research, I could picture my family's history evolve.

EDUARD'S BUSINESS SUCCESS on Geburtsstrasse has not happened overnight. He made the cross-country move from the large eastern German city of Berlin to the small western city of Bocholt in 1910 and started working as an employee in a clothing store across the street from his future wife, the widow Selma, and her nine-year-old daughter, Hilde.

Eduard and Selma marry and have their only child, a son, Kurt Herzfeld, in 1913. Eduard purchases the building and business where he had been an employee, and he rebrands it, calling the clothing and textiles store Herzfeld. Later, he expands Herzfeld, purchasing the adjacent building to accommodate his business success. He affixes his name to the front of the building, as other shop owners in town do.

Customers travel from all around the area, including from neighboring towns across the Dutch border, to purchase clothing off the rack or to be fitted for a special custom-made outfit, or to select items for a dowry or communion-wear or masquerade costumes, or to choose from the locally woven textiles to sew their own clothing. Being near the town center, where the Rathaus, churches, and farm marketplace attract many people, Herzfeld welcomes numerous customers each week.

Resources in the interwar years are not plentiful. Yet, the Herzfeld family does well enough. They live in a neighborhood whose diversity is reflected in the religions represented and thus the primary public schools available to attend. There is the Protestant school, the Catholic school, and the israel-itische, Jewish, school.

Neighbors meet one another at the farmer's market, at the Gymnasium activities once the children are old enough to attend the public high school, or while riding bicycles to run their weekly errands.

One neighbor who lives behind the Herzfeld store is a coffee roaster. Next door on one side of Herzfeld live the Löwensteins, a Jewish family related to Selma by marriage. Buchbinder owns the bookstore next door on the other side of Herzfeld, and one more door beyond is the Kekse bakery. A few blocks away is another bakery with a big door, Kempers, which would become one of Walter's favorite places to visit and where he would devour the creamy delights.

In 1925, at the age of fifty-six, Eduard is ready to step back and locate a partner. He finds one in Oberhausen. His name is Moritz Stern.

OR PERHAPS MY OMA and grandfather, Hilde and Moritz, found each other first, and then Eduard decided to create the partnership.

I pieced together bits of my family's life from 1926 to 1927 based on photos and documents. Moritz was a go-getter. He was someone who knew what he wanted. It's possible that he simply embraced the path on which he found himself, a path he followed with a full heart and presence of mind. And planning. He didn't realize that his personality, stamina, insistence, and persistence would enable his family to survive, and for his granddaughter to document this history.

Though I never knew my grandfather, I ached to know him, to talk to him, to breathe the air he breathed. To understand the business savvy he had acquired with no formal education, but rather from his sales experience starting at the age of fourteen. And his experience a few years later fighting for his Heimat, then as a prisoner of war in France during World War I.

Soon after joining the Herzfeld business and family, Moritz was likely the one who made some changes. Work commenced with the architect W. Hallen to modernize the façade of the Herzfeld store and the family's home. The two adjacent and touching buildings would now appear as one entity, one building.

Shiny letters adorned the new façade above the storefront windows: HERZFELD. "Our house."

The local newspaper, *Bocholter Volksblatt*, reported on October 8, 1927:

Business alteration on Geburtsstrasse ... [T]he Herzfeld manufactured goods of Geburtsstrasse opened its new business today. By ... putting up a modern façade, the architect Mr. W. Hallen succeeded in giving the house an artistic, contemporary impression with function and beauty in harmony. The individual doors and windows merit special attention, as do the new, modern features. The modification contributes, to a high degree, to the beautification and modern decoration of the cityscape. It is proof of the industriousness of the Herzfeld firm ... We wish it much success in its new building!

Another photo in my acquired collection features Oma and my father, a young Walter, around ten years old, dressed in a pullover long-sleeved shirt, shorts, and shiny leather shoes over socks that reach his midshin. Hilde and Walter stand, each gingerly holding one of the blossoms that cover a cherry tree. It must have been May or June, cherry-blossom season. Walter sports a sweet, happy, boyhood smile as he gazes at the blossoms they hold. His hair neatly combed to one side shows off one ear, sticking out slightly.

On the bottom of the photo, Oma subsequently wrote in English, "Our cherry tree in the garden."

Perhaps it was during the 1927 renovation that the family's beloved cherry tree was planted.

On Google Earth, I could get close enough to see a tree near the reconstructed building. It didn't look like an eighty-year-old cherry tree. But I held on to the fantasy for a while that it just might be.

CHAPTER 6

ELECTION

I FOUND MYSELF REGULARLY IMAGINING my father's life. Had he enjoyed the cherries from his tree and the gorgeous blossoms produced each spring? To what degree was that young boy aware of the events unfolding around him? Pondering these and other details, I was mortified that I did not know the history of a country on the verge of dictatorship and what led up to my family's need to flee everything they had ever known.

I started reading about Germany after World War I and especially the goings-on of the early 1930s. On January 30, 1933, President von Hindenburg named Adolf Hitler chancellor of the German cabinet. Two months later, on April 1, supposedly in reaction to an international boycott of German goods, the Nazi Party declared a boycott of Jewish-owned stores, and they prevented Jewish lawyers and judges from reaching their places of work. They committed acts of violence against Jewish people and Jewish property. In the early hours of that April morning in 1933, the windows of the Herzfeld shop were shattered for the first of many times. The next day, the Sturmabteilung, storm troopers, stood in front of the Jewish shops and denied entry to those willing to buy.

IN APRIL 1933, further civil rights are removed. Jewish people are being fired from their public service jobs. Soon, trade unions are banned. Political parties other than the Nazi Party are also banned. Germany leaves the League of Nations. Political prisoners and "undesirables" such as homeless or unemployed people are sent to concentration camps, the first of which, Dachau, had opened its gates in March 1933.

After the death of President von Hindenburg in August 1934, the office of president is abolished. Hitler becomes the Führer, leader, in addition to his previous role as chancellor. The Schutzstaffel or SS, a paramilitary protection squadron, reports directly to him. People all over Germany, not only Jewish people and Communists, begin to live in fear, especially if they are not wholehearted supporters of the Führer and his party.

Moritz is fortunate to still have some loyal customers whose children are getting married and need items for the dowry, and they still need clothing for themselves. However, they no longer feel safe coming to his store. He devises a plan to keep his family afloat.

Moritz straddles his bicycle and pats his pocket to confirm he remembered the paper and pen. "I go now," he says. Hilde watches, brows knit, as her husband rides off.

If the customers can't come to the store, Moritz can go to his customers. He cycles to their homes, mostly on farms, to take their orders. He returns by bicycle a few days later to deliver the merchandise.

I SOAKED UP THE HISTORY of that time in any way I could. I read Holocaust memoirs, history books, and websites devoted to aspects of the era. I watched Holocaust documentaries. I attended Holocaust survivor presentations and conferences for families of survivors. I joined a 2G group, where other second-generation members shared their experiences growing up with a Holocaust survivor parent. I learned a lot, including to consider more deeply what it must have been like for my family in 1930s Germany.

As I envisioned my family contending with the events of their day, I considered how neighborly relationships would have changed in those challenging years. Early on, did residents have the courage to speak out against antisemitic acts perpetrated against their neighbors? Or at least quietly help them? Did they align wholeheartedly with the Nazi Party and its ideals? Or did many neighbors disagree with the government yet choose to keep quiet to protect their own loved ones? I would come to realize the latter might have been more likely than I cared to consider.

In the aftermath of the 2016 election, as the United States left the Paris Climate Accord and hateful rhetoric proliferated online and on the streets, as refugee families were placed in unclean and dangerous camps, the two periods of history collided in my mind. *Where would I hide? Who would I trust if my family needed help?* I considered what I would do—or what I might have done—if my neighbors asked for help to hide their family. To do nothing was still an action. It was complicity. Maybe I would help my neighbors so that they could earn an income. I'd like to believe—wouldn't we all?—that I would be brave enough to offer others protection from violence. I hope that conviction will never be tested.

CHAPTER 7

SCHOOLS AND BULLIES

EVERY SO OFTEN, even before I revisited my father's testimony video, I would sit at my desk with an iced coffee. The brooch would be nearby as I searched online for "Bocholt" or "Herzfeld" or the too-common "Stern" to see if something new had been added to the vast internet.

In April 2007, my "Bocholt" search had a hit. A Florida-based newspaper article included an interview with a man named Harry Berg, who had grown up in Bocholt. I reached out and we talked on the phone, but Harry had only spotty memories to share.

Harry was born in Bocholt in 1924 and spent his early childhood there. He vaguely remembered Walter Stern and the Herzfeld store. Greta, the woman who would become Harry's wife after the war, lived across the street from Herzfeld in 1938 and had witnessed the Kristallnacht destruction of the store. Later, I would meet Harry and Greta's son and daughter and piece together the relationship.

Through 1933, Jewish children attended the israelitische school on the north side of town, and Harry told me Jewish schoolchildren were still able to participate in the annual St. Nikolaus Day parade.

Once Hitler came to power in 1933, it became acceptable, even preferred in some circles, to taunt Jewish people, whatever their age. Things started changing. Slowly at first, then more intensely.

Through the first part of 1933, my father walked to his israelitische school each day. It would have been a short walk, maybe twelve minutes for a young child. Less if he were taunted and had to run.

My father's walk to school changed after October 1, 1933, when the regional government abolished the israelitische school as a public school. Although the Jewish children could attend the Protestant or Catholic public elementary schools, some Jewish parents decided instead to create a new israelitische school in a room on the south side of the town, near a railway station, where three boys and eleven girls attended from 1933 to 1938.

During his testimony video, my father spoke of being taunted by the neighborhood children even from the age of seven.

I listened to his explanation about the israelitische Volkschuler.

We had only about twelve or fourteen children in all of the classes from first to sixth grade. There was one teacher who was teaching every grade. We also got a Hebrew education there at the same time.

This Hebrew school was created by our parents in order to save us from the hazards of being with non-Jewish children in the same classroom. Many a times, many a times, teachers would discriminate against Jewish students, which happened at many other schools. And not only that but also acts of violence were directed against the Jewish students by their classmates. In order to avoid this problem, we had our own israelitische grammar school. Not a high school, just a grammar school.

WALTER MAKES HIS WAY to the new school. It is still a short walk. He moves nervously down streets lined with flags of the Third Reich, each one slanted toward the street from each residence and business. Soon, the Nuremberg Laws of 1935 would officially forbid Jewish people from flying the Nazi colors. The street is a canopy of hatred, a sea of death-black swastikas in white circles on blood-red backgrounds, imposing itself overhead, flapping unpredictably in the wind or hanging quietly in wait. Inescapable and unforgiving.

On his way to the new school location, Walter passes directly in front of the oversized image of Hitler lording over him high on a building to his right. The Rathaus looms directly in front, across the market square through which the military parades would pass. Towering over him from the roof of the Gothic-style Rathaus growls the motto: "Ein Volk. Ein Reich. Ein Führer." One people. One country. One leader. The slogan of the Third Reich. The definition of nationalistic tyranny.

Walking on the street is treacherous for a Jewish child. As Walter and some of his schoolmates round the corner on the way to school, non-Jewish children lay in wait and throw rocks at them, spit in their faces. But that's not as hurtful as the words the children throw: "dirty Jew."

The Jewish children walk through the humiliation toward their school. "Stay calm, don't do anything," one of the older children reminds Walter.

Walter stiffens, his anger and fear wound tightly inside. Their parents had warned them, "Don't answer, don't retaliate, don't throw rocks back. If you do, your father might be sent to the concentration camp." The first concentration camps had opened in 1933. It was known that political prisoners and others who were perceived as enemies of the state were sent there. Walter believes that, if he makes a wrong move, he might be personally responsible for his father's death. All he is permitted to respond is, "I am proud to be a Jew."

Bullies attack the store as well. Numerous times between April 1933 and November 1938, in the dark of night, they heave rocks into the plate-glass windows of the Herzfeld store. Each time, there is a tremendous crash and they scream "dirty Jew" and other hateful words.

Sometimes, instead of breaking the windows, they paint large swastikas on them using tar.

Walter is eight and the anxiety he would experience for years took root here.

I PAUSED THE VIDEO, closed my eyes, head in hands, and imagined my grandparents holding their son closely, trying to comfort him after his run home from the Jewish school, unable to control his shaking. I could imagine the neighborhood children's fresh saliva dripping from his face, the emotional wound caused by the words "dirty Jew," and perhaps the sore spots on his skin—soon to discolor into purple bruises—where the rocks had made impact. Afraid to reply lest his own father be sent away to a bad, bad place. Such a burden for a child to carry.

A bullying experience from my own childhood flooded me. During my elementary school years, two afternoons a week, I made the twenty-minute walk from public school to Hebrew school, where I learned all the important Jewish prayers, holiday customs, and daily rituals.

One day, I encountered a group of bullies, probably a little older than me and certainly a lot meaner. I don't believe they were Jewish and, as far as I knew, they did not know I was. This had nothing to do with antisemitism. They were simply bullies taking advantage of someone with less power than they had at that moment, perhaps as a way to be in control of something in their lives. There were three or four of them. They grabbed me. I was unable to pull away as they mashed snowballs into my face. They seemed to relish my struggle. I don't recall telling my parents about this incident. Somehow, there was an undercurrent of "you shouldn't say anything." I knew it was better not to tell them.

Lifting my head, I resumed the video.

Now this situation was going on and on, and as a child it was doing a great deal of psychological damage because we had a feeling to be different, to be inferior to other people. You developed a very, very deep-rooted inferiority complex, and you were called "dirty Jew." You were not the same person as a normal person, in a normal society.

In the video, my father raised his shoulders in a small shrug, as if to ask, *What could you do?*

"Evidently, this situation led to a deep-rooted inferiority complex, haunting me through the latter part of my life." I found this phrase in an account my father wrote in a document he titled "Detailed description of persecution."

The bullies my father had encountered were driven by hate. They were children themselves, and so they learned that hate after hearing their own parents or teachers talk about the "dirty Jews." Or from the leaders of the Hitler Youth, of which they were members. How could the culture have changed so suddenly, from a community of neighbors to a place of hate, fear, and violence? Or maybe it had been there, unspoken, all along.

Two of the books I'd read for my research provided me with insights about Jewish life in Germany leading up to and during Nazi rule: *The Pity of It All: A Portrait of Jews in Germany 1743–1933* by Amos Elon, and *Between Dignity and Despair: Jewish Life in Nazi Germany* by Marion A. Kaplan. Did my family, and other Jewish families, live in denial of the undertones and the unspoken true nature of people, as I read that Jewish people in Germany had? Or was Hitler a cunningly manipulative and evil master of psychology, for years planning ways to create fear and hate so that, when he needed people to act inhumanely, that fear and hate would not be so hard to access? I realized, after reflecting on these books, that this phenomenon would not be such a preposterous leap of expectations.

Contemplating my experience living in America, I rationalized that things would be okay. I had chosen to live in a "safe" place, a quiet, liberal town in the northeastern United States, where diverse religions are represented, where acceptance and mutual interest are demonstrated. I didn't need to be proactive. But "safe" places aren't always safe. Things aren't always okay. And they never have been.

At the same time I was reading about Germany in the 1930s, there was an amplification of hate speech in current-day America. Almost daily, news stories reported an increase in acts of intolerance toward Black people, Jewish people, and other groups. The impact of centuries of inequities and racism was on full display. The preference by so many of us to focus solely on ourselves, to not accept or help those perceived as being "other," had created an unhealthy culture of selfishness in America. During and after the 2016 election, I started questioning my own beliefs about the safety of where I lived. Would I need to devise an escape plan? When and how did my grandfather in 1930s Germany first realize that he might need an escape plan?

CHAPTER 8
SMUGGLING

OVER THE YEARS, my husband, Seth, and I have driven to Canada a few times for vacations, crossing the border and coming back over it again. Seth is slim, with all gray hair and, even wearing glasses, his green-gray eyes remind me of my father's. I'd describe my husband as an engineer-type, analytical and detail-oriented. Seth cannot be described as a risk-taker.

So, I always laughed at the questions he would ask me before talking to the border agent. "Is that bottle of wine packed away?" "Did you hide that half sandwich?" I decided Seth would never make a good smuggler—even before learning from my father's testimony video about my family of origin's history of smuggling.

My father was smuggling his own money into Holland on weekends on the bicycle!

IT IS ANOTHER NICE SUNDAY in 1935 Bocholt, and Moritz continues to assemble his plan.

"Come, we go now for a ride, the bicycles are all ready," Moritz says to Hilde and Walter, as he does on many Sunday afternoons. By the age of eight, Walter is used to these rides to visit a rabbi-friend in Holland, though he doesn't know what has been secreted away in the metal tube under his father's bicycle saddle.

The family cycles from Bocholt to Aalten, a forty-five- to sixty-minute ride through forest and flat green farmland. They travel across the border from Germany to Holland, where Moritz would need to lie to the border guard and claim that he carries no goods or money.

Finally, they arrive near the Aalten synagogue at the rabbi's home. Walter is kept occupied while Moritz retrieves the special rod with a hook at the end that he keeps in Aalten. Moritz removes his bicycle saddle and uses the hooked rod to pull out a rubber tube filled with money that he had slid all the way down into the hollow post that supports the saddle.

The next day, the rabbi deposits Moritz's funds into an account managed by Moritz's nephew, Harry Slager, who lives in the Dutch town of Enschede. This routine is part of Moritz's elaborate plan, smuggling funds as a kind of insurance in case the need would arise.

TAKING A BREAK from my father's testimony video, I located the manila folders filled with financial papers that I'd brought home with me from Florida after his death. At least these documents were in English.

Resting my eyes on his Swiss bank account statement, I wondered why my father would feel the need to secret away some funds. Not a lot of funds. He didn't have much. But it was enough. Enough to leave this country with his family and start a new life somewhere else.

Perhaps it shouldn't have been a surprise. Still, this find reminded me that, years earlier, my father had told me we always needed to have funds somewhere safe, just in case. He had explained that that was the reason he bought us Israel bonds each year. Though he was an ardent supporter of Israel, and he hoped to enable us to pay for airfare to Israel, to take a trip for fun, it was also an investment—for *just in case*.

Conducting my research in contemporary America, I listened to the news of neo-Nazis, white supremacists, and the racist rallies people attended. *Did I need to make plans like Moritz did, like my own father did?* Denial, lack of planning, lack of facing reality had not worked out so well for many in 1930s Germany and throughout Europe. Each day, I tried to convince myself that things were different now, different here in the United States. But then I'd listen to the news, or read it, and the hate-filled events taking place around the country continued. It felt as if they would be never-ending.

CHAPTER 9

ROSH HASHANAH

AS I REVISITED my father's early life—what I knew and what I'd imagined—I recalled certain celebrations from my own childhood. Each Rosh Hashanah, my father drove my mother, brother, and me from Long Island to New York City. Oma lived in the city, as did Aunt Mathilde. So, we went to be with family—a family that would have celebrated together in Germany had history been different.

The journey into the city seemed particularly stressful for my father. The traffic approaching the Throgs Neck Bridge was typically terrible. He was so tense that he would pull the car over to get out and take a few full breaths before continuing on. His behavior didn't seem normal to me. He kept his thoughts to himself.

As a child, I sat in the back seat, feeling bad for my father, unable to understand why he was so tense on the eve of a holiday. Yet this was how it was, and I absorbed it as part of our life. *One must push oneself to the point of discomfort, to achieve or please, and to never stop moving.* I absorbed this lesson well.

At the Hebrew Tabernacle, a synagogue in Washington Heights, we listened to the cantor and the choir and sang the Shema, the quintessential prayer of the Jewish faith proclaiming one God, the prayer one recites morning and evening. And upon preparing for death.

Through my research, I learned what had happened in the weeks before and after my father's final Rosh Hashanah in 1938 Bocholt. Eduard, the creator of the Herzfeld store and patriarch of the Stern-Herzfeld family's household, had died on August 18, 1938, and was buried in the Jewish cemetery under the Wasserturm, water tower, near Solly, Selma's first husband. The following month, the family ushered in their first High Holidays without Eduard.

WALTER IS ELEVEN YEARS OLD. A couple of weeks after his Opa's death, he reaches for his colored pencils and draws a Rosh Hashanah card for his family, trying to bring them some light. He embellishes the paper's edges with images of the holiday—a prayer book, two loaves of bread, an open Torah scroll, a kiddush cup and bottle of wine, scales of justice, and the Jewish year 5699. In the center, he writes in brown Hebrew lettering, "l'shanah tovah tikaseivu"; and in German, "Wünscht Euch Euer Walter." Wishing you a good year, your Walter. These words are surrounded by orange water paint that brightens up the page.

Little does the family know that their days would soon become even darker. That this would be one of the final times the Jewish people of Bocholt would enter their synagogue, passing under the two tablets of the Ten Commandments that sit atop the entrance doorway.

HAD MY FATHER BEEN SO STRESSED on our drive to the city because he associated Rosh Hashanah with the upcoming anniversary of his synagogue's destruction, and that of their very lives? And the destruction of the Ten Commandments tablets above the doorway? They couldn't have known—as I came to realize through my research—that these tablets would be destroyed and removed less than three weeks after the end of the holiday season. The shattered tablets would be found again about forty-five years later, but there is no mending something so utterly broken.

CHAPTER 10

THE UNTHINKABLE
JOURNEY HOME

BY EARLY 2018, I was deeply immersed in my father's story and the stories of my ancestors. Using Google Maps, I plotted most of the path my father and his family had taken from Kristallnacht through liberation. Now, I wanted to see those places, breathe the air, and talk to the local people in person. I needed to get as close as I could to touching my father's life and the lives of his ancestors.

In April, I purchased roundtrip plane tickets to Frankfurt, Germany, for Seth, our twenty-eight-year-old son Josh, and me. Josh had finished up his school year as an art teacher. Jonah, a few years younger than Josh and starting a new job, was not able to join us. I made reservations in hotels and inns in my ancestral hometowns. I planned our route to retrace my father's footsteps, from escaping his German hometown to his arrival in Holland, where they lived in safety, then in hiding, always in fear. My brother and sister-in-law decided they would join us for the most critical couple of days of our journey, when we would physically retrace my father's escape and survival route.

In May, before traveling to Germany, the cherry tree in my yard blossomed, and its pink double petals gave me pause. I'd planted this tree a few years earlier, before I realized my father had a cherry tree in his childhood garden in Bocholt. And before my brother reminded me of the cherry tree my father had planted at our Long Island home growing up. Had I somehow unconsciously chosen to perpetuate an invisible intergenerational theme? Similarly, did I get giddy on April 1 because my father did, even before I understood the significance of that date to him? Did my joy, my compulsion, to make deviled eggs for New Year's Eve as my father had done when I was a child stem from his own childhood, something that had brought him comfort?

Every few days during my cherry tree's short bloom, I clipped a small branch, a twig really, and placed it gingerly, tenderly, into a low crystal vase. Each twig I clipped stood upright, supported by clear glass marbles, and drank up its nurturing water. While the snipped twig reached upward, the blossoms themselves hung heavily downward, carrying a burden even in their beauty.

Each time I walked past them, I was reminded to be happy that I could remember my father and his family, and their home. Then, I felt sad that it was a place and time and people I could never really know, or touch, or talk to, or hug.

Finally, taking in the cherry blossoms that became my symbol of hope, I accepted the bittersweet feeling that I was doing what I could to learn about my family of the past. And I would continue to learn. Soon, the flowers would fall from their branches, yet my labor would yield fruit.

Before we left on our trip, I shared with Seth and Josh a view from Google Earth showing the building that now existed on the land where my family's Bocholt home once stood, where I could vaguely discern a tree. Was this the cherry tree they had planted so long ago?

I could not yet say the words: "I am going to Germany." I could barely formulate them in silence. This was a dream I'd had, yet now that I was about to visit my ancestral places, it was difficult to reconcile my decision. *Me*, a Jew, going to Germany. *Me*, a Jew of German descent, a descendant of people who were killed by Germans for the crime of being Jewish. Ringing in my ears were my father's words, spoken in his testimony video, as he moved hands from left to right, signifying "never."

I have never gone back to Germany.

I will never go back to Germany. I will not give them the satisfaction or for my own pride. I just wouldn't do it, I couldn't.

My father's insistence in the video forced me to grapple with my choice. I wanted to believe that he would have approved. I told myself that if he were still alive, given the changes in Germany, he would have traveled there with me. But in 2018, I was still wrestling with my decision.

I wondered—rightfully, it turned out—how often I'd be interrogated by friends and family about going, as it was tacitly understood by so many that, as a Jewish person, you simply didn't go there. And I worried that, from up above somewhere, my father and Oma might never forgive me.

Nevertheless, thanks to the gifts of my father's testimony video and the many photos and documents I had examined to that point, plus the research I had completed, the time had come.

Packed away in my aching heart was some baggage I could not shed, my father's words, echoing every step of the way. Stowed in my luggage would be almost one hundred Tikvat Yisrael markers that Josh, the always-creative art teacher, had made for our trip. Well before we left, he had asked, "Don't we want something to leave at the gravestones we visit? I can make coin-sized tokens."

My father might have cringed at the idea of our bringing reproductions of the brooch into Germany, the brooch that he'd made while in hiding in Holland. Still, I liked Josh's idea, and before we left, I sent him a photograph of the wooden Tikvat Yisrael brooch my father had gifted to me.

Josh had spent hours screen-printing one hundred images onto an aluminum sheet, then punching them out one by one, into half-dollar–sized rounds.

When we met up at the airport in Boston, Josh handed me the tokens. As we waited to board, I turned a couple of the tokens over between my fingers. I read the words I had asked Josh to print on the back: "In remembrance of our family Stern, Sternberg, Herzfeld, 2018." It included my email address.

I imagined the power of returning a piece of my father to his ancestors, as my plan was to leave a token at each ancestral gravestone we would visit. In retrospect, I wondered if Josh was channeling my father as he performed this labor of love.

As the plane's gear extended for our landing in Frankfurt, I focused on the last German lesson I'd be able to fit in. It wasn't a language I cared to hear, much less study, as I associated it with Nazis and Nazi ideals and the shattering of my family and millions of lives. Yet, I wanted to learn enough to be able to talk with the people I was most nervous about meeting—the owners of my family's former home and business.

I'd learned how to say, "I have a flat tire" and "That is boring" and "I would like a piece of black forest cherry cake, please." I remembered the German Schwarzwälder Kirschtorte from my childhood. And I had learned two more practical phrases: "My great-grandmother married my great-grandfather and lived in Bocholt." "My grandparents and your grandparents were neighbors." I shuddered, imagining myself speaking those last two phrases to the person for whom I learned them, the person whose family now had possession of my family's home and business.

We deplaned directly onto the tarmac. "Did you expect this in an international airport like Frankfurt?" I asked Seth.

We were directed to a bus. I felt it was more of an order: "To the transport. That way."

The bus was already packed, but people were still coming off our plane, so the driver waited for everyone. Each person was required to stand upright. There was no room to move, to sit, to rest. I couldn't see how more people could be stuffed in. But more could and more did. I could barely conceal my shaking or control my impulse to cry out.

"Achtung," the transport speakers might have screeched. I honestly couldn't recall the exact words, only my shock. I tried to find air to breathe as people continued to crowd the space.

Breathe, steady the shaking, I repeated silently. *Why had I dragged my husband and son here?*

Breathe, our transport is going to the terminal, I reminded myself. Still, I wondered, *why in the world was I here?*

Was my father offering an *I told you so?*

I talked myself down. *Breathe, this anxiety will leave once our transport arrives at the terminal. I will get out. I will proceed to retrieve my luggage. I will continue on my journey, unlike others before me. Breathe.*

I tried to rationalize that my anxiety was because of a history I was getting too close to. How did those in charge know how to pack an airport bus full of airplane travelers so efficiently? Didn't they know what their ancestors did to my ancestors? Was this a recent past they'd inherited, or more innocently, a cultural desire to be uber-efficient? Still, how dare they?

Of course, we did arrive safely at our terminal, where we retrieved our luggage. Next, we arranged ourselves in our rental car and began our drive, learning new vocabulary as we traveled. I proudly pieced together that Ausfahrt meant an exit, the combination of the words for "out" with "drive."

We drove for three hours through cities, hillsides, and farms, stopping at one of the occasional Raststätte, rest stops, along the way. The road signs, announcing the approach of Bocholt, sung out as we got closer, a beckoning and a caution all at once. Like a "panoramic view" sign where you know there's something breathtaking to behold if you will stop and look, while being wary of getting precipitously close to the edge of the viewing area.

Our view of the farmland receded. We finally arrived at Bocholt, a small city with approximately seventy thousand inhabitants on the Dutch border. Bocholt is dotted with modest homes, grocery stores, restaurants, and hotels. We checked into our hotel and immediately began the mile walk to Geburtsstrasse #35. The first road we crossed was the busy Willy-Brandt-Strasse. Waiting for the walk signal, we faced a block of red brick chain stores and restaurants that reminded me of the city's long-gone medieval walls I had read about. In the center was the Neutor, new gate, which would lead us into Bocholt's older section.

Once inside the gate, we passed buildings—businesses with homes above—rebuilt after having been largely destroyed in Allied bombings near the end of the war.

Soon, we crossed the Bocholter Aa River, necessary to the textile industry that Bocholt of the nineteenth and twentieth centuries was known for. We crossed Südwall, then Südmauer, both words for south wall.

It was late afternoon. Cyclists reigned on the car-free roads as they rushed past us on their way home from work or school or on an errand before the shops closed. Our fifteen-minute walk turned into thirty as we tried to determine the rules for pedestrians in the bustling street. "Watch out!" Josh cried, pulling me back as we tucked ourselves alongside a light pole, safe from those cyclists.

A set of chimes on the brick façade of the building directly in front of us greeted us with a song. I didn't know the melody, didn't know why they were playing. They simply appeared, ten small bells hanging vertically and, to their left, six smaller bells horizontally, grounding me in the present and leaving me contemplating the past. It was as though their song was a portal to long ago, somehow telling us we were on the right path. Had these chimes played out years ago for my family to hear?

We were getting close and, as I knew from my virtual travels up this street, the alte Rathaus, old town hall, was on our left, now an ice cream shop and café. The Gothic-style building was set at the back of a large, open plaza that was filled with small tables and chairs. The air was filled with the sounds of forks and spoons clinking on coffee cups, ice cream dishes, and small plates. We could see the green copper steeple of the St. Georg Church peeking out from behind the alte Rathaus. We turned and walked three blocks farther.

Finally, we had arrived at Geburtsstrasse #35, where my family had lived and from which they had escaped eighty years earlier. I stood on the cobblestones in front of a rack featuring brand-name men's clothing that was placed just outside the shop doors. This was the spot where the glass lay shattered on that cold November morning. No evidence of that era remained.

PART II
COURAGE

GEBURTSSTRASSE #35, BOCHOLT, GERMANY

IRENE STERN FRIELICH: JUNE 2018

I STOOD, FROZEN. I could barely believe I was physically in this place I had both dreamt about and dreaded seeing.

"Here." I pointed at the sidewalk in front of the shop. "This was the spot where the glass windows lay shattered," I managed in my shaky voice. As if Seth and Josh hadn't already figured that out.

"I cannot remember first hearing my parents' war stories.
It seems to me that I always knew. Shards of their past
lodged themselves inside me at birth, if not before."

–Elizabeth Rosner, *Survivor Café: The Legacy of
Trauma and the Labyrinth of Memory*

CHAPTER 11

DRAGONFLIES

IN 2018 BOCHOLT, I stood in front of my family's former home. My impressions from a months-ago virtual neighborhood visit via a YouTube video were confirmed. This building must have been rebuilt after the war years, its façade newer, brighter than that in my family's photo of the address. "The Weber store of today was updated since the war." I explained the obvious to Seth, who was supportively waiting to follow my lead, and Josh, who was eager to enter the building of his ancestors, the place that we all had only heard about in stories. I was overwhelmed by my own apprehension of the place and time that I was about to step into.

I stood, frozen. I could barely believe I was physically in this place I had both dreamt about and dreaded seeing, standing in front of the clothing display outside the doors of the shop. Men's clothing. The current owners had continued the business that once belonged to my family in this space. How extraordinary and, well, awkward and uncomfortable, that there was continuity of a sort.

"Here." I pointed at the sidewalk in front of the shop. "This was the spot where the glass windows lay shattered," I managed in my shaky voice. As if Seth and Josh hadn't already figured that out.

I felt like an interloper. A spy.

Now shaking, I walked through the glass doors, entering this sacred space for the first time, the place where my ancestors walked, worked, worried, slept, sewed, sat silently. My peripheral vision melted away as the shell of my body and the vessel of my soul tried to contain the spirits that now joined me.

I could focus only on what lay directly in front of me in this realm, yet I was deeply connected with some other dimension. My father and Oma could never have imagined that I would find this place, would have the audacity to return to the scene of the crime. I stood in the place to which they had vowed they would never return, never to "give them the satisfaction."

It was like entering a forbidden place. Was I letting my ancestors down? Would I find healing or was I reopening a wound? Despite my fears, I knew I had to be there.

Approaching a display of neatly folded shirts, then moving left toward the hanging shirts, I imagined how this place looked on that night. Here is where the glass pieces had been cruelly strewn. And there, deep in the clothing. And over there, in those racks, which I passed as I slowly floated toward the back of the store. The shards would have been crackling and crunching under my feet, the fragments falling out of the clothing as I brushed past. I could not absorb the enormity of the shattering that had happened here eighty years earlier or the magnitude of this visit and the impact it would have on me.

The glass might have also been at the back of the store, where a small section of children's clothing was on display. Perhaps this was where my family's Singer sewing machine sat, eighty, ninety, one hundred years ago, operated by Oma or a hired worker as they tailored men's suits to order.

And there, in the center of the building, where the stairs now are, glass would have cracked under my feet. This wide staircase was not the original, of course, though it still took us to the second floor. Vaguely aware of one of the store clerks watching me, I drifted upward and entered the space of my family's onetime living quarters.

Was this the living room? This the kitchen? A bedroom?

There, along a wall, I stood one or two floors below the area where there was once a porthole-like window. The place where my family gathered in the early-morning hours of November 10, around the stepladder that awaited its last use by this family of soon-to-be escapees.

I recapped the story for Seth and Josh. And I reminded myself.

ON NOVEMBER 10, 1938, Moritz ushers his family, still in their pajamas, to the rooftop after the plate-glass windows of their shop have been violently shattered by the brownshirts. It was a noise so savage and piercing that it awoke the household. Now, the family stands in the cold darkness on the rooftop. They can smell smoke from the not-too-distant fires they can see—the burning of some Jewish homes. Moritz disappears, then returns with coats in hand for his family to don over their pajamas. He tells them about his encounter downstairs with a man holding a pistol and how quickly he was able to escape to their private quarters and lock the door behind him, before returning to the roof with the coats.

As the sound of the mob dissipates, around two or three in the morning, Moritz ushers the family back into the house. He is ready to enact his escape plan. He brings them all into the attic, on the fourth floor, to a wall where there is a hidden window. The one he had put in, just in case.

I WALKED TO THE BACK OF THE STORE, to the area where I imagined there was once a hidden window in the attic above. Sometimes the power of the moment—the conflation of what was, and what it could have been, what it should have been—was too intense for my heart to reconcile without tearing up.

Before the trip, I'd read the following line in Elizabeth Rosner's *Survivor Café*: "I cannot remember first hearing my parents' war stories. It seems to me that I always knew. Shards of their past lodged themselves inside me at birth, if not before."

I finally understood the essence of Rosner's sentences. Standing in my ancestral home, this was the moment the shards of *my* family began to crystallize. I could start to put words to the torment. I could feel the sharpness of their pain, rather than a dulled and masked anguish. The tear in my heart deepened.

Being propelled from below my imagined attic window location, now toward the front of the store, I asked the well-dressed suit salesman, "Sind Sie Markus?" Are you Markus?

"Nein," he answered, followed by other words I didn't understand.

It was Markus Weber I was seeking, the store's owner.

Markus hadn't replied to my multiple email attempts prior to our visit, so I decided to show up and ask for him in person. Half of me expected to find him working on the shop floor, as my grandfather had done, and like the suit salesman was that day. The other half expected I wouldn't find him at all.

I turned away from the salesman, whose eyes followed me curiously. The open window beckoned me to view Geburtsstrasse, to experience the view our family once had from their dining room. I peered into one of the windows across the street, where, I had learned, fourteen-year-old Greta, the daughter of a prominent Jewish Bocholter family, had been awakened by a loud commotion that night in 1938 and witnessed about a dozen men outside the Herzfeld store on November 10. She watched them destroy the shop before her mother pulled her away from the window.

This was a trauma, I later learned, that Greta would need to cope with, along with the loss of her own parents, when she eventually arrived in America, an orphan. I wondered if Greta's own children struggle with the same inheritance of trauma as I do? Do they also think about where they would hide? Just in case.

Moving away from the window and continuing my circular path around the second floor, I noticed Josh examining white polo shirts with black somethings on them. "This would be perfect," he said, pointing to the display, "if only they had extra small."

"Why?" I asked, barely able to tolerate the thought of making a nonessential purchase in Germany, much less in this place. In my family, in much of the American Jewish community, it was an unspoken rule that you do not purchase German-made goods. Of course, I had broken that rule, and so had my father once, significantly so, when he purchased his tan Volkswagen van for camping trips he would take with my mom.

"I love dragonflies," Josh answered. I noticed the dragonflies adorning the shirt. I was pleased they didn't carry his size. Months later, I would learn that dragonflies symbolize change, courage, our ability to triumph over adversity. I realized Josh is not encumbered with the same sense of inherited family trauma I had to deal with. I was thankful for that.

With Markus Weber nowhere in sight, I reluctantly pulled myself away from the space of my family's living quarters to descend the stairs and toward the salesman at the cash register. He listened to my question, my voice shaky, "Ist Markus Weber hier?"

His response, concise and in German, informed me that he was the store manager, that Markus was away on a trip and would return in two days. He didn't smile. I'm certain I wasn't smiling either. Breathing deeply, I tried to calm my heart rate, now at speeds reserved for biking uphill rather than wandering around a clothing store.

I explained in German. "I believe my grandparents and his grandparents were neighbors." I could not discern a reaction, could not read his face. Perhaps my sentence structure or pronunciation left doubt as to my meaning. Perhaps it left no doubt.

With nothing left to explore inside for now, Seth, Josh, and I headed outside, to the area behind the store where my family's yard had once been.

The place where we hoped to find a tree filled with cherries. But this tree, the one I had found on Google Maps, was not a cherry tree.

Two days later, we headed back toward the Weber store. This time, there was a farmer's market in front of the former Rathaus, locals bustling about, purchasing their favorite fruits, vegetables, and flowers. The dark-red cherries next to the yellow-green gooseberries, red currants, and other juicy and delicious-looking small round fruits called to us. We had to purchase a bagful and, before walking a few more blocks to enter the store again to find Markus, we visited our tree in back.

I watched as Josh bent over to tie his shoe at the patch of dirt where our family's cherry tree might have once lived eighty years earlier, the only patch of dirt in the area where the not-cherry tree now grew. Josh wasn't actually tying his shoe, I realized. He was enjoying the sweetness of a fresh cherry we'd purchased, discarding the pit, and gently inserting the pit into the soil. Then another. And one more.

In that moment, I imagined my possible return in three years. I hoped for a miracle tree.

Together, we walked around to the front of the building. The cobblestones. Racks of men's clothing. Plate-glass windows. There was a stability in this place, a predictability.

Now familiar with its layout, we entered the store.

"Yes, I am Markus." The stocky, blond-haired, blue-eyed man cautiously greeted us.

"I think your grandfather and my grandfather were neighbors."

Markus shared, in fluent English, "Jews used to live here."

Markus, we learned, lives upstairs on the rebuilt upper floor, in the same space that my family's rooms had once been. The building had been reconstructed on top of the existing foundation, avoiding the legal requirement to excavate what lay beneath.

I had come this far, taking risks, and displaying my own brand of courage.

I weighed the idea of asking for an invitation to my family's—to Markus's—private quarters, in order to get a little closer to touching my family's life. It had been rebuilt, but the space my family once inhabited was still there.

No, I decided. It would be too much for me to bear. And, I figured, the building wasn't going anywhere. I settled for exchanging email addresses with Markus.

I asked, "Do you carry the polo shirt with the dragonflies in an extra small?"

"No, we don't carry that size."

Throughout my time in the shop, I could feel Oma watching our conversation. I could feel her anger. One year later, during a visit to the regional Münster archives, I would find dozens, perhaps hundreds, of letters spanning years after the war. The letters were between Oma, Markus's ancestor, and the local authorities. The outcome was not clear to me. But the volume of letters told me enough about the bitterness my grandmother held. About her fight over who rightfully owned the store.

CHAPTER 12

HEIGHTS

SETH, JOSH, AND I left the Weber store and walked around the block, to the area behind the shop. I wanted to look at it again, get a sense of the height of the building as it might have been. To see the roof.

"It would've been somewhere up there," I said, pointing out the top of the Weber building to my husband and son. The highest part of my family's Bocholt home was, essentially, the fourth floor. "That's where the hidden window was. It overlooked the Röster home."

I remembered my father, in the testimony video, saying:

Mr. Röster made a living with burning [roasting] coffee. They had these old-fashioned coffee burning machines.

MORITZ HAS OPENED THE ATTIC WINDOW, in the dark, chilly, early-morning hours of November 10, 1938. He had been calling throughout the night, "Röster, Röster, please help us."

Finally, Mr. Röster awakens. He hadn't heard the earlier shouts and crashes one street over. He doesn't yet know what's going on. "Yes, Stern, what is it?"

"Help us! We have to come to you and hide."

"All I can do is put a big ladder up here on that window and get you down."

Röster disappears for a few minutes, returning with a long wooden ladder, which he props up at the window where Moritz stands waiting. Family members take their turn climbing out the window onto the ladder. Selma first. Then Mathilde, who is afraid of her own shadow, grabs the ladder and climbs down. Kurt, Hilde, Walter, and then Moritz follow. The ladder takes on a complex identity of its own, an instrument of fear intermingled with safety.

Röster ushers the family into the horse barn, waving his hands for them to hurry.

"There," he says, pointing to the hay in the loft above. "Rest there until daylight."

NOW, IN 2018, I stood staring at the back of my family's former Bocholt home thinking how impressive the ladder must have been. Four rungs up was my limit. I'd never gone higher. I most certainly could not have climbed down from a window on a ladder at that height.

I knew this because, a few years before, I decided to try gorgeneering. For some reason, when I signed up for this adventure, I pictured myself wading through the low and slow waters of a picturesque rocky gorge. I had no idea that first I'd have to rappel into it, alongside a raging waterfall.

I thought I'd found the perfect challenge and a surprise for Seth, but it terrified me. I don't know how I was able to force myself over the edge. But once I'd started down, there was no going back. No one to rescue me but me.

Our two guides were brilliantly patient and helpful as I navigated through the gorge, shimmying over smaller, yet not insignificant, waterfalls that roared ferociously due to the opening of an upstream dam. We paused for a break here and there, our guides moving ahead to scope out the gorge and to determine our best and safest way forward.

About halfway through our adventure, I stood solidly on the stone foundation of a cliff, which provided safety from the rapids below. The only way forward was to jump off the cliff, six feet down, then make the quick swim across the raging waters to prevent being swept downstream over the next waterfall. I mustered my courage to proceed the only way to exit.

I did it. And I vowed *never* to do it again.

My fear of heights had been confirmed. And the guided gorgeneering adventure did nothing to help me overcome it.

Looking up again at the height of the Weber building in Bocholt, I wondered if Aunt Mathilde had overcome her fear of heights, her fear of her own shadow.

Then I remembered my father's description of his experience that night.

When you are in panic, and you are afraid, you do anything to survive. It was high.

CHAPTER 13

MR. RÖSTER

IN 2018, I WAS STUNNED to find the Röster shop. It was located behind the building that had been my family's home. I peeked into the shop window and looked at Seth and Josh. "I can't believe it's still here. Do you think it's open?"

"Let's see," Josh said. "Try to open the door."

I'm not sure why I was surprised, but the door did indeed open. We walked slowly across the wooden floor, taking in displays of gift items. In the back was an old wooden counter with drawers and shelves that held a vast array of freshly baked goods for sale. The tea and coffee selections overwhelmed me. There was only room for one table that seated four people.

Examining the coffee styles for sale, I tried explaining to the saleswoman why we were visiting. That my family once lived in Bocholt, and that the Röster family had helped mine during the war.

IN THE RÖSTERS' BARN, Hilde gently rubs Walter's cheek. He stirs, after having spent the remaining hours of that November morning in hiding.

"Come, we are invited into the Rösters' home for breakfast," Hilde says, softly.

Walter follows her inside. The familiar rich smell of coffee beans, heating in the metal roasting machine, greet him. He looks around the dining room table. "Where is Aunt Mathilde?"

"Aunt Mathilde already went to the Bocholt train station to return home," his mother says. Hilde motions for Walter to take a seat. He's still a little groggy and definitely hungry. He fills his plate with items from the beautiful breakfast Mrs. Röster has prepared, the finest of cheeses and eggs.

As Walter wakes fully, he notices that Mr. and Mrs. Röster are crying. They had just heard what happened.

THOUGH MY EXPLANATION of long-ago events was incomplete, the Röster saleswoman seemed to understand on some level how important this place was to me. I purchased four bags of Bocholter-style coffee beans to take home.

I sat on one of the wooden benches along the wall so I could take in every inch of the shop. Our saleswoman busily prepared our cappuccinos near the prewar coffee-roasting machine that displayed bags of Röster's Bocholter coffee. My eyes moved from the floor displays to the drawers of tea, to a wall of coffee bags, to the back corner, upward to the tall white ceiling.

"This could be the same space where my family ate their last breakfast in Germany as guests of the Rösters," I said to Seth.

I felt myself floating atop my bench perch, not entirely in the present. "They might have looked at this same ceiling."

Perhaps the same antique machine a few feet away was actively roasting coffee that morning when my father awoke. From my seat in the Röster coffee shop, I realized that my family probably had no appetite to enjoy the lovely food prepared for them. Was my father aching to know when they would return to their shattered store and home? Did he know about the plan his father had devised?

Like my family's former home next door, the Rösters' house was a sacred space to me, but in a different way. In this place, I didn't feel fear or anger. I wasn't nervous about my conversation with the saleswoman. I simply felt gratitude—the deepest sense of appreciation I had ever felt. The tears in my heart began to repair themselves.

Since I wasn't sure if I'd be able to return to the Röster coffee shop, I needed to absorb as much of the place as possible. I wanted to package up and take the sights and smells of the moment home with me.

Thinking of my father and his family at their breakfast at the Rösters' home, I sipped my cappuccino from one of the Röster coffee shop's white mugs. Its stylized coffee-bean logo on the inside greeted me each time I tipped it. I purchased four identical mugs so that I could forever sip my morning coffee from one of them. And I would take all of them out for guests. It would be one way to continually express my immense gratitude for that family.

Once Josh, Seth, and I finished our cappuccinos, we carefully arranged our coffee shop treasures in our backpacks. I took my time to ensure the safety of my mugs, and to linger in the shop a few minutes longer.

CHAPTER 14

TOHUWABOHU, CHAOS

BACK OUTSIDE, nearby the Röster coffee shop, in the empty parking area, I wasn't the only one trying to inhabit my father's story as we knew it.

"Is this where the limo picked them up?" Josh asked.

"Yes," I said. "It was somewhere near their home, tucked back from the street. This could've been the spot where the driver that Mr. Röster found picked up my family."

MORITZ IMPLORES RÖSTER to get them a taxi of some sort. "We want a ride to the Dutch border. I know exactly how to escape into Holland. I have mapped the route." Moritz's stomach churns as his indigestion flares up.

"Here, take this." Mr. Röster hands Moritz a cigarette to help calm his nerves. Moritz has not been permitted to smoke since his angina started. This is his first cigarette in years, and it makes Walter realize even more the enormity of the moment.

Mr. Röster makes some calls and, not long after, a black limousine pulls up outside his home. It is still decorated with flowers from a wedding the day before.

"Come, quickly. Get in, get in," Moritz whispers to his family, as he ushers them into the limousine.

The unnamed chauffeur drives them safely away from the Rösters' home, passing by their own home, where they silently witness their store's shattered display windows—the windows they had replaced multiple times in the years since 1933. Their beautiful clothing is scattered in the street. The doors to their home have been smashed.

The limousine driver tries to avoid the glass shards that reflect crackles of the morning's light. Moritz and Hilde sense they will never again repair their Herzfeld shop windows. Walter hopes he will never again have to walk the streets among taunting children calling him names.

They drive past some of the other Jewish homes and businesses that were ransacked the night before. So many other Bocholt Jewish people were not as safe nor comfortable as Moritz and his family were during that night on the roof.

Mr. Seif, the synagogue's Jewish caretaker who lived next door to the building where the Jewish congregation met for worship, had been beaten. The rioters broke into his house and their leader said, "Get him down and slash his stomach, then I'll invite everyone for a drink!" Mrs. Seif had been beaten on the head with a wooden club and officers passing by took her by bicycle to a hospital.

The roof of the Friede villa, south of the Rathaus, had been destroyed. No one who was watching the destruction told the men to stop. Broken chairs and jars of preserved fruit lay smashed on the floor. A local friend had, on hearing what was happening and aware that Mr. Friede was away, arrived at the Friede villa that night to help protect the family.

On the north side of the town, club-wielding men had shattered the

Metzgers' windows and took the family's belongings into the street to destroy them.

On her way to church for the St. Martin's Day service—what would be the last one before the war—one witness passed the Herzfeld shop. She observed the store's textiles and clothing in Tohuwabohu, chaos and disorder. At the local high school, there was talk of what happened in the town. One student was shocked that her peers spoke supportively of the prior evening's destructive and violent activities. Another expressed a sense of shame and observed that a known Nazi-member teacher was wearing a new suit. It was one that the student and his friends suspected he had stolen from the Herzfeld store during the night, after the windows had been shattered.

WALKING THROUGH THE STREETS of present-day Bocholt, I repeated my father's recollections to Seth and Josh, even though they had heard them before. I tried honestly and completely to consider each piece of testimony I had listened to or read, attempting to recreate with words the images of Kristallnacht. The horrific things that happened.

There were some rays of light—a few people who had demonstrated courage and compassion, or who had at least felt shame and sadness. It was a challenge to hold these polar extremes in my head, in my heart. But the fact was, not everyone behaved badly. Not everyone was a silent bystander.

From time to time, certain realizations would hit me. My great-grandmother would never again be able to visit her first husband in the cemetery. Nor would the family be able to visit Eduard's grave to unveil a gravestone, a Jewish ritual to gain closure, to fully say goodbye to the patriarch of this family. The man who had purchased their family home and built their family business.

But I could. Before continuing on my family's escape route, I could visit Eduard.

CHAPTER 15

CEMETERIES

AT THE OFFICE of the nearby Christian cemetery, I again had an opportunity to practice my German. The young man dressed all in black, with black and red tattoos covering every visible inch of his skin, did not speak English.

I recited one of the first sentences I'd taught myself in preparation for our journey: "Haben Sie die Schlüssel für die jüdische Friedhof?" Have you the key for the Jewish cemetery?

"Ja," he answered, as he handed me the key. This moment felt uncomfortable.

Did he realize we were Jewish? Did he think it silly or unusual for there to be visitors to a cemetery not in use for decades, since well before he had been born?

No matter. Seth, Josh, and I arrived at the green metal-barred gate to the "new" Jewish cemetery, key in hand.

We opened the lock to this cemetery, created in 1940 so that the graves could be moved from the "old" Jewish cemetery. We closed the gate behind us and approached the large, granite, rectangular monument in front of us. The stone, dating from the late 1940s, sat guarded between two rhododendrons, fully leaved yet past their bloom, in a bed of green ivy, which provided a soft covering over the entire cemetery except the walkways. The face of the gray stone appeared sponged in beautiful shades of old and newer green moss, behind which some text was carved in old German writing. "Zum Gedenken an Die jüdischen Mitbürger der Stadt Bocholt Die in den konzentrationslagern ihr Leben lassen müssten." In memory of the Jewish citizens of the city of Bocholt, who were forced to give their lives in the concentration camps.

Three rocks sat evenly spaced atop the left half of the memorial, indicating visitors had been there. Who were these visitors? I noticed a fourth, smaller, flat rock that sat alone at the other end of the top of the memorial.

"Sie starben für ihr Volk und ihren Glauben." They died for their people and their faith.

The inscription was signed by those remembering, "Die Stadt Bocholt," the city of Bocholt.

We continued up the path, viewing each gravestone we passed, guided by the cemetery map that the town archivist had given us earlier in the day. The map showed where each person was purportedly buried in this cemetery and whether a gravestone marked the location of their remains.

I told Seth and Josh that I hoped the map wasn't accurate. That the mapmaker had somehow missed the tombstone of Eduard Herzfeld. I hadn't yet realized that he likely wouldn't have had a stone, since my family had fled so soon after his death, and the Jewish tradition involved waiting a year to do so.

"Maybe Solly Stern is here somewhere too," I said, longing to locate both of Selma's husbands, both of their grave markers.

But we found no family tombstones. Instead, we used the map to locate the approximate site of Eduard's bones.

"Right there," Seth said, pointing to a spot in the ground. "That's where this map says Eduard is buried."

The soft quilt of ivy covered what we presumed to be the location of his remains. I approached the gravesite. I placed one of our Tikvat Yisrael markers from the stack that Josh had made, pushing it gently into the ivied soil. Eduard would be remembered, and there would be evidence of his visitors there.

We stood for a few moments, silently paying our respects.

I had thought this would satisfy some deep need to get close to my family and their story. Yet I was far from satisfied. I knew the locations of my ancestors' graves in five other towns, where the cemeteries had been maintained, even repaired after gravestones had been vandalized.

In time, in all, I would visit the marked graves of fourteen direct German ancestors, including that of a fourth great-grandmother. But the grave of Selma's first husband, Solly, was nowhere to be found.

On the day of our visit to the new cemetery, we returned to our car. "I read about an 'old' Jewish cemetery on a street called Auf Der Recke. The street is near here."

"Let's go," Seth said. "Maybe we'll find something. Tell me how to get there."

The cemetery on Auf Der Recke had not been described clearly on any website I could find. The town archivist hadn't mentioned this place to us.

We parked on the corner, then walked along the largely residential Auf Der Recke on that misty and cool summer day, looking for I had no idea what. Some kind of a sign.

Auf Der Recke wasn't a long street and, almost immediately, we were attracted to the Wasserturm on our left, a towering, cylindrical, red brick structure rising above all the buildings that surrounded it. Its tall and narrow windows contributed to the Wasserturm's imposing and almost fortress-like appearance. Not knowing yet what it had become, nor what it had been, what had been under its guard, we walked across the asphalt toward the structure to a plaque mounted on the bricks. The plaque included a sketch showing the Wasserturm's location and a building we had walked past that faced the street. The diagram showed a square around that building a little larger than the building itself, one side along the street Auf Der Recke.

We slowly translated the words on the water-tower-turned-classroom-building. Dated 1998, the plaque was more of a historical marker than a memorial. It explained that, by 1940, 304 Jewish souls' bones had been buried at this cemetery, within the outline depicted. This area had been an active Jewish cemetery for 118 years.

On June 12, 1940, burials had ceased. A decision had been made to relocate the Jewish cemetery, presumably to make way for a temporary garden. The remains were exhumed and moved to the "new" Jewish cemetery, the place we had just visited.

More precisely, 133 sets of bones were moved, along with 94 monuments. The year was 1940. The Nazi Party was in power. They had ordered their Polish prisoners of war to perform this labor. How diligently did they work to ensure all the bones were properly exhumed and moved, together with their matching gravestones, under the silent watch of the Wasserturm?

We learned that some of the missing gravestones might have been repurposed as part of a roadway or other structure in the 1940s and were not in good enough shape to be relaid with those they memorialized. And so, the final resting places of as many as 171 Jewish souls, wherever they might lie, remained unmarked in a graveyard off Auf Der Recke.

As I was doing the math, I pieced together that my great-grandfather Solly's bones were not among those moved and that was why his name did not appear on the town archivist's map of the new cemetery.

This "old" Jewish cemetery would have been the place Selma came to visit her two husbands after they died, Solly in 1902 and Eduard in 1938. It was only a ten-minute walk from their home.

"Selma might have visited Solly's grave each October or November, on his yahrzeit," I said. "The family might have visited many times a year, but certainly on the Hebrew calendar's anniversary of his death." Perhaps Selma would tend the grave and offer a Mourner's Kaddish, a prayer recited in memory of lost close relatives, sometimes accompanied by her daughter and grandson.

This was how I chose to picture the scene.

ONE NOVEMBER MORNING in 1931, five-year-old Walter accompanies his mother and grandmother to the cemetery to visit the grandfather he never knew. It is Solly's yahrzeit, twenty-nine years now since his death, and Selma visits his grave faithfully, checking on its upkeep.

After pulling some stray weeds that grow above Solly's grave, Selma opens her prayer book to the Mourner's Kaddish and recites the ancient prayer, even without the requisite minyan of ten men. Finally, she places a small rock on his gravestone, marking the visit.

She looks around the cemetery, expecting that she will be buried here one day too. It is a peaceful place, filled with greenery in the spring and summer, brown and rust in the fall. Taking a breath, Selma looks at Hilde and Walter, "Come, we go home now."

As they walk past the Gymnasium, Hilde turns around to look at the school building. "Look, Walter, you will go to school there one day, when you are older."

Walter smiles. He looks forward to the time when he will be grown up. "Ja, Mutti, I would like to learn there!"

"Wait, then." Selma stops them. "Walter, go stand in front and I will take your photograph."

Walter does as he is told, standing in front of the triplet arches that shield the entry doors. The granite stones' smoothness is interrupted by divots and pock marks, giving the façade a weathered but sturdy appearance that would be apparent in the photo many decades later.

IN THE CEMETERY, I brought myself back to the Wasserturm of today. I moved my eyes over the area, left to right and around again, finally resting on the site of the "old" cemetery with disbelief. It had been dug up to make room for one in a series of new school buildings on this block. On the section of land, now asphalt, that comprised most of the former cemetery, a black, rectangular, now-apocalyptic-and-sterile-looking school building stood, as though it belonged on this land.

Under our feet, where we stood at that moment, could be my great-grandfather Solly's remains. The man who died too young, well before the Holocaust, who was buried and visited by family. A man whose name had never been mentioned to his only two great-grandchildren, possibly because his own daughter, born only nine months before his death, would not remember him. Did he lay interred under the asphalt where we stood? Or under the asphalt a few steps away, where we saw a series of six rectangular, grave-sized asphalt patches, possibly where the utilities could be accessed? Or was he under the school building? Or below the small patch of garden, where a delicate white flower blossomed close to the ground? The bloom called to me, and so in the ground where he could be, waiting for someone to visit, I nestled one of our metal Tikvat Yisrael tokens. Like Eduard, Solly would be remembered. Our token, that piece of my father we brought to Germany with us, would be evidence that Solly, too, had visitors!

Needing to sit alone for a few moments, to mourn the loss of a man none of us knew, I found a nearby bench from which I could look out over the once-upon-a-time Jewish cemetery, trying to understand. We knew the impact of the Holocaust extended beyond the 1930s and '40s to our current day. It extended back in time as well. There was no record of Solly's gravestone, much less a gravesite we could visit or tend. My relatives who were killed in the Holocaust were memorialized somewhere. But Solly, who died in 1902, has no surviving memorial. And Eduard's death three months before Kristallnacht meant there wouldn't be time for a gravestone to be made to mark his resting place.

For me, remembering my great-grandfather Solly and my step-great-grandfather Eduard, the Mourner's Kaddish would not suffice.

CHAPTER 16

MONIKA

I BREATHED IN THE BITTERSWEETNESS of this place. The sterility of the building atop my ancestor's bones coupled with the gift of having located Solly's cemetery and being able to share this experience with my son—Solly's second-great-grandchild. I wasn't ready to leave the mourning bench overlooking the onetime cemetery. It was time to go, yet I needed to be alone with my thoughts for a while longer before returning to the car.

Finally, I spoke. "Let's walk the rest of the way down Auf Der Recke and around the block." Seth and Josh agreed.

We proceeded back past the rectangular asphalt patches in silence, looking for more signs as we walked, open to whatever might come. The mist hung in the air, shrouding us as we turned left, then left again, passing two more school buildings that stood behind the Wasserturm. Cyclists, oblivious to my heartache, rushed among the cars, all following the traffic rules, stopping at the light, and waiting until it was their turn to proceed. All as though life were normal.

Approaching our final turn, we came upon one more school building.

The large metal lettering, standing out two inches from the building's granite stones, spelled out St. Georg Gymnasium. I wasn't searching for this place, even though I had learned of it earlier that morning.

At the end of our visit with the Bocholt archivist, I had pulled out one of the old unlabeled photos I'd brought with me and showed it to him. "By the way," I said. "Do you have any idea where this is?"

The young child in the photo looked to be five or six years old. I'd guessed it was my father, dressed in a belted, double-breasted winter coat and a cap. The child looked straight at the camera—or at a loved one holding the camera—that captured him standing in front of triplet arches that shield the entry doors of a grand-looking building. The granite stones appear old and worn in the black-and-white photo, giving the façade an aged and solid appearance.

The archivist, who had already provided us with a map of the new Jewish cemetery and had showed us Oma's birth certificate, immediately identified the building in the picture as the St. Georg Gymnasium, the public high school in Bocholt.

I was pleased to have this information, impressed at the archivist's knowledge of all things Bocholt. I also knew that my father had not attended this school, so I didn't ask where it was located. We had cemeteries and a synagogue site and a museum to see, and we needed to get lunch at some point.

Yet, there we were, standing in front of that school. A place that wanted to be found, or perhaps a place that found me.

Had my family of 1931 also visited the cemetery and then stopped for a photo in anticipation of my father's future education there? Had my father wanted to stand in front of the school he might one day attend—if only things had been different?

"Take a picture, Mom!" Josh didn't lose a moment positioning himself in the same location where my five-year-old father had stood in 1931. Josh, a young man who looked so much like the young-adult version of my father, posed here. I took the replica photo. I imagined the granite stones' smoothness, interrupted by the divots and pock marks that covered the façade and that would be apparent in this photo eighty years in the future.

As we marveled at this coincidence, Josh urged us on. "Let's go inside and look around."

"No, we need to head to the synagogue and the town museum. I want to have time to see everything before they close." I needed to be sure we visited all the sites on my list. "Besides," I added, even more adamantly, "I really don't want to end up in a German jail for trespassing."

Josh's persuasiveness won out.

With guidance from a janitor and some English-speaking students, we made our way upstairs, and through a maze of halls to the office. The ladies in the office, who spoke almost no English, understood enough to be excited about our visit and the 1931 photo I showed them.

One tall woman climbed a precarious step stool to unlock a cabinet high above the office doorway. She reached inside to retrieve the list of St. Georg Gymnasium graduates from the years 1899 to 1929. They asked my father's name. We shared it, along with his birth year, knowing full well they would not find it there. Nor did they find an entry for Uncle Kurt.

Nevertheless, in their excitement, the office ladies continued to engage. "There is someone you should meet," one woman communicated to me. She proceeded to make a phone call, and I heard her say, "Monika."

The history teacher was also the teacher of Holocaust studies. Monika greeted us with a warm smile.

To our relief, Monika was fluent in English. She toured us around the school for two wonderful, history-filled hours. We saw the school's museum, visited the auditorium space, and explored the old-style classroom display. My techie-husband enjoyed examining the antique items in a glass-paned cabinet. "Wow, you really have some old instruments!" Seth said.

"Do you know what that one is called?" Monika asked.

"That's a galvanometer, a volt meter." Seth's answer delighted Monika.

We moved on to examine the photos and newspaper articles in one of the stairwells where Monika shared some of Bocholt's history.

It was in this moment that I started realizing there was another point of view. They, the German people, had a connection with the past—the distant past, and the more painful recent past. Their history was not entirely based on textbooks. They lived inside the pain and the shame.

Monika shared that, as a Holocaust educator, she had volunteered at Yad Vashem, the World Holocaust Remembrance Center, a memorial and museum in Israel that remembers those who perished and those who were persecuted during the Holocaust. Yad Vashem also honors the heroic Jewish people and righteous gentiles who fought Nazi oppression and helped protect Jewish people in need. There, Monika and other German educators learned how to teach the Holocaust from the perspective of the victims rather than that of the perpetrators.

As we circled back to the starting location of our tour, one of the women in the office shared more about Monika's work. "You know, she is also the coordinator of the exchange program between Bocholt and a school in the United States."

The program the woman referred to had been started forty years earlier by a teacher in a US school who grew up in eastern Germany. She sought to replicate a similar successful exchange program between a school in America and one in France. "This American school is in Massachusetts," the woman said.

"Oh? We're from Massachusetts," I said. "Do you know the name of the town?" The words came out of my mouth at the exact moment my eyes made contact with a plaque that answered my question.

"It is called Canton," she said.

"No, really?! We live in Sharon, Massachusetts," I said. "In the town next to Canton. We've lived there for thirty years, and I didn't know."

Word spread through the Gymnasium about our visit. The principal left a meeting to find us, to say hello, and take a photo together.

My father did not attend a public secondary school in Germany. Nevertheless, this Bocholt school in front of which his photo had been taken would forever link many people. Across oceans and generations, some of us would meet again.

This experience was one of my most healing moments in Germany. And the set of events that happened before it—my visit to the old cemetery—was one of my saddest. Somehow the sadness and the joy intertwined in my heart, the beauty of one moment, together with its burdens, highlighted the other.

I wanted to believe that the photo of my father in front of that building I could not at first identify had been planted there for me to discover. A moment of beschert, a gift, meant to be. A photo of fate. My father's family perhaps stopping on their way back home from a cemetery visit to snap a photo of young Walter in front of the St. Georg Gymnasium in anticipation of his attending school there one day.

I wondered how many school children and their teachers in the 1930s looked out of their school windows to view the old Jewish cemetery where both Solly and Eduard lay at rest.

Before we left, Monika and I exchanged contact information.

We planned to stay in touch, though we would not yet know the extent to which our lives would intertwine.

Back home, as the days and months moved on, I pondered why I had met Monika. I made up stories and imagined reasons. Perhaps she would be my key to Bocholt. Perhaps she would invite me to share my family's story with her students every year or two, and my family would, in some small and entirely inadequate yet meaningful way, be remembered in the town of my ancestors.

I wondered, too, if Monika made up her own stories about the purpose of our first meeting.

CHAPTER 17

THE SYNAGOGUE

AT HOME, THE FIRST TIME I noticed the clipping from the newspaper *Aufbau*, I disregarded it because I hadn't yet connected it to my father's story. But the next time I journeyed through the documents he'd left me, I finally knew what I was looking at.

As I touched the yellowed page, my finger traced the outline of the Ten Commandments remnant that appeared next to the article. The hairs on my neck prickled.

My father and Oma had read the German-language *Aufbau* with great interest when I was a child. They would chuckle at the cartoons while, I'm sure, they also anguished privately at other news. My father had ripped out page fifteen of the January 20, 1984, edition. I could picture him tearing it, not cutting it carefully with a pair of scissors. Perhaps, out of surprise and excitement, he had left the rough edges. With a sense of incompleteness, he had then stored it with his German and Dutch documents and photos. All for me to find, but only after my first Bocholt visit.

The short article included a photo. I placed this artifact in my view as I cued up my father's testimony video:

And I have a photograph of the fragments of the tablets, of the Ten Commandments, which was on top of the door, the entrance where you walk in ...

My father looked upwards, to the left, as though imagining his synagogue as it once was. He lifted his right hand high, then his left hand to meet it. With his forefingers, he traced the outline of the tablets.

... which was recovered after the war, and they are still there, somewhere.

WHILE MORITZ BEGINS to execute his escape plan in the Rösters' dining room that morning of November 10, 1938, he is vaguely aware of the scope of devastation of Jewish homes and businesses throughout the town. The early light reveals the violence done to the Bocholt synagogue and the destruction of a 140-year-old Jewish community.

The Torah scroll, the holiest object in Judaism, the item that requires people to fast for forty days if it even touches the floor, is no longer in its ark of protection. Instead, it lies helpless, torn, and vulnerable, each holy letter and the holy white space surrounding each letter, all left to rot, on the floor. Outside the synagogue, charred items lie in the street amid the broken glass from the smashed windows. Inside, the benches are destroyed, and prayer books are strewn about, many of them torn.

About 267 synagogues are destroyed across the country overnight, most burned to the ground. In Bocholt, the brownshirts had gotten as far as spreading gasoline on the synagogue floor and setting a small fire. But before they could see the building engulfed in flames, one of the men, a carpenter, had ordered, "Put out the fire immediately, or I'll beat you to death." His shop, next door, was filled with wooden window and door frames and other lumber products and would be at risk if the synagogue caught fire.

The marauders dismantle the set of stone tablets inscribed with the Ten Commandments from its home above the synagogue's entrance and break them.

AT THIS POINT IN MY JOURNEY to understand what happened to my family—my father's lived experience—my research and my visits to Germany began to intertwine. I'd heard Avivah Zornberg, a Torah scholar and author, once say something that resonated deeply with me: "You tell a story to get some sense of meaning."

One day, as I viewed my father's testimony video, it was as if time collapsed. I imagined my father telling me about his life, as if he were still alive. Instead of sitting in his flowered armchair recording his testimony, my father was in my living room, in my house in Sharon.

"The tablets, they are still there. Somewhere." My father looked directly at me.

I moved toward my father, eager to share some monumental news. "I know where, Dad! How I wish I could share this with you. And if only I could ask you a few questions."

He looked at me, expectantly. "Ja?"

"How did you feel when you read in the *Aufbau* that the synagogue building was entirely destroyed, having fallen victim to Allied bombings in 1945? That the tablet fragments were excavated from near the old synagogue entrance in the early 1980s? What did you feel when you learned there are no longer any Jews in Bocholt?"

"The building. I don't know what happened to the building," my father continued, though he had learned about its destruction. He looked into the distance. "They did never burn our synagogue because behind it, adjacent to the synagogue, was a lumber yard that belonged to a Nazi. He prevented this from happening, so they just demolished the synagogue instead."

Breathless now, I was eager to share more with him. "Let me show you the video I took from a place on the cobblestone sidewalk. On my first trip to Bocholt, I stood right where the inside of the synagogue would have been, where you attended services as a boy. Dad, look! See how the Bocholters 'remember' the location of the synagogue with dark gray rectangular stones, marking the footprint of the lost sanctuary space." I traced the outline of the image with my finger, in case it was not immediately apparent to him.

Then, hesitant to remind my father of the memories he could never forget, with a softer voice I added, "And I can show you how they commemorated Kristallnacht on its eightieth anniversary. Candles and stones mark a visit, and wreaths dot the area in front of the memorial stone. A list of the Jewish residents forcibly taken from Bocholt and, ultimately, killed is also there."

My pace evened out, but I was still tense, frustrated. "I paid my respects at the memorial stone. But your father and uncle are not listed on it since they weren't deported from Bocholt to be murdered."

I sat next to my father's feet, on the ottoman, leaning in toward him as he slumped forward at this reminder.

"Uncle Kurt had not been commemorated. Anywhere. And your father was commemorated only on a single Page of Testimony in Yad Vashem, submitted by Oma. But now, there's also a book listing those Bocholters who perished in the Holocaust, which includes a short biography of each of the 178 Bocholter victims."

To transport my father with me to the Bocholt synagogue site, I took his hand. "Let's go inside the building that replaced the synagogue. See, it's now an insurance company office."

My father and I walked toward the service representatives seated at their desks inside, awaiting customers to assist. They moved out of the way to make space for us as we viewed the large bulletin board display about the former synagogue. The board was prominently titled: Synagoge der Jüdischen Gemeinde Bocholt, Synagogue of the Bocholt Jewish community, (1798–1942).

One drawing on the bulletin board depicted the small yet stately building as it once appeared or had been planned. A fence surrounded the property and lollipop-shaped trees adorned the street edge. Decorative pillars flanked the entry door, which was topped by a Magen David and a menorah. A tablet-shaped adornment appeared near the roof, above a wall that separated the two tall windows that open to the street.

"Dad, do you remember it this way?" I asked.

My father responded by pointing to the photograph that took our breath away. It was the one that showed the inside of the synagogue.

"Uncle Kurt made that photo," he said.

My father told me what I had already learned. In the photo, sconces filled with tall white candles were affixed on the geometrically patterned wallpaper on either side of the ark. In front of the ark was the reader's table, where the Torah would be placed when it was read, until it was returned to its ark of protection.

I added to the photo's biography. "This was the only photograph known to Bocholters of the inside of the building. Perhaps they will add due credit to Kurt Herzfeld for the photograph next time they update the display."

"Ja," my father said. He was otherwise quiet, taking it all in.

Underneath the bulletin board we saw a large, green-covered book, a monumental undertaking by Josef Niebur, with Hermann Oechtering. "This is the book in which your father and Uncle Kurt are commemorated, three information-packed pages about each of them," I said.

My father enjoyed watching me turn the page, open to that of Salamon Seif, a neighbor of the synagogue and its caretaker, to that of his own father,

Moritz Stern. Perhaps the next school group that would go through might ask who this man was before the teacher turned the page back.

Then the flood of questions came, swirling in my head, some I didn't know I had. "Dad, what was it like to attend services? To celebrate holidays? To be Jewish in your home while being persecuted everywhere else?"

Now I slumped my shoulders, while still I watched my father. It would take more real-life trips to Europe and years of imagined conversations with him to learn everything I wanted to know. But in that imagined moment, I stopped myself from asking more. Slowly, I raised my finger to point at the central image on the bulletin board, above the synagogue rendering, to the drawing he noticed long before my barrage of questions. It was a photo of the Ten Commandments tablets.

"Ja," he said. "This was the image I saved from the *Aufbau* for you to find, finally!" My father smiled broadly and nodded his head, his eyes glistening. He noticed, in this image on the bulletin board, the outline surrounding small areas within the tablets that were found and replicated in a memorial outside this building. In the place next to where the Holy Ark once stood.

In my fantasy trip with my father, we walked back outside the synagogue-now-insurance- company to the former location of the Holy Ark. We wanted to view the memorial together—father and daughter.

Only two complete words remained of the shiny granite tablets: both the short, two-letter Hebrew word "lo," which we usually translated as "Thou shalt not," and the most complete commandment #6—where "Thou shalt not" is followed by the first two letters of the next word, *murder*. Thou shalt not murder. More accurately, *thou shalt not mur* ...

The irony was not lost on me, as it was not lost on the person who wrote about it on the Bocholt town's website. The commandment to not murder had been broken.

"This is a replica. Where are the originals?" my father asked.

"I'll show you." I floated with my father across the old part of town to the Bocholt City Museum, into the basement, to the farthest corner, in order to stand in front of the Holocaust-era display case. Amongst the Nazi items, we saw the remnants of the original Ten Commandments tablets from the Bocholt synagogue.

Then my father no doubt noticed the shelf under the tablet remnants, the one containing a book called *Mein Kampf,* with the face of the book's author, his eyes glaring upward from the book cover to the remnants of the tablets. Or maybe he stared directly at us. I was not quite certain.

The other items in this museum case related to the Nazi era and did nothing to dissipate the shock waves that still reverberated in me. Next to *Mein Kampf* were other Nazi items, including a small book with the title: *Gott Mit Uns, God with Us.* Though not directly a Nazi saying, it has been used over centuries. Yet, I wondered, who *was* God with during the war years?

I moved my gaze to an empty wall. I weighed if I would have shared this troubling experience I'd had in the Bocholt City Museum with my father.

Instead, I imagined us floating together, back to America. My father landed softly on the chair that enveloped his body, the chair arms supporting his arms. The ottoman similarly supporting his legs crossed at the ankles.

I took his hands in mine and breathed in deeply. I gazed straight ahead at the ghost of my father. He was not crying on the outside. But it was time to close our conversation with a collection of words I could not say aloud to him.

"Your sadness is too deep for me to bear. Though you are always with me in spirit, I will not take you back there with me. I will not show you the videos I took. And I will not ask you all my questions. Whether you actively or passively taught me this, I will not discuss this with you. It is all too painful."

I ended my imagined time with my father by hugging him tightly. I kissed his warm, comforting cheek, feeling the hints of stubble catching my lip. And then I let him go.

As much as I wanted the distance to close between us, for me to be with my father again, truly in his presence, it was not to be. My father was unable to talk to me about his pain when he was alive. And I was fully aware that his corporeal self was gone now. I was left to learn about his life on my own.

I would continue to seek answers to my questions. To explore the pain he must have experienced. The pain I now felt. I wanted to name it. I needed to talk more with German people in our ancestral hometowns, especially in Bocholt. I longed to hear that there were courageous people so that I could continue the healing process for our family. For our children, grandchildren, great-grandchildren.

One day I wanted to take my father's grandchildren—some of whom he never had the chance to meet—to see these sites. I'd begun to visualize something new. My version of the Stern-Herzfeld Bocholt walking tour.

CHAPTER 18

LIMOUSINES AND LUNCHES

ESCAPE DAY. That's what we called our journey to retrace my family's escape route of eighty years ago. In June 2018, Seth, Josh, and I entered one rental car. David and Robin, my brother and sister-in-law, got into another—our respective personal limousines.

David and Robin had joined us midtrip for a couple of days to visit the most profound of the survival locations. My brother, with his curly, graying, dirty-blond hair, hazel eyes, and freckled face had always been a hard worker, a serious person who lived his life to the fullest after having suffered two heart attacks in his thirties. The connection between his health and my grandfather Moritz's heart ailment wasn't lost on us.

Robin had a huge camera around her neck, so large that she had to hold the long lens in place as she walked so it wouldn't bruise her body. A generally fun person who laughs a lot, she was uncharacteristically quiet that day.

In our caravan, we drove the fastest route to Vehlingen, the town that my grandfather had told his limousine driver to head toward on that long-ago

November morning. Passing farmland, with the Dutch border in the distance, I was aware this wasn't the exact route my family had taken, since this highway probably hadn't been built yet. There would have been a more direct route. A ride I tried to imagine as I peered out the window at the passing scenery.

I'd been in a limousine only one time with my father. It was also the only time I ever saw him cry. My brother, father, Oma, and I were being driven to the funeral home where my mother would be eulogized, then taken to the cemetery to be laid to rest. She'd succumbed to her second round of breast cancer at the age of fifty-seven.

I couldn't begin to imagine, even decades later, how Oma coped with seeing my father, her only child, in such great pain. That day, my father reached for my hand as his tears fell. I was twenty-three at the time of my mother's death, and David, at twenty-one, hadn't graduated from college yet. I showed my outer strength at that moment, as I held my father's hand tightly. Back then I was not aware of his own childhood limousine ride or the gravity of the trip he and his family had once taken.

IT'S 1938, and the limousine driver follows the directions provided by Moritz, making his way through the farmland on the outskirts of Bocholt, toward the Dutch border. Hilde looks out the window at the passing fields. She reaches for her twelve-year-old son's hand. As she sheds silent tears, this mother wonders if she will ever again see her beloved Heimat, the only town and the only street she has ever lived on.

Walter takes her hand and holds it tightly, his own fear and sorrow milling about in his head.

As the farmland approaches the edge of a forest, Moritz points to the window. "Here! We get out here."

Moritz ushers the passengers out with hushed urgency. "Run through the forest. That way," he says, pointing toward the border.

The five family members don't think. They simply do as they are told. Everyone runs through the dense forest with their pajama pants hanging out under their winter coats.

Moritz catches up, positioning himself in front of his family, leading the way. Suddenly, he turns to face them and holds up his right hand. "Wait!!" The forest edge now confronts them.

Moritz explains the next phase, as he outlines the shape of a nearby ditch in pantomime. "Go, down in that ditch there. Stay low."

The family members squat in the dry ditch and catch their breath as they await the next instruction. Moritz knew there was a German gendarme, border guard, nearby. After a few minutes, the border guard bicycles home for lunch. In fifteen minutes, his replacement will arrive.

Moritz marvels, momentarily, at how his bicycle trips to customers across the border have enabled him to become familiar with this gendarme's schedule.

Once the gendarme is out of sight, Moritz scrambles out of the ditch, and everyone follows behind him. Selma has some difficulty, but still she manages, thanks to the heavy dose of adrenaline coursing through her body.

"Run to that farm." Moritz again points out the next location. "It is owned by a customer of our store."

The five family members run past the barn, toward a horse fence. As soon as they walk through the horse fence's gate, on the same farmer's property, they are in Holland. The German police cannot arrest them here. Only the Dutch police have jurisdiction.

OUR TWO RENTAL CARS aimed for the tree line we'd found on Google Maps satellite view. We estimated that this tree line was now the edge of what was once the middle of a dense forest.

We turned right onto Pferdehorsterstrasse, the street that runs along the woods, and searched for a suitable picnic site. We decided we would need sustenance before crossing the border somewhere near these woods.

"Wait, stop!" I cried. "Pull over!"

I knew we were in the right place. A picnic table, large enough to comfortably accommodate the five of us and our fixings appeared in front of the first home we passed. The site came complete with a municipal-strength trash barrel.

"Have you ever seen a picnic table in front of someone's property like this?" I asked.

Josh responded. "Clearly, it was meant for us. Our family must have been in this spot."

"Do you think the woods across the street once reached to the border?"

"Probably. They had to reach far enough to give them cover to get very close to the border," my brother said.

David offered us some of the cherries we'd bought that morning at the Bocholt farmer's market, and I divvied up the slice of Schwarzwälder Kirschtorte, the black forest cherry cake we had purchased from a bakery in Bocholt around the corner from my family's former home.

I took a cherry. "I know I've done a lot of planning for this trip, especially escape day, but I couldn't have planned something like a picnic table, right in this place. It's as though it popped up here for us in the exact moment we needed it."

"I wonder what other signs we'll find," Robin said.

After we ate, we packed up and returned to our cars. Seth drove the lead car as I navigated us toward the Dutch border on the northern part of this town of Vehlingen. We turned onto a street conveniently called

Sternenbuschstrasse. Another sign, we decided, the family name Stern neatly contained in the street name. We passed horse fences, and then a sign directed us left toward Megchelen. The road was narrow, in retrospect, probably not intended for cars, but rather for walkers and cyclists, of which there were many on this sunny and cool, early summer day. The border gate appeared in front of us.

Although the borders were now open in Europe, this particular crossing was closed to cars. We pulled to the edge of the pathway, leaving enough room for pedestrians and cyclists to pass.

"Do you think we might get a ticket?" I asked.

"I don't think so," Josh said.

I silently worried that my son was wrong, or worse, that we might be towed. I said, "I don't care." Nothing was more important to me at that moment. "This is our family's escape route," I said. "We need to be here. Doing this. Right now. Let's go."

Stepping out of the cars, we walked toward the border. It wasn't much of a border crossing, just a white gate, about four feet high.

I searched for a ditch of some sort. The place where my grandfather had told the rest of my family to "Wait!"

The ditch, as my father had described it, was a wide, shallow depression in the ground. I tried to imagine how my family could have hidden in such a place undetected. They could have covered themselves with leaves or other debris, while they trembled, whimpered softly. They had to have been afraid for their lives, though I believed they must have trusted Moritz's plan. Even as they worried that this was the end for all of them.

I approached the white gate, looking left and right along the border, taking in the green and tan farmland and a cluster of tall trees a couple hundred feet away.

There. I saw it. Next to me, extending to the left and the right sides of the pathway. A ditch. A dry ditch. Surrounded by tall grasses. It was deeper than

I had pictured, deep enough for me to squat low and not be seen by, say, a German border guard whose job it was to watch over this crossing.

Suddenly it made sense how my family could squat down in this ditch that looked like a dry riverbed, or perhaps a hand-dug irrigation channel, waiting for the gendarme to bicycle off to lunch. The shock, I realized, was a combination of seeing the spot where my family might have crossed the border and also seeing the ditch where they might have hidden. I was amazed that we were able to locate that spot, and stand right there, right then. We stood there in safety and in warmth. Joy at the discovery was mixed with deep, deep sadness.

Still transfixed by my surroundings, I leaned on the border gate. I looked down the path in front of me. The path into Holland—the path to freedom. The gray pavement, wide enough for two cyclists to ride side by side, was a long welcome mat. It beckoned me toward a tan brick home with white shutters a quarter mile away. A broad carpet of green, spread out widely on either side of the pavement, was punctuated by early summer stalks of corn and a stray tall evergreen. The farm we stood in front of seemed to be entirely in Holland.

I was getting so close to my father's story. And yet, I needed more. I needed to know if this was truly the right place. Though there was an abundance of horse fences, and their respective horses, on our cautious drive toward the border, there was no evidence of horse fences or barns in the green expanse in front of me in Holland.

Our family walked down the path, passing the tan house, then a smaller white home next to a silo.

"I'm not sure this is the right path. It looks like this farm is fully in Holland, doesn't it?" I asked my family.

"Does it really matter?" Robin said. "If it's not this farm, we know we are within a half mile of the location, right?"

"I suppose," I said. But I remained stuck in my desire for precision. I needed to know the exact location for certain. So I could walk on the same ground my father had run on during his escape.

"Let's knock on the door of this house," Josh said. "Maybe they know something."

"I don't think so," I said. "I don't think they would be able to help us. Plus, we don't even know if this was the correct entry route of our family."

And so we continued, bypassing our opportunity to knock on the door of the tan house or that of the white house.

We didn't know which direction to head, yet signs propelled us forward. One pathway sign was in Dutch and German. It cleverly depicted the outline of a red heart that was also two hands clasped together, as though shaking in friendship. At the top, four red arrows pointed us forward, the words below "Auf dem Weg zur Freiheit" in German, "Op weg naar de vrijheid" in Dutch. On the way to freedom!

Later, I would learn that this was the trail the Allied forces had followed in 1945 as they liberated the region, but we were accepting this as our family's liberation trail.

Sensing that we were on the right path, Josh unpacked his drone, which he had brought in order to take aerial photos. "I feel so connected to Sabah's story," he said, using the Hebrew word for grandfather. "I'm glad we're retracing his path!" He sent up his drone to capture this moment, this place.

The drone's camera photographed the farmland below it, the tan house and the white house, and the silo. It took pictures of the landscape and the bucolic roadway occupied by an occasional horse and rider or cyclist. And it documented our family of five searching for something, seeking to walk in the footsteps of the flight of my father's family of five.

A local man approached Josh, speaking Dutch. "Goedendag," he began.

I watched from a distance, conflicted and concerned that we were overstepping by sending up a drone. Yet, I also wanted to engage with local Dutch people to learn if it was possible that my father had run along this road.

Josh smiled and packed up his drone, unsure if the man was interested in what he was doing or annoyed that his contraption was flying close to the silo. All of us were unaware that we would meet again.

JOSH AND I RETURNED to this idyllic village of Megchelen five months later, in November 2018, to explore an alternate escape route. We tried a different entry point, along a spot I had found on Google Maps, near what appeared to be structures on the German side of the border a few feet from structures on the Dutch side.

It was Thanksgiving morning, and I wanted to find out if this could have been a farm at one time, with horses and a barn on the German side.

Josh and I drove to the property that was on the Dutch side of the border. We walked from there through the border gate into Germany, where we found more ditches. Even deeper than the ones we saw a half mile away on our prior trip.

"I'm going to take some pictures," Josh said. He hopped into one of the ditches and squatted down. He'd be able to see what my father would have seen eighty years earlier. Dirt, dried grass, stray leaves.

When I got closer, I could clearly see my twenty-eight-year-old son. And I could also imagine my twenty-five-year-old uncle Kurt and his family in that spot eighty years earlier. From a distance, the family would have been hidden well enough.

That morning with Josh was windy and cold. The kind of weather for which I had purchased my silver, knee-length coat with a hood. The kind of coat that kept the wind from penetrating the fabric and attacking the skin, the insides of the body. I zipped it up to my chin as I walked along the small, paved path back toward Holland.

To my left was the set of structures I had found. Defunct buildings that could have included a horse barn, I decided. Then a fence. Then a home, in Holland, a stone's throw from the German structures.

I looked at Josh, who had caught up with me. "It was in this spot! Eighty years ago, this month, our family ran across the border. Right here!"

"I think you're right," he said.

Overcome with emotion on that day of thanksgiving, it was hard to speak more words, but I tried. "I give thanks that we are able to be here."

"Look. The people who live here are watching us," Josh said.

We approached, but the couple did not understand my English question, so we attempted a conversation using my phone's translation app. "Did that used to be a horse farm? Part of this property?" I pointed out their backyard window toward the abandoned structures, a few feet away over the border.

There was no cell service, and all I could understand was, "Nee," no.

Convinced I had the right location, but frustrated that I could not be absolutely certain, Josh and I thanked our momentary hosts and continued on our way.

This was not the end of my fascination with this place. Nor was it the end of what I would learn about it.

IT WAS DURING OUR THIRD TRIP, in June 2019, that we confirmed the truth. Through a series of unlikely—but not unexpected, given how my journey had played out—events, we met a woman named Sonja, who lives on the outskirts of Bocholt. Sonja had joined us for part of a day we spent exploring my family's "places" in the downtown area. I had told her about the border crossing and how I yearned to know the correct crossing point.

Sonja smiled. "I know someone who will show us. I will pick you up from your hotel tomorrow at four and we will go there."

I had learned to go where fate would bring me, without making a fuss. Seth, Josh, and I hopped into Sonja's car at the designated time. We got out at a spot in Germany and met Betja, who walked us along the border until we came to a gate. "Here is where they crossed," she confirmed.

We arrived on foot at the same border crossing Josh and I had explored in November 2018, but from a different direction.

"We talked to the couple in that house," I explained with disbelief, pointing.

"I know them," Betja responded. We knocked on their door. No one answered.

"If only they were home! They would have been so amazed!" I said. I was disappointed—even surprised—that they weren't waiting for us.

"Would you like to come to my house for tea? I live close by," Betja urged. We graciously accepted.

As we approached her home, I understood a little more of the complex, interwoven paths that had been set before me. We had walked past Betja's home during our June 2018 exploration of the border. It was the white house with a silo.

I was giddy with excitement. As we took a seat in Betja's living room, I busily searched for a photo, then handed them my tablet. "I have a picture for you."

"That is our house!"

"Yes, Josh took that from his drone last year when we were here."

"Ah!" Betja's husband became excited as well. "I remember you, with your drone. I said hello to you. I was interested in your drone."

There must have been a dozen, maybe a hundred, tiny events that had occurred to bring us to this moment of confluence.

Betja handed me something. "I would like you to have this, Irene."

She couldn't have known that I had started collecting tree images, beech trees, trees of life, one of the symbols of this personal journey I was on. Or perhaps she did notice the tree necklace I wore. But that she happened to have this gift for me was beyond comprehension. I looked at the three-strand bracelet, a series of beads on pieces of leather and string, accentuated with a round charm of a tree, its branches stretched tall and wide, extending out as far as it could reach.

CHAPTER 19

ONE LETTER

THE FIRST TIME WE ATTEMPTED to recreate escape day, in June 2018, all signs had pointed to us being on the right track. The signs would keep on coming. On that summer day, however, the five of us—Seth, Josh, David, Robin, and I—were, unknowingly, on the wrong path. Still, it was where we were meant to be, as we stood at the intersection next to the white house and silo.

A group of cyclists had stopped to talk to us that day. One man spoke German, so I attempted to explain what we were seeking: a horse farm that my family had walked through on their way from Germany to Megchelen in 1938.

"Mein Vater über die Grenze von Deutschland zu Holland in die Welt Krieg, zu ein Bauern mit Blücher. Wo ist eine Blücher Bauern?" I asked in my fractured German: My father over the border from Germany to Holland in the World War, to a farm with horses. Where is a horse farm? David and Robin stepped aside and giggled through the interaction. Apparently, David realized that "Blücher" didn't mean "horse" but was a humorous allusion to an old movie.

The kind man conferred with his friends, but they had no idea what I was talking about. He directed us: "Biegen Sie hier links ab. Gehen Sie zum Camping auf dieser Strasse und erbitten Sie weitere Auskünfte." We understood enough: Turn left and stop at the campground, where someone might have more information.

I worried that some local people might call the police on us. The thought of the cars we had left behind in Germany was also distressing me. Would they still be there when we returned? Even with all my worries, for now, our mission hung more heavily on me. But we could use another sign.

We weren't disappointed.

A table appeared on the side of the road, with a red-and-white-checkered tablecloth. As we came closer, we could see what was for sale on the table. Bowls of juicy, sweet-looking, dark-red cherries. Cherries! We still had our bag from the farmer's market in Bocholt in the car, unfinished from our picnic lunch. We didn't need any more cherries. But my father's cherry tree in the garden was never far from my mind. I insisted we stop and buy another kilo.

The cherry seller, a Julia Child look-alike, spoke no English, but still I managed with my scant German. "Meine Familie kam von Bocholt nach Megchelen in neunzehnhundertachtunddreissig." I had learned my numbers well and "1938" rolled off my tongue.

Understanding enough of what I was saying, Julia held up one finger. *One moment.* She rushed inside to retrieve something she insisted was of interest to us.

When she returned with a book, I could see it was about Megchelen during the war years. It was titled *De Moezeköttel.* I didn't know what that meant and couldn't pronounce it, but the photo on the cover showed some sheep grazing in front of a brick structure. Alongside a ditch.

It looked like the area where we were standing. Julia flipped to the page with a photo of a school building that had been used as a hospital for those injured in the war. It was clear. I had to purchase this book even though I could not understand it. We paid Julia who, it turns out, was the owner of the campground the cyclist had directed us to.

Five euros for the cherries, and another twenty euros for the book. One day I would get it translated and seek out the names of locals who might have helped my family, I thought. Or perhaps I would simply look at the photos and captions and remember this trip. Somehow, I decided, it would assist me in my quest to grow closer to my father.

"Let's go back to the cars," I said. In part, I felt satisfied that something auspicious had just happened. Partly, I yielded to the pit in my stomach about needing to claim our vehicles.

As we retraced our steps back to the car, we talked about this path.

"Let's get a picture of us in front of the 'freedom' sign." Robin raised the camera she wore around her neck. "I can't believe this sign is here. Whatever it is for!"

The five of us paused during our leisurely walk along a path toward freedom so Robin could snap some photos. My family of 1938 had had no time to linger. They ran. Once again, I was forced to hold contrasting feelings. Deep sadness and deep gratitude. My heart simply did not know what to do with it all. My family of 1938 must have battled fear and the uncertainty of their next steps. They had to keep moving, with no time to reflect. My family of 2018, too, had to move on.

A few minutes after managing our respective seven-point turns to avoid the ditch we had parked astride, I continued to navigate the long way around, the drivable way, toward the Megchelen town center. We passed cute brick and stone homes with neatly manicured yards. We located the stately clock-topped Catholic church.

We needed a respite. Just as my father and his family probably did after running through woods, squatting in a ditch, and running across a farm into this village. My intuition directed us to the smaller of two cafés. But it was closed.

We parked across the street and walked to the larger café a block away and sat at an umbrella-shaded outdoor table.

The waiter brought us our coffees and teas and served Josh the peach ice cream he'd ordered, with a dash of liquor on top.

I looked around. "I don't see any gray-haired people to talk to about the horse farm."

"Neither do I," Robin said. "But let's relax for a few minutes before we continue on the escape route."

I gave in, mindful of this street along the Liberation Route. Sipping my cappuccino, I kept thinking about my father and his family. According to my father's translation of the local police report, on the morning of November 10, 1938, they'd arrived at the home of a family named "Düring."

I'd surmised the family had lived somewhere near the town center. I tried to visualize the experience, and I recounted the standoff as my father had described it in his testimony video.

FROM THE FARM THAT STRADDLES the Dutch border with Germany, Walter and his family run up the street toward the Megchelen village center. The brisk air of November 10, 1938, stings their pajama-clad legs. Two sets of police approach the family, both prepared to arrest the refugees.

"Come in here." A baker steps out of his house and calls Moritz inside. "What happened?"

The man sees panic on Moritz's face as he looks down to see the pajamas underneath the coat Moritz wears.

Moritz explains, briefly, but enough for his momentary host to understand that the family is in grave danger.

The leader of the first group of police steps up to the door. "We are arresting you. It is for the better." Wiendels, the village veldwachter, policeman, speaks to Moritz, but he is looking over his shoulder, nodding toward the quickly approaching Dutch Marechaussee, federal police, now within earshot.

"No, we arrest you," the lead marechaussee calls out. "You crossed the border illegally."

Walter stands behind his father, who in turn stands behind the host. Both are close enough to hear the ensuing argument between the two sets of police.

Wiendels responds. "Nee, they are under our jurisdiction. We got to them first. We're arresting them. They are in our custody."

"You can't do that," the federal officer says. "The state is more important than your little town."

"You will have to take it up with the Congress. Take it up with the queen. We have the law. And these people are in our custody. Over our dead bodies you will get to these people."

The lead marechaussee sneers, addressing Moritz. "You know, you may call yourself lucky. I wouldn't arrest you. I would call up the Gestapo or the SS and hand you back to them at the border."

I TOOK THE FINAL SIP of my coffee at the outdoor café and shuddered to think of how things might have turned out. "They—we—were so lucky the 'good cops' arrested our family."

"Boy, this whole story sinks in so much more when you put yourself in their shoes for a few hours," David said. "When you can picture more of what it was like for our family." My brother looked up the street again. It was as though we both half expected to see the police appear.

But there were no police nearby. No one to argue with us about being in their country. We rose from the comfortable seats. It was time to leave.

Still, something urged me toward that other, closed café. The small park across the street, in front of our waiting cars, drew me in, pointing me toward something important, pulling me like a divining rod, except I didn't understand why.

The smell of white hydrangeas, with their tint of green on this warm and sunny day, filled the air. I imagined my father and his family standing on the street, or in this park, on a cold November day.

I wished my father and his family could be there with me, to take in the sweetness of the petaled, bright-yellow spots of sunshine growing on nearby vines. I longed for them to feel the softness of the fuzzy, pink balls of flower happiness.

In my father's reality, his family was escorted into a police vehicle. Perhaps with a little force to show the marechaussee who was in charge. In his translation of the police report, my father had identified the baker as Mr. Düring. I imagine Mr. Düring would have been relieved that my father and his family were in the custody of these local police, whom he knew would treat them well.

"Come on," Seth said. "Let's go. We've been here long enough." My husband pulled me back from my daydreams, though if I'd had my way, I would have sat on a bench and imagined a conversation with my father about this place.

I would have asked him, "Exactly where were you and your family arrested?" Perhaps he would have walked me to the exact spot.

Sliding back to reality and into the front passenger seat, I shared my unexplained need to return to this park, and to its guardian: the quirky bronze statue of a worn farmer with his two cows.

AFTER RETURNING HOME TO MASSACHUSETTS from the June trip, I resumed my research in preparation for my next visit in November 2018. Opening the Dutch book I'd purchased from the Julia look-alike, I scoured it for the family name "Düring." Perhaps one family member had been injured, or worse, killed during the war. An address might be included. No luck. But I was certain the book had to be the key to something. All those signs had brought the book to us.

I emailed the book's author a cautious message. I left out family names in my request for his assistance. The author shared my message with a Megchelen friend, who replied, "You are talking about the family Moritz Stern, who fled in 1938 from Bocholt to the 'safe' Holland."

The only clue I had provided was my name in my signature line, including my geboren, birth, name of Stern.

The message continued. "The family crossed the border at Megchelen. They found a place at Jan Bernard Düking. He was a baker and grocer in the village."

A small typo in my father's translation of the police report, an "r" instead of a "k." This tiny mistake might have kept me from knowing the name of yet another person who had helped my family to survive. One typo could have kept me from acknowledging the name, and it could have caused me to postpone my visit to the spot where my family had stood for a few hours, perhaps only a few minutes, until their arrest.

My new Megchelen friend shared with me that most of the Düking children had died, but that the oldest, who was ninety-three years old, knew they had had refugees in their home. So many from my father's generation were gone by the time my search was getting started. That wouldn't stop me from doing whatever I could to keep all these stories—especially my family's—alive.

My correspondent emailed me a photo of Jan Bernard Düking and his house circa 1938. Düking was a serious and calm-looking man, wearing a suit, white shirt, and a tie. His dark-rimmed round glasses obscured his eyes as he looked off to the side.

And my correspondent shared one more piece of information: the address of the Düking house was Millingsweg #12.

From my home in the United States, I immediately visited the address virtually. Using Google Street View, I looked around. My eyes widened as the image revealed itself. Directly across the street was the lovely park marked by the quirky bronze statue of a worn man with his two cows.

Next door to the former Düking home was the closed café I had wanted to visit.

WITHIN A FEW MONTHS OF MY DISCOVERY, I would again visit the park with the bronze statue and the house across the street that had belonged to Düking.

I would stand in front of Düking's former home, comparing the photo I had with the current structure. Many of the details were identical, even though it had been rebuilt. A cold wind nipped at me as I tried to sense what it might have been like for my father to stand in the street in front of this house, awaiting arrest. And the unknown next step in his father's escape plan.

CHAPTER 20

WILHELMINA, QUEEN OF THE NETHERLANDS

OVER A PERIOD OF A COUPLE OF YEARS, I worked to piece together my family's movements from Bocholt, across the border into Holland, and finally to the United States. In all, I took three trips to Europe, and I performed countless smaller actions that allowed me to follow in their footsteps. My attempt to map their journey was not as linear as their actual journey was. At times, I would read a document or view a landscape and only a part of the story was revealed. An example of this happened on my second trip to Holland in November 2018, with Josh.

Josh and I explored downtown Gendringen, a more robust town than Megchelen, though still small. Over a late-afternoon snack of vegetarian bitterballen, I told Josh that my research hadn't turned up the place mentioned in the police report, where my family had initially stayed. The deep-fried meal was surprisingly satisfying given that I had been feeling quasi-guilty for not making myself go hungry for the day. After all, I reasoned, my family surely experienced many days of hunger.

Searching for the hotel Het Posthuis, I led us across a street called Bringenborg, whose significance I didn't yet know. I had a yellowed, fray-edged letter that had been sent to my great-grandmother on November 24, 1938. It had been sent to her at "Hause Alex Cussel, Gendringen," but it excluded the street address on Bringenborg.

My quest was to locate the home in which my father said he had first stayed. That I knew I could find. In addition to his testimony video, my father had recorded a video of his only trip to Holland, in 1991, which included his visit to Gendringen. He'd been specific.

"There are two churches around here," I said to Josh. As we walked, I was alert, looking for signs. "My dad videoed the churches, then zoomed straight in front of where he stood. To a large estate-type home, where he said he had lived in Gendringen. There was a flagpole in front of the house."

"Do we know their name, the people who lived there?"

"Yes, my father said it was Spier," I told Josh. "What's really odd is that our family stayed in Gendringen for a few months until their 'furniture was cleared' and they 'had a place to go to.' My father said they were like 'poor people at the time.'"

"Their furniture?" Josh asked, engaged in the mystery I was attempting to resolve.

"I still haven't figured that one out. I know some photos from before Kristallnacht had made it safely to them somehow. But I can't figure out how their things were moved across the border."

"Well, what are the options?" Josh always got me to expand my thinking, to unlock the possibilities.

"Maybe an uncle still in Germany with connections? Or Harry Slager, the Dutch relative who managed Moritz's money?"

"Could Moritz have gone back himself with Kurt to help him?"

"I can't imagine that. Perhaps a neighbor. I've fantasized that Weber himself was responsible, but I quickly ruled out that possibility."

"You never know, maybe it *was* the man who 'bought' our family's business."

Josh left me feeling uneasy about this unknown. I would not uncover the mystery of the furniture's relocation for another year, after translating some of the eight hundred documents I would photograph in the Münster archives, on what would be my third visit to Germany.

But on this day, in Gendringen, Josh and I positioned ourselves in the spot my father must have stood to shoot his video decades earlier. In a parking lot between two old churches, we looked northeastward as my father once did.

Directly in front of us, through the trees, was a flagpole. Behind it was a large, estate-type home. We took a closer look. Unlike my father in 1991, we rang the doorbell. At this point, my son's risk-taking had rubbed off on me. I fidgeted, ready to run, but waited for the resident to open the door. My father would have been proud of our boldness.

The current resident, a woman a little older and a little taller than me with short, wavy hair, listened to our story. She told us that she'd recently moved in after retiring and was renovating the home. Hospitably, she invited us into the backyard, where we took in the plant-filled landscape, barren in November as it would have been for my father when he first arrived in 1938. The gardens, she told us, were much larger back then.

"Can you picture my father walking around back here when he was twelve?" I asked Josh.

"Of course! Do you think there were fish in this little pond? Maybe he fed them. I don't think he could have imagined what would happen next."

"I don't think anyone could."

Pleased with our discovery of the location where my father had videotaped the home between the two churches, Josh and I headed back toward our rental car. I felt a lump in my throat, experiencing my father's absence. "I can feel him looking down on us right now."

"He would really enjoy this," my father's look-alike grandson said.

Even so, as much as I had walked in my father's footsteps, I still needed more. "I wish I knew the location of Het Posthuis."

We paused to cross the Bringenborg street again. I noticed a bright-yellow, oval sign topped with a crown shape on the two-story brick building in front of us. "Look at that." I pointed to the sign. "Het Posthuis!"

But the doors were locked, and there were no people around to ask about this building.

Pleased that we had retraced what we could of my family's steps, in this town where they were not quite free but not yet imprisoned, I let it go. I took a deep breath and we continued on our way. My father was looking down on us that afternoon, as he had each day of our journey.

But that afternoon was different. I felt him watching us continue to unravel his story, slowly peeling away each layer. One step at a time. Savoring each moment of discovery. With each of those moments, my heart sensed a healing feeling, a wound closing.

Back at home, months later, I would be able to create a timeline of my family's first month in Holland based on the documents I had discovered. Filling in details where I needed to, I imagined complete scenes, aided by my full heart, its scars mixed with trickles of blood, augmented by tears.

IT'S 10 NOVEMBER 1938. Het Posthuis is a modest hotel in downtown Gendringen, two or three floors high and, like many buildings in the area, made of brick. It is here that the pajama-clad Stern-Herzfeld family sit in a room on the second floor. Their coats still covering their bodies for added warmth, they wonder how they will obtain their clothes, not to mention their precious photos and documents; blankets, pillows, and tablecloths; dishes and silverware; their beds and sofas and tables and chairs.

Kurt stares out the window at a scene of barren trees and fallen leaves stirred up by an uneasy wind. He yearns for his camera and mourns the loss of the photos he's left behind.

Hilde sits close to her husband, thinking about the Singer sewing machine they were so proud to have purchased. The journal of her holiday trips she might never see again.

Selma weeps quietly. She thinks about the synagogue she can no longer attend and the only home she's known for the past thirty-eight years. Her Heimat on Geburtsstrasse and the cemetery she can no longer visit.

Walter, newly twelve, yearns for a shred of comfort—the sketchpad and colored pencils he had used to make a holiday card for his family a couple of months ago. He worries about the children here and hopes they will not chase him, throw rocks at him, call him awful names.

Moritz, of course, is preoccupied with the next steps of his plan to keep his family safe. He is thankful to the village veldwachter, Wiendels, for placing them under house arrest. The man has posted police surveillance downstairs so no one can enter Het Posthuis and forcibly return the family to Germany. As Moritz fingers the meager Reichsmark in his coat pocket, he is relieved that he had had the foresight to smuggle cash across the border for just this eventuality. Although he isn't surprised it has come to this—that his planning had been necessary after all—he is horrified at what lies ahead. Both back home in Germany, where he vowed to never return, and in this new life he will build for himself and his family in another country.

"We will never return," Moritz says to the resigned and tacit agreement of his family.

In another part of town, Wiendels reports the situation to the burgemeester, town mayor, Jan Beaumont. This was an unusual situation, and Beaumont weighs his options: send the family back to Germany or protect them, at least for now, in Gendringen. The latter seems the only proper choice, even though the family had, after all, illegally crossed the border.

Burgemeester Beaumont consults with the attorney general and the acting director of police in Arnhem, the seat of the province in which Gendringen is located. After careful deliberation, he contacts the Department of Justice; someone there promises to get back to him with guidance.

In the meantime, Wiendels directs a trustworthy man to make the short trip to Bocholt to verify the account Moritz had shared at the Düking home earlier in the day. This person returns to Gendringen in the evening to report that the statement was absolutely correct. The large display windows of Mr. Stern's building had been nailed shut, covered with planks, and the place was guarded.

While the family awaits word of their fate, Moritz contacts his nephew. Harry Slager drives ninety minutes from his home in Enschede. He is an outspoken man and a creative and savvy insurance agent and house broker, who, when attending an evening of theater, had himself paged as a marketing gimmick to give the impression he was a highly sought-after advisor.

Harry is well dressed and has strikingly sad eyes; his left eye droops a bit, and his left ear sticks our further than his right. He tells Wiendels, "I will make two thousand Guilders available from Moritz Stern's bank account that I manage for him." He is referring to the funds Moritz had smuggled over the Dutch border to Aalten. Harry continues, "And I will make an advance payment toward the family's hotel bill at Het Posthuis. I have space for this family in Enschede. I would like to take them with me."

Because it had been established that Moritz "received favorable responses from the Argentine Consul in Stuttgart," it appears that the family will remain in Holland for a short time before proceeding to Argentina. But the mayor is not ready to release them from house arrest as he awaits direction from the Department of Justice.

11 November 1938. In the afternoon, the burgemeester speaks with the attorney general by telephone. The attorney general says, "You may grant the refugee family a temporary permit to stay in Gendringen. Provided that the family is not a burden to the municipality or more generally to the government."

Burgemeester Beaumont issues a permit for three days under the conditions that the family remain in the town and that Moritz report to the mayor's office each morning to ensure they have not left. The family is granted "some freedom of movement, inside the Village of Gendringen," and is given the option of remaining at Het Posthuis or living with one of the Jewish families in town.

Selma and Kurt move in with Alex and Saartje Cussel, up the street from Het Posthuis on the Bringenborg. Walter and his parents move in with the Spier family, whose home is a short distance from the two large churches in the town, a two-minute walk from Het Posthuis. The Spiers provide them clothing, warm bedding, and comforting foods. There are no children for Walter to interact with at this house, but he was used to being the only child in the home. He would, no doubt, find ways to occupy his time, working on art projects. And, in the warmer weather, walking the gardens nearby.

18 November 1938. Burgemeester Beaumont types up a report: "The Inspector of the Border Guard has today made the telephonic request no longer to grant a resident permit to the family Stern, but simply grant a stay without the necessity of a residence permit." Although Moritz is required to continue his daily reporting to the burgemeester's office, this is a temporary relief as the family enters the weekend.

21 November 1938. It is Monday morning. Selma dates the letter she is about to compose. The family is making plans to move to Enschede, but she feels the urgency of first recovering the personal belongings they've left behind in Bocholt. Sitting at a writing table, looking out one of the tall windows toward the cow barn in the backyard, Selma feels her host's clothing, still foreign on her body. Material unwanted yet appreciated. She thinks of her twenty-five-year-old son relegated to wearing the shirt and pants of a much older man as she gazes out at the young birch tree, its barren branches reaching upward as it prepares for the cold winter ahead.

"An den Oberbürgermeister Irrgang," she writes. Selma considers the best words to convince Bocholt's mayor to send her family's possessions to Gendringen. Twenty minutes later, the church bells chime, and Selma hands the completed letter to Kurt. She asks him to post it.

24 November 1938. A letter arrives, addressed to: "Frau Eduard Herzfeld im Hause Alex Cussel, Gendringen, Holland." The Bürgermeister's response is typed on a half-sheet page with the embossed beech-tree insignia of the city of Bocholt. It's a response that will eventually yellow and fray with age, as it would sit in Hilde's, then Walter's, possession. And later find its way to his daughter.

"Ihr Schreiben vom 21. ds. Mts. gelangte in meinen Besitz ... "

I have received your letter from 21 of this month and have passed it on to the responsible office. Your possessions are still available to you and I only put your apartment under lock and key to prevent unauthorized persons from entering.

It is your fault that you are without linens and so on. It is up to you to collect the key to your apartment from me personally.

Selma clenches her teeth as she feels her face redden. She is incensed, if not surprised, at the response. Later, she will inform the rest of the family, but first she needs fresh air. Her fists are tight and her lips drawn. She walks out the back door, along the hedges, toward the barn. The gentle cows might console her. As Selma notices the remnants of the wren's nest made the previous summer in a pair of trousers that hang on a wall inside the barn, she thinks of her own flight. *Where had the wrens gone? Where would she go?* But the barn was no place for a proper lady, and overcome by the stench, she makes her way back to the house, ready to show the letter to Moritz, Hilde, and Kurt, to decide on the next steps.

Moritz reads the letter. "No. I refuse to return under any circumstances. It is not safe. You heard the gunfire that night. You know I could have been shot, right there in my own home."

Shaking now, trying to steady herself, Selma knows that Moritz is right. "But I don't want to be a burden on Harry and his family. We need our things. What are we going to do?"

"I have an idea." Moritz's wheels are already in motion.

25 November 1938. Moritz writes a letter in German to Burgemeester Beaumont.

Regarding our relocation to Harry Slager … who gives us free food and lodging here in Holland until we move to America, we ask Herrn Bürgermeister to make it possible for us to move to Enschede in the short term. In advance, thanking you for your effort. Respectfully, Moritz Stern.

26 November 1938. Burgemeester Beaumont writes the attorney general, requesting permission for the family to stay.

… In the case of the family Stern, it may be desirable to conduct a careful survey by the Department of Justice especially since the arrival of several more refugees. At first, I had expected that according to regulations the admission would be officially acceptable.

Apparently, since that is not the case, I kindly am asking you to take the necessary steps in that direction.

In addition, it should be taken into account that Moritz Stern (head of the family) has made a request to settle in Enschede, where he will live in the house H. Slager … as to where he and his family will enjoy free room and board, while he is required to make cash payments for miscellaneous items.

It would appear to me that granting this request may offer no objections, and that in fact it is desirable to approach these refugees in a favorable manner.

I DON'T KNOW HOW MUCH of these negotiations my father overheard. But what he didn't hear directly, he learned at some point, and he shared this information in his testimony video.

In November 2018, in our hotel in Holland, I replayed a short section of the testimony video for Josh, so he could hear the emotion in my father's voice.

The mayor would try to legalize our stay in Holland, and of course, if Congress turned us down, we would have to be sent back to Germany. And the Dutch Senate was saying, "No," and they would send us back.

The Justice Department said, "No," we could not stay, and we will have to be sent back to Germany.

And ultimately, the mayor said, "I'm appealing to the queen."

In the video, I heard my father carefully enunciate, "Queen Vil-hel-mina." Each syllable separated, as though he were invoking a sacred name. He paused briefly, to smile broadly and share the words of Mayor Beaumont to the queen.

Alright, now [the mayor] said to [the queen], "I will send these people back over my dead body. I refuse to do it. My conscience does not allow [me] to do that. If yours does, please say so."

And she says, "No, I can't send those people back."

My father's voice changes suddenly. He smiles and nods, and he sounds as though he's about to cry for joy and gratitude.

And she gave us a stay.

In the meantime, thousands and thousands of Jewish people fled Germany under the same circumstances and entered Holland.

After months of blocking refugees, the Dutch government granted my family's appeal. They, together with thousands of others, were permitted to remain in Holland.

The challenge was finding a suitable location for these people without a home—one that would not impact the citizens of the country. The goal was to minimize the refugees' integration into society and prevent them from taking jobs away from local Dutch people.

At the time of my family's arrival in the Netherlands, Wilhelmina was the fifty-eight-year-old monarch who had been queen since the age of ten, when her father had died. Her mother, Emma, was named queen regent until Wilhelmina was sworn in, in 1898, at the age of eighteen. She was unaware of the significant role she would play in history.

NEEDING TO LEARN MORE ABOUT THE QUEEN, at one point Seth, Josh, and I took a side trip to Het Palais in The Hague, which was one of the homes of Wilhelmina's Queen Mother Emma.

Het Palais, a museum now dedicated to works of M. C. Escher, housed an exhibit of the royal mother's life there.

We explored the museum and marveled at the art. Het Palais had many rooms. As we visited each one, I focused more on the description of the room and what the queen mother did there, listening for mentions of Queen Wilhelmina. Seth and Josh focused on the Escher art.

The neutral-colored walls of the front drawing room were once lined with red silk, the museum signage explained. There had been fancy carved molding with golden decoration in the ceiling and along the walls and doorways.

In this room, the Queen Mother Emma lay in state in 1934. Also in this room in 1945, Queen Wilhelmina received General Dwight D. Eisenhower, who had led US forces in liberating the western front of France and Germany.

Escher and Eisenhower, one an artist, one a military man, both conceptualizing and executing intricate plans, one to create art and one to enable the freedom to enjoy the art. In this exhibit, we read about the techniques Escher used in his printmaking.

My research would spotlight the complexity of Queen Wilhelmina's decision to locate homeless refugees to Westerbork, a desolate area in the north. I recognized how complex this world had been, where up was down, where left was right, and where we traveled forward, seemingly unable to progress until we ended up back where we'd started.

The journey, sometimes, led me to places I didn't intend to go. The best of plans led to outcomes that could not have been expected or even wanted.

Over time, I learned that Camp Westerbork would shelter about 750 refugees in 1939. The desolate place would eventually become the Westerbork transit camp, conveniently providing the Nazis, upon their 1940 invasion of the country, a stable of Jewish people already congregated. Barbed-wire fences would soon keep the prisoners in, under careful guard from the watchtowers.

By 1945, over 95,000 of the almost 102,000 Jewish and Romani prisoners in Camp Westerbork would be herded into one of sixty-eight transports to their deaths. Most to Auschwitz-Birkenau and Sobibor.

"Was our family ever there? In Westerbork?" Josh asked, as we toured Het Palais.

"No," I said, taking a breath. "Because of their connections in Enschede, they had a place to live."

Yet another way that Moritz had helped our family survive.

CHAPTER 21

ARYANIZED

EARLY IN MY RESEARCH, I came across the only family property document passed down to me from my father. It was dated July 18, 1939. I fumed for months over the document that signified the finalization of my family's life in Germany.

It was the only clue I had that my family's property had made its way into the Weber family's possession. The document didn't explicitly state that my family sold the property, only that Ernst Weber obtained it "by reason of abandonment." The fact that this document survived, and that my father had held on to it all those years, still takes my breath away.

Yet, it was there for me to discover, so many years after my father's death. And it was one of many keys that unlocked the richness of a story that had never been told to me. Thrilled that I could confirm the exact location of my family's home and business, and shocked that the store in the current location still carried the Weber name, I considered how I could face the descendants of the Weber family without anger. In a way, I felt I had to hold on to some outrage—the betrayal—on behalf of my father and Oma. I'd inherited trauma, though I didn't yet fully realize this. If there was a possibility of finding any sort of reconciliation in this story, it would take me a while to get there.

In June 2019, during a heatwave, I sat in an unair-conditioned room in the Münster archives. There, I would locate hundreds of pages of documents related to my family's property, from as early as 1918 through its sale in 1938, and then resuming from 1945 until the 1960s. The documents were mostly in German. They included the 1925 partnership agreement between my grandfather and Eduard Herzfeld that went into effect on January 1, 1926; the marriage certificate between Oma and my grandfather; and a copy of a July 1938 five-year lease between Herzfeld and Weber that was supposed to go into effect in 1939. In the pile was also a copy of the December 1938 sales document of the Herzfeld store to the Weber business. Hundreds more documents represented the correspondence between Oma and Weber and their lawyers and government officials from 1945 through the 1960s.

I weighed the value of having them all translated. Perhaps I'd be able to deduce what brought these neighboring families, with a seemingly cordial relationship prior to 1938, to a relationship of animosity after 1945. I wanted to locate information that would clue me in to the reason none of this was mentioned to me nor shared in my father's testimony video. I followed my gut, or my heart, or whatever it was that guided me. I selected documents that most called to me, roughly translating them on my own in the follow-ing months. In time, I had enough to stitch together the timeline, though I remain uncertain about the players. It could have been Weber or his attorney talking with Moritz alone. Or any number of variations. But that the legal transactions transpired on these dates, I have evidence.

IT'S 30 NOVEMBER 1938. Ernst Weber, a tall man with blond hair, arrives in Gendringen at Selma's request. They had been longtime neighbors and colleagues and were in a similar business selling clothing. Ernst holds his tall frame erect as he climbs the steps to the front door of the Bringenborg home. Saartje Cussel welcomes him, takes his coat and hat, and shows him to the living room. His shoulders relax for a moment as he breathes in the pleasant aroma of the freshly brewed coffee and cooling apple cake. Ernst graciously accepts Saartje's offer of Kaffee und Kuchen and stirs sugar into the cup of coffee with shaking hands, causing the spoon to collide loudly with the sides of the cup. He anticipates new requests Moritz might make as they would conclude sale negotiations on the Geburtsstrasse home and business.

Moritz sits across from Ernst, too agitated to take a bite of his apple cake, his indigestion again flaring up. He leads the negotiations on behalf of the property heirs, his wife, Hilde, and his brother-in-law, Kurt, who sit nearby.

"We can no longer live in Bocholt or in Germany," Moritz says. "Instead of leasing the shop to you, as our parents had agreed to a few months ago, we will sell it to you. We will sell you the entire building."

Before Eduard's death in August, the family had realized they would be unable to earn a living any longer, because customers were not permitted into their store, and it would be increasingly difficult for Moritz to visit his customers by bicycle in winter.

On June 12, 1938, they entered into a lease agreement with the Webers, to become effective on January 1, 1939. The Webers would pay rent for use of the store space while the Stern-Herzfelds would continue to live in the upper floors. But now, their life in Germany was gone and this sale an inevitability, not a choice.

Ernst's mind races. He is eager for this, to purchase the entire business and integrate it with his own, and he is prepared with a sale price that would be practical, fair to him if not to the seller. Jewish businesses throughout the town, and all towns across Nazi Germany, were becoming "Aryanized," a process that had started in 1933. The Stern-Herzfelds are fortunate to have held out this long. Ernst has mixed feelings about his role in the inevitable.

"Thirty thousand Reichsmark," Ernst says, a little too loudly.

"Nein. That is far below the value. You know it's worth at least four times that amount."

A plate drops in the kitchen, shattering, heightening their collective agitation.

"I can't afford that. Remember, the mortgage must be paid off, and I need to replace all the windows and clean the inside of the store. The glass is in all the clothing. In everything, still."

"Ja. I know. But you get all the business, all the inventory. You have your customers and my customers come to one location now. You will do well."

"This is difficult. You know I am just now taking over, helping my widowed mother."

"Look around," Moritz says, somewhat louder, on the edge of defiance, as he motions to his wife and brother-in-law. "I help my family to survive. We have no life in Germany."

Kurt blinks hard to fight back tears as he hears the truth he knows but is still trying to deny. Hilde straightens herself in her seat, stretching her spine, slightly pushing out her lower lip. It's a look Moritz immediately recognizes as an expression of distaste.

Ernst observes the body language too, trying not to make eye contact with Kurt and Hilde. "Ach, I can go up to thirty thousand and seventy Reichsmark," he counters.

"I will accept that amount." Moritz knows it is useless to push for a higher price. "But I need one more thing."

"What is it?" Ernst peers over his glasses as he sets down his coffee cup.

"We need all our personal belongings. Our furniture, clothes, and kitchen goods."

"That is a great hardship for me. A lot of work and a great expense."

It was true, it would require extra effort and some careful workarounds, especially since the new regulation of November 12 had completed the process of Aryanization, prohibiting Jewish people from having retail stores. Yet Ernst would be getting the business he wanted, and the entire building on top of it. It is a good business deal.

"You know we cannot return to collect our belongings ourselves," Moritz adds.

"I do." Ernst stares into his plate, at the crumbs he left behind, at the piece of apple he could still scoop up to enjoy if he had the stomach for it. His head reels at the thought of the work ahead. "Alright, then. I agree. But it will take a few months for us to get you your things."

They prepare the agreement, which includes the sale price:

... on condition that the whole private property of the families Herzfeld and Stern (move commodity like beds, furniture, linen, clothing, porcelain, knives, forks, and spoons and household items) is to transport to Gendringen Netherlands, Haus Bringenborg. Cession can only be after the whole private property Herzfeld and Stern have arrived here. The firm Weber is liable to all costs of this contract. Mortgage will be reduced from buying-price.

After retrieving his coat and hat, Ernst leaves the Bringenborg. Hilde immediately writes a succinct note to the family lawyer. "We have today sold the house to the Weber company. The conditions are set out in the contract."

One week later, Ernst is asked again to come to Gendringen to finalize the legal document, to seal the deal. That was the last he would know about the well-being of Moritz's family until after the war.

Some months later, on July 18, 1939, the land would be registered in Weber's name "by reason of abandonment." A copy of the registration document made its way to Hilde in Enschede, and her son Walter would hold this document until his own death.

OF COURSE, this chapter of their lives must have been immensely painful for both Oma and my father. They could not talk about these troubles, at least not in English, with me or David around, when we were young.

Whether this was a topic of conversation in German at the dinner table, or over a game of cards, or late at night after we were tucked into bed, I will never know.

Subsequent research and connections I made brought me deeper into information about the Cussel family as well as the anecdote about the wren's nest in a pair of pants inside the barn during the summer of 1938. And about the Spier family's actual home location a street away from the estate where my father claimed the Spier family lived. If only he had faced south instead of northeast when standing between the two churches, he would have recorded the correct location. And about the details of some of the dealings between Weber and my family.

All I could accurately piece together before my trip to Gendringen was that my family stayed with Jewish families as they awaited their furniture. The Bocholt mayor would not send their things to them. They lost their home and business to Weber. And their furniture somehow arrived in 1939, allowing them to move to Enschede.

Perhaps the details I imagined in my retelling of my family's first month in Holland were spot on. Perhaps not. But I had enough of the facts to know I was very, very close.

CHAPTER 22
ENSCHEDE

DURING EACH TRIP, I was able to fill in different pieces of the story. The day we retraced my family's escape day—the June 2018 trip that included Seth, Josh, David, Robin, and me—we made the drive from Gendringen to Enschede in two cars.

After such emotional activities, we welcomed a pastoral, hour-long drive through flat, green land with few buildings. In the passenger seat, I reviewed the map of Enschede even though I'd already memorized it. I said, "After we check into our Airbnb, let's head to the four addresses where my father and Oma lived. Then we'll have dinner near the Slagers' former home. After that, let's walk to the synagogue."

Seth and Josh were used to my intense organization. They knew that my overplanning might be turned upside down if new findings popped up out of nowhere. Either way, our schedule was going to be tiring.

As we drove into Enschede, a tall, defunct smokestack greeted us. "That must be a remnant of the textile manufacturing in the town. Back in the 1930s, there were many mill owners, both Jewish and non-Jewish." I shared only a small part of what I'd found in my research.

What I'd also learned was that the town had begun absorbing thousands of Jewish Polish refugees as early as 1923. As many more Jewish people found refuge beginning in 1933, this time from Germany, the German Refugee Committee was established. This committee was led by Sieg Menko, a member of the Enschede City Council and the Enschede synagogue. He was involved in the textile industry and owned a large factory.

ON A MILD SPRING DAY in 1939, Walter and his family are driven to Enschede, toward the house that Harry had arranged for them to live in on Soendastraat. This is where they will make their home until they can emigrate.

Walter looks out the open window as they drive, noticing the sunny skies over the gray fields. If he begins a new school in Enschede, he wonders how he will manage when he doesn't yet speak the language of the country. He hopes this next phase of his life will be less stressful than the last few years have been. His daydreaming is interrupted by his grandmother's sudden outburst.

"That stinks!" Selma wrinkles her nose as she rolls up her window, even in the stuffiness of the crowded car. Walter and the entire family also notice the smell. There must be a dozen smokestacks spewing their gray haze over the town.

"Ja, those are the textile plants," Harry says. "You get used to it. They are good for business in our town."

"Look at that smokestack!" Walter points to the first one they pass. It reaches high into the sky.

"That belongs to Mr. van Gelderen. His family has owned De Nijverheid now for three generations. They employ one thousand people!" Harry speaks proudly of his town's success as he pulls up in front of Soendastraat #31. "Here is your new home. It is modest sized, and I hope you will find comfort inside. Your furniture should be here, and all your things. You get yourselves set up, then come over for supper. My Hilde makes something good for us."

IN REVIEWING DOCUMENTS and speaking with historians, I'd learned that Moritz might have told the Gendringen authorities that the family planned to live with the Slagers, though I could find no evidence that they moved into the Slager home. Perhaps that was their "story" and they moved into their own place with the help of Harry, their house-broker relative.

Perhaps the Soendastraat home was owned by Harry as a rental property. The first address that appeared on Hilde's Dutch identity card was Soendastraat #31, which was not far from the Slager's Haaksbergerstraat home. Had Harry exaggerated in his statement to the authorities, knowing he'd find a place for my family to stay? Was he so similar to Moritz in doing whatever was necessary to survive? I suspect it might have been a bit of both.

CHAPTER 23

REMINISCENCES

WHEN I FIRST SORTED THROUGH my inherited treasures, before scanning and placing them in archival sleeves, I spread them all out on my dining room table. I examined each one, trying to engage with a life that wasn't mine. A life I longed to know. There were photos, letters, and other documents that would take their time to reveal their meaning to me.

I contemplated how these items had made it to Enschede. I liked to imagine that Weber had had them boxed up with the furniture and other possessions. That he'd been a kind friend to collect and send them to my family.

Closing my eyes, I imagined my family finding the box after settling into their Soendastraat home in 1939. A place some of them would live until 1942.

HILDE OPENS THE HUTCH DRAWER to put away the last of the linens she's unpacked from among their Bocholt possessions, the white napkins with the letters "HS" embroidered in the corners. Many of their belongings made their way to this new home in Enschede, a home that isn't quite their home.

"Ach, would you look here, what I found!" Hilde places a small box on the dining room table, as if she's found a treasure chest. "Come, everyone."

The family gathers around the table quickly, unsure of what's made Hilde so excited. She holds up a photo of their home and business, or rather their former home and business.

"Our Heimat." Selma speaks softly. "Eduard worked hard to build up that business. You know, he started with one address, then expanded to two."

"Ja." Moritz stands behind the women, pointing at his pride and joy. "That is the photo from 1927, from right after we did the renovation."

"Eduard found in you a good partner to manage the business, Moritz. Of that I am pleased." Selma offers a heartfelt, though infrequent, compliment.

The next few photos in the box catch Moritz's attention. He spreads them out on the table and points out the tree in each of them. "Look, our cherry tree. It always brought me happiness in the springtime. See the blossoms, Walter. Do you remember this photograph?"

Walter examines his image from a few years prior. He remembers how he enjoyed wearing that pullover long-sleeved shirt. He is quietly embarrassed, now, about his one ear that sticks out slightly. His mother and he stand, each gingerly holding one of the blossoms that cover the tree.

"Look how you are smiling," says Hilde. "You are so happy in this photo."

"Ja, I remember," Walter says. "You told us to look at the blossom we were holding. I had to stand there like that for a long time."

Moritz smirks at his son's impatience while posing for photos. "Ach, I miss our cherry tree in the garden." He rifles through more of the photos and documents, placing them around the table.

"Ach du Lieber, I forgot about this." Moritz carefully unfolds a letter, and it tears at the seams where it was folded. "My reference letter from Gebruder Alsberg, from 1909. Bring me some tape to fix this."

"What does it say?" Kurt asks.

"It says: 'Mr. Moritz Stern of Montabaur was present in our houses from 1 August 1905 until 1 August 1908. He was zealous and has trained as a good sales assistant.'" Moritz smiles and scans his audience, standing up straighter. "'We are happy with his accomplishments. We are able to endorse Mr. Stern as a young sales assistant. Our best wishes for his well-being to accompany him. Oberhausen, Rheinland, 1 May 1909. Signed Brothers Alsberg.'"

"How old were you then?" asks Walter.

Moritz sits down to apply the tape along the tears.

"Let's see." Moritz looks up for a moment as he quickly calculates. "I was fourteen years of age when I left my parents' home in Montabaur in 1905 for this work in Oberhausen. So, I was seventeen when I went back home again for a while before going into the Great War."

"Then you came to Bocholt?" Walter tries to piece together his father's timeline.

"No, not yet. First, I went back to Oberhausen to work. I lived there near the train station and worked again as a Kaufmann, a salesman. It was January 1926 that I officially became a partner in the business with your Opa, Eduard."

Selma takes on an expression that is less of a smile than a longing. "Then you came to Geburtsstrasse and married our Hilde. That was such a happy time."

"Who is this?" Walter points to another photo.

A baby's sparsely haired crown peeks out of a baby carriage, which is being pushed along by his nurse. His twenty-five-year-old mother, stylishly dressed in a drop-waist, long-sleeved V-neck dress, touches the carriage with one hand as she walks beside it. On the other side of the carriage is his thirty-five-year-old father in a three-piece suit, tie, and fedora, holding his walking cane, an accessory all his friends had at the time.

Hilde's eyes sparkle. "This is you, Walter. It was your first walk on the Geburtsstrasse, just outside our store."

"Ach du Lieber, my Max! My Dinchen!" Selma interrupts, holding the postcard that her sister-in-law had written to her family in 1919. Selma had known Dina, Dinchen, as a little girl in Bocholt. She had grown up and married Selma's beloved brother, Max, who had died in 1934. "I pray that Dinchen and Alice are managing safely."

Selma reads aloud the short note on the back of the photo. "Meine Lieben! So that you won't forget us completely, I'm sending you this postcard. Hopefully you're doing fine as we are. Businesswise we're content. When do you want to go to Berlin? Cordial greetings, Dinchen."

"Mutti, look here." Kurt tries to get his mother's mind off dear Uncle Max and Aunt Dinchen. "We still have the photos of the inside of the synagogue, the ones that I took after the renovation!"

Selma smiles, proud of her son. She carefully lifts the next item from its box. "This was from last year, the High Holy Days. 'L'shanah tovah tikaseivu,' you wrote, Walter."

Walter smiles, pleased with this sketch he'd made. He had written the Jewish New Year's greeting in neat Hebrew block letters with all the dots—the vowels that help with proper pronunciation of the words—meticulously placed. He had signed it, "Euer Walter," your Walter. The perimeter is decorated with symbols of Rosh Hashanah. At the bottom he had added the Jewish year about to arrive: "5699."

Selma looks at Walter. "This brought me a little joy in my sadness after your Opa died."

Walter sees his mother pick up some smaller pieces of papers with childlike handwriting. His curiosity is piqued. "What are those?"

Hilde looks up at him, the seriousness of a mother guiding her child through challenging school requirements. "These you wrote home to your father from our summer holiday to Bad Oeynhausen. You were six or seven years of age and practicing the new Sütterlinschrift script, perfect handwriting for such a young child!"

"Ja, I enjoyed reading these letters, even with the misspellings I found." Moritz winks at his son and smiles. The expression conveys *I know you are learning and will do well in life.*

"Let me read one," Moritz says.

Meine Lieben! My dears!

In the express train, it was very nice. It was not coupled to each other like other trains, but there were thick iron plates between the wagons and folded leather like a photographic machine. The furniture in our bedroom is white and the wallpaper has a rose pattern. And children here still are going to school. And when Mama was at the dactor's [sic], I got two small boxes. And Mama got a bath application today.

Bad Oeynhausen is a health-spa town in the same state as Bocholt. The healing qualities of the mineral waters is a destination, one that young Walter and his mother once enjoyed. Memories fill Hilde, who picks up another of the letters and reads.

Meine Lieben!

It is very nice in Oeynhausen. And today I was in the bathhouse with Mama, and it was very nice in the bathhouse. And I even saw an airplane. And yesterday I got a ship. We were also on the sluice. And on the sluice, I was also in the water with my feet. On our way back we saw pretty swans. And we came through a pretty forest. Many greetings, your Walter

"Do you remember that, Walter?"

"Ja, I do a little. The airplane was exciting to see. Read that one, Papa." Walter points to another letter.

Moritz reads:

Meine Lieben!

How is it in Bocholt? You should all stay healthy, especially you, Papa, with your gall … Yesterday I played with three children. The sun is shining today … Here you are stung by a lot of bees and wasps. And heartfelt greetings, your Walter

"Ja, even then you knew I had indigestion." Moritz places his hand on his stomach, reminded once again of his stress. He tries to comfort himself.

"Even then, the bees and wasps came out," Selma says.

"Now, one more photo before bedtime," Hilde says, placing another photo on the table, as if she is making a final play in a card game. "Look, Kurt. You remember taking this photo of our family on New Year's Eve?"

"Ja, I remember that well," Kurt says.

In the photo, a young Walter is seated at a white-clothed table that is populated with nuts, a glistening layer cake, and crystal wine glasses. Selma sits close to him. Eduard sits at the head of the table, one hand resting gently on the bottom of his wineglass stem, as if he's almost ready to lift the glass for a sip. They all look toward the camera, posing for Kurt. A print hangs behind Walter and Selma, showing two young women at the beach looking dreamily away from the sea toward something happening near the viewers.

Kurt remembers asking each adult to take a position, and he coaxes Walter to smile for the camera. Yet Walter's wide-open eyes and slightly downturned lips seem to express surprise, or perhaps disdain, as he glares to the left of the camera.

Between Selma and Eduard stand Moritz and Hilde, smiling and looking directly into each other's eyes, seductively, as they lift their wineglasses in a toast.

"Ach." Selma shakes her head once again. "That was a special New Year's Eve party in our German Heimat."

I OPENED MY EYES AGAIN, shaken by the depth of sadness my family must have felt, leaving their Heimat and knowing they'd never return. As I examined the photos one more time before placing them in the archival sleeves, I looked for more hints, for clues I hadn't noticed yet that would tell me more about their lives in Germany.

The one of my father in a baby carriage with his parents flanking it was labeled in Oma's handwriting but in my father's first-person voice: "My first time seeing the Geburtsstrasse." I could tell, comparing it to another photo, that it was taken in front of their home.

Oma had labeled the photo showing the family gathered around a festive table: "New Year's Eve Party in Germany Homestead." Underneath, there is a purple stamp: "Kurt Herzfeld."

Oma must have hoped that her son would remember these places and people from his youth in the old country, even with the pain mixed in.

CHAPTER 24

THE BARMITZWOH

I VIEWED MY FATHER'S TESTIMONY video countless times, and I watched his recorded 1991 trip to Holland almost as often. I'd learned that he had attended Hebrew-school classes and prepared for his barmitzwoh, Oma's spelling of "bar mitzvah," in the Enschede synagogue. Not a far walk from his new home, it was conveniently located next to the public school he had also attended.

Continuing my research in my home office, I typed "Enschede" and "synagogue" into the Google search field. "Welkom in de mooiste synagoge van Nederland," it boasted. Welcome to the most beautiful synagogue in the Netherlands.

How could this Jewish building, a synagogue no less, have survived German occupation? I would have to wait until I got deeper into my father's story to find out. But on that day, I cued up my father's 1991 video of his visit to this site.

The synagogue was a brick building with an enormous copper dome set back behind the entrance doorway. Two smaller copper domes anchored the front of the building on the left and right of the entrance. Stained-glass windows adorned the front of the building along its entire street view.

I watched intently, listening for any details I might have missed the last few times I'd played it. My father moved the camera so slowly that the building's every nook and cranny were visible. For almost three full minutes, he recorded memories to take home with him, pausing over the particularly pleasurable spots, and periodically enlightening his audience.

Now this was the synagogue in Enschede where I was barmitzwo-hed and where I learned all the evil things you could learn in Hebrew school with the other no-goodniks. It's a beautiful building.

The video dwelled on the light-green oxidized copper roof, zooming in first on the largest dome, then on the smaller ones. My father explained about the use of the rooms under each dome. For twenty seconds, he zoomed in and panned out, periodically resting on the large wooden entrance, a bed of pansies, the stained-glass windows, the intricate brickwork above the windows, and another bed of pansies.

Copper, solid copper.

This was the main dome over the sanctuary and the main entrance.

One of the most beautiful shuls in Holland, well known for it.

It nearly was bombed during the war. The Germans wanted to blast it and blow it up and the Dutch government here in the city suggested to use it as an ammunition dump for the German army, not to blow it up. And they listened.

My father lingered, shooting more video than most viewers would want to see. As I watched, it became clear to me that *he* needed this footage. This sanctuary must have brought him comfort in a time before hiding, a time of innocence growing into knowing—into too much knowing.

From a different angle, he zoomed in yet again.

See the contour of the sheet metalwork? Beautiful windows.

Unfortunately, I cannot get inside. The doors are locked and there is no minyan on Shabbos tomorrow because the chazzan is away on vacation and there are not enough people to do these sort of things.

The footage lingered on the front door, on the flowers outside the building, on the windows my father had already shown viewers. He was not ready to leave quite yet.

My father's video jogged my memory of a poem I'd found among his photographs. I removed it from the album where it sat decaying. Before scanning it and placing it in an archival sleeve, I read it aloud to calm my nerves, the rhyming lyricism made even more striking because of my limited German comprehension. Its title translated to "On the occasion of the barmitzwoh of an expatriate boy."

Zur Barmitzwoh eines ausgewanderten Knaben
Ernst ist das Leben heut', wir wissens alle,
wir wissen, dass die Zeiten sehr betrübt,
drum sind wir froh, wenn im besonderen Falle
es einmal wieder was zu feiern gibt.
Und wenn auch Wehmut wohnt in unseren Herzen,
und wenn auch Trauer um verlor'ne Erde
um Hab und Gut uns packt mit neuen Schmerzen,

wir hoffen doch, dass es einst anders werde.

Barmitzwoh ist es, die wir heut begehen,

drum lasst die Freude ein in Herz und Haus,

Barmitzwoh, wenn wir richtig sie verstehen,

so füllt sie reinsten Sinn des Lebens aus.

Du Knabe, stehst an einer Lebenswende

und aus dem Kinde wird ein junger Mann,

der Kindheit Paradies ist nun zu Ende,

der Ernst des Lebens tritt an Dich heran.

Im Elternhaus von allen treu gehegt

empfandst das Judesein Du nicht so schwer,

und was die Zukunft Gutes in sich trägt,

das gaben Segenswünsche heute her.

Doch blick mit Mut und Kraft und Gottvertrauen

ins Leben nun, was es auch bringen mag,

die Zeit geht weiter, immer vorwärts schauen,

und Segen ruh auf Dir an jedem Tag.

Although there was no record of my father's barmitzwoh in Enschede, nor any details of it in his testimony video, I imagined how it might have gone with the help of that poem Oma had written for the occasion. My best estimate of a barmitzwoh date was November 16, 1939, the first Shabbos after my father's Hebrew birthday.

Once I had the poem properly translated, I was able to understand more of the complexity of emotions Oma must have been balancing during these first few months in Holland.

ON FRIDAY NIGHT, November 15, 1939, after dinner, Hilde sets out Walter's favorite dessert, a Zwetschgenkuchen, in honor of his becoming a barmitzwoh the following morning. She serves her family one slice each, one a little larger for Walter. "Before you eat, I read to you the poem I wrote for your barmitzwoh."

Hilde begins with the title, "On the occasion of the barmitzwoh of an expatriate boy." She sits up straighter in her chair and continues, proudly, "by Hilde Stern, November 1939."

Walter smiles, pleased his mother has found the energy to write poems once again. He puts his fork down and listens intently.

Life is serious today, we all know this,
we know that times are very troubled,
so we are happy when there is a special occasion
once again there is something to celebrate.
And even if melancholy dwells in our hearts,
and even if we are gripped with new pain
by grief over lost earth and our belongings,
we hope that things will change one day.
Barmitzwoh is what we celebrate today,
so let joy enter into our heart and home,
Barmitzwoh, if we understand it correctly,
fulfills the purest meaning of life.
You, boy, are at a turning point of life
and the child becomes a young man,
the childhood paradise ends now,
and seriousness of life approaches you.
Faithfully cherished by everyone in your parents' home
being a Jew didn't seem difficult to you,
and good things the future is carrying for you,

are named by blessings today.
But now look to live with courage and strength and trust in God
whatever life may bring,
time goes on, always looking ahead,
and blessings rest on you each day.

"Thank you, Mutti," Walter says before lifting his fork once again to devour the plum cake. He loves his mother's poems. He finds comfort in them even if the rhymes sometimes seemed forced. They remind him of nursery rhymes like, "Hoppe hoppe reiter; wenn er fällt, dann schreit er … Fällt er in den Sumpf; macht der Reiter plumps!" A violent little rhyme, as many nursery rhymes are. This one means, "Hoppe, hoppe, rider; When he falls, he screams … If he falls into the swamp; The rider makes a splash!"

November 16, 1939, has finally arrived. Walter and his family are greeted by a crisp and mostly overcast mid-November morning as they begin their walk on the narrow side street.

Moritz and Walter take the lead with Hilde, Selma, and Kurt following. Moritz marvels at how his son has grown in the year since they escaped from Germany—both physically and emotionally. No, this is not their Bocholt home, but the community accepts them well enough, and it will have to do for now.

Moritz breathes in the cool air and looks up to sun rays that peek through clouds from time to time. He glances at his son, who is smiling, looking down, keeping pace on their way to synagogue. After a few minutes in silence, they approach Haaksbergerstraat and Moritz turns to his son. "You, my boy, are at a turning point of life as you become a young man. Your childhood paradise is now ending, and the seriousness of life approaches you."

Walter lifts his head, looks at his father.

"I know that you've worked hard to prepare for today," Moritz continues. "Keep working hard. It is how you will succeed."

Walter adjusts his glasses, knowing what's coming next.

"Remember, I went off to work at fourteen years of age. That's how I was able to run our store all those years. It is important that you finish your schooling and consider a vocation. Harry can help you, with all his connections."

"Ja, ich weiss." I know. Walter can't focus on that right now and looks back at the ground ahead. His father often brought up ideas about his future in this new place, but he isn't quite ready for that yet.

Hilde catches up to her son while Moritz slips back to walk with Kurt and Selma.

"How are you feeling? Are you a little nervous this morning?"

"I'm fine." Walter fibs, as his stomach lurches. He worries about tripping up on the memorized Torah trope, the cantillation marks absent from the Torah scroll itself, which keep challenging him. He knows that wouldn't be the worst thing, though, because no one would need to correct a cantillation mistake. His immediate concern is mispronouncing one of the words, which would require correcting. In public.

"Life is serious these days. Ja, we all know this," Hilde says, observing her son's puzzling facial expression. "We hope that things will change one day. A barmitzwoh, if we understand it correctly, fulfills the purest meaning of life."

In the few months since the family has lived in Enschede, Walter has prepared to read a short section directly from the Torah, in its ancient Hebrew letters, which omits the vowels and trope. He worked hard in the Hebrew-school classroom, under the smaller dome across the hall from the sanctuary, aiming to please his teacher and to make his family proud. He also learned the choreography of the Torah service and his part in the ceremony that would mark his legally becoming a man in the eyes of the Jewish religion and his new Enschede community.

"Remember the ending of the poem I read to you last night?" Hilde watches her son's face closely. "'But look now to live with courage and strength and trust in God; whatever life may bring; time goes on, always look onward; and blessings rest on you each day.' I know you'll do great, Liebchen."

They arrive at the synagogue. Walter, as has become his habit on approaching this building, lifts his head to view the large central copper dome and the two smaller ones. This place is a home to him. It makes him feel safe.

Hilde and Selma say "Gut Shabbos" to the men and approach the separate entrance to the women's balcony. In this synagogue, as is typical in Orthodox communities, there is a separate seating section for men and women. Walter, Moritz, and Kurt enter the large wooden front doors to approach the main sanctuary. Hilde and Selma move toward their seats upstairs, on the aisle in the fourth row, on the left side, which will give them an ideal view of the men in their family, below.

Entering the prayer space for the last time as a child, Walter looks across the sanctuary past the dozens of men already in prayer, upward toward where the choir sits. They are singing one of the morning prayers. He moves his gaze to the right, in time to see his mother and grandmother taking their seats in the balcony, nodding their heads and smiling supportively. He smiles back nervously, ready to please them as he always has.

Hilde and Selma lean forward, stretching their necks as if the extra inch will provide a binocular view, peering precipitously over the balcony's banister, as the Torah service begins. The barmitzwoh boy removes his tallis—a distinctive black-and-white-striped, fringed prayer shawl—from the cabinet in front of him, opens it wide, and recites the requisite blessing, then wraps himself in it. Each man does the same with his own tallis, which then sits atop the owner's shoulders for the remainder of the service.

Selma whispers to Hilde. "I have such melancholy in my heart, even as if mourning for lost earth and belongings. I'm so grabbed with new pain. This should have taken place in Bocholt. It is wrong that we must mark this day here, as expatriates."

"Ja," Hilde says. She understands her mother's bitterness. "But barmitzwoh is what we celebrate today. We should drum with joy in our heart and our home."

The Torah is removed from the ark and marched around the men's seating area. Walter follows the lead of others, kissing it by way of his tallis fringes, while the choir sings out, "Etz chayim hee … " The Torah is a tree of life. The Torah is placed on the reading table, open to the reading for the week.

One man recites the blessings, then the designated reader chants the words of the Torah for that week's portion. Walter's eyes follow the now-familiar choreography. He awaits his turn. His foot quivers. Six more men are called. Each man rises as he is summoned, recites the blessings before and after the Torah reading, then accepts well-wishes from the other men as he returns to his seat. As each man takes his turn, the queasiness increases in Walter's belly. His turn is getting closer.

Hilde's eyes remain fixed on Walter. She doesn't want to miss a moment, a movement, even as she resumes the whispered conversation with her mother, trying to push aside her sadness and fears for a few hours. "Ja, we know that times are very troubled, but let's be happy on this special occasion. Once again there is something to celebrate."

A pressure builds behind Hilde's eyes and nose as something strains to be released. She fights back tears of joy, or are they tears of sadness that relate to what her mother insists on reminding her about? Intermittently, she closes her eyes tightly, then opens them wide. She will stay strong, as she has been brought up to do. She will keep her deepest emotions tucked under the surface to maintain her composure.

Finally, the cantor calls Walter's Hebrew name, a loud, piercing call, for this final Torah reading aliya: "Alexander ben Eliezar haKohain, bachor ha-barmitzwoh!" Alexander, son of Eliezar the Kohain, the barmitzwoh boy! Walter rises, shaking yet smiling. He adjusts his round glasses, pulls down on his almost-too-tight suit jacket, and readjusts his tallis as he approaches the Torah to recite the blessing.

Hilde looks upward now, toward the domed ceiling, to prevent the water that is collecting in her eyes from escaping to form a river down her cheeks. She blinks hard, staring toward the ceiling at the intricate zodiac mosaic radiating from the sun, at whose source are the Hebrew letters chet and yud, spelling chai, life. She can't read the letters through the blur, but she knows they are there.

Walter completes his rise to adulthood as he recites the final blessings. He descends the bimah, the altar, and, as his father taught him, he firmly shakes hands with the men seated nearby, then with his own father and uncle. He smiles broadly now, still shaking, but with relief.

"Good work, little man." Kurt smiles knowingly, remembering well the stress and exuberance of his own barmitzwoh experience in Bocholt shortly before Walter was born.

"Danke, Onkel Kurt."

"Not that difficult, you made it look easy." Moritz presses a reassuring palm on his son's shoulder.

Walter nods, smiles, once again glances up to the balcony.

Quickly, surreptitiously, Hilde dabs her cheeks with her white handkerchief, and she turns to her mother with words of optimism. "And what carries the future good in itself, that gave her blessing today."

Selma offers a half-nod, a little less hopeful about the future on this day's brief ray of sunshine peeking through the storm.

THOUGH I MIGHT NOT FULLY KNOW the details of my father's barmitzwoh day, I could return to my father's beloved synagogue, this time to enter the green-domed building to finish what my father could not in 1991, because the synagogue doors had been locked.

In June 2018, my family and I arrived at the Enschede synagogue on a comfortably cool day, under a cotton-ball sky that, at times, turned steely gray. The building looked exactly as it had in my father's 1991 video, with one striking exception.

"This can't be," I said, my disappointment palpable. "This dome is different. It's supposed to be a green copper roof, like in my father's video and photographs, not this dull brown." It did not stand out against the overcast sky.

"They must have replaced it," Seth surmised.

I would learn that copper roofs had a life expectancy of about eighty years and, since the synagogue had been constructed in 1927, the roof had been replaced sometime after 1991. Although I was seeing the roof as it had appeared when my father became a barmitzwoh, I needed to see the roof exactly as my father had captured it in 1991 so that I could have the full experience he could not have had.

Once inside the building, Evertjan, the man who had replied to my email inquiry and invited us to visit, took us on a private tour of the synagogue. We visited the large sanctuary. It was truly one of the most beautiful synagogues I had ever visited. The intricate zodiac mosaic in the ceiling radiated from the sun, at whose source are the Hebrew letters chet and yud, spelling chai, life. This I could see clearly, my eyes not yet tearing up. The gold and blue tiles sparkled in the light. The image was both intensely beautiful and unusual for a synagogue.

Visiting the women's section in the balcony, I turned to my brother. "Where do you think Oma and her mother sat?" Without a word, we proceeded together to the spot we both imagined they prayed, said Kaddish for Eduard, listened to my father recite his barmitzwoh prayers, and talked with the other women of the community, whom they had befriended. We sat there for a few minutes, looking down at the men's section, the ark, the bimah, up to the domed ceiling and around the rest of the balcony.

We headed back to the main floor and visited the rooms across from the sanctuary, already knowing that the farther room had been the boardroom.

In my father's video, he had zoomed in on the front-left dome. "Under this dome, the board meetings were held," he had said.

Evertjan explained the background of the architecture of the room and the reproduction of the original stained-glass windows portraying names and related symbols of various biblical prophets. We viewed portraits of men important to this Dutch Jewish community, including Sieg Menko, onetime head of Enschede's Committee for German Refugees, and later head of the local Joodse Raad, Jewish Council, which reported to the central authority in Amsterdam.

Next was the small sanctuary, where Shabbos services were held these days because the congregation was small, and cooling or heating the large sanctuary was unwarranted, not to mention unaffordable. "This was the prayer room," Evertjan told us.

We nodded at each other. I already knew this. When my father had zoomed in on the front-right dome, he'd recorded, "Under the other small dome, we had our daily minyan. Now they don't even have a minyan on a Shabbos."

Earlier, I'd asked in an email if Shabbos services were still held there and received the reply: "The cantor is in Enschede only every other Shabbos and will not be here during your visit."

My father's sadness reverberated in my own heart. I yearned, as he had, to experience Shabbos services in this place. I felt the loss of something I'd never had but somehow knew I needed.

Evertjan's insightful, inspiring, and—for me—bittersweet tour of this most beautiful synagogue ended at the synagogue's café, where we were treated to lunch.

"This area," Evertjan said, pointing to a corner of the room near our seats, "was the jail used by the Sicherheitsdienst, or the SD, the security service of the Nazi era. The imprisoned locals were forced to stand for hours or days, the cells were so small."

We continued our conversation over our lox and cucumber sandwiches that had been prepared by another Irene. This Irene was the synagogue fundraiser, and I told her that we wanted to make a donation to the synagogue in my father's honor. The synagogue was understandably financially challenged, given the city's small Jewish community. The space was large and cost a lot to maintain and heat. I felt driven to help keep my father's beloved synagogue a place others could enjoy for a long time to come.

After working out the details of how a payment could be processed, the synagogue fundraiser handed me a gift-wrapped package, about the size of a sheet of paper. "Here is a gift for you, as a thank you for your donation," the other Irene said.

My head pulled back for a moment, in shock. I'd almost completely fulfilled one of my dreams, and I did not need any more gifts. Nor did I did wish to dilute the moment with this one.

"Thank you," I said, accepting the package graciously. Its weight was surprising, considering its almost paper-thin flatness.

"Open it," she prodded.

I undid the tape that held the wrapping closed. As I unfolded the paper, a beautiful, soft shade of light green peeked through. It reminded me of the color of Lady Liberty, the statue my father would have seen in the harbor of New York City, lighting the way to the land of opportunity. The gift was a piece of copper. On it was etched an outline of the synagogue.

"That is a piece of the original copper roof from our synagogue," the other Irene said.

My tears could not be restrained, and I felt no need to prevent them from flowing down my cheeks. I now held what was my own piece of copper roof, sky schmutz and all. It had been part of the building when my father had become a barmitzwoh, above the space where my family celebrated and mourned and prayed when they had still been free to do so. The roof my father had seen and recorded years earlier. I would forever be able to see it. A beautiful piece of copper roof I could hold close each day of my life.

As we left the synagogue, I shared my emotion with my family. "I'm overwhelmed with all the 'gifts' we've received in just two short hours. But—"

Seth, Josh, David, and Robin looked at me as if to ask, "What else could there be?"

"There is still one thing I need to do," I said. "I still need to attend services here as my father had wanted to in 1991."

I had walked in my father's footsteps, learned stories of his past. Yet, for every fragment of my father's life that I unveiled, ten more questions arose. My obsession to get still closer gripped me. And so, I added an item to my list of unfinished business: Attend Shabbos services in the Enschede synagogue, the most beautiful synagogue in the Netherlands!

CHAPTER 25

HUGO SLAGER

SETH, JOSH, DAVID, ROBIN, and I faced the school building on our June trip. It was next to the synagogue. I explained, "My father attended this school when he lived in Enschede."

There were times during our trips when I would describe portions of my father's 1991 video. Of this location, the video had shown a two- or three-story brick building with six tall windows on the second floor and three on the bottom left. To the right of the doorway were three smaller windows. An oval dormer window jutted out from the red-tiled roof, as if keeping a watchful eye on the schoolchildren below. A fence and tall brick posts surrounded the building, marking the walkway that led to the front door.

"Now look at this," my father had said in the video. "This was the school I attended … B2 in Enschede." He panned the camera right to show a wing of classrooms, still there today.

"Openb. Lagere School B2" was painted in gold lettering on black with a decorative blue, white, and gold border along the sign's perimeter. As my father repeated, "B2," a car horn beeped in his video.

169

I chuckled as I imagined my father standing in the middle of the road with his video camera, unaware of anything but his old school—the car horn a perfectly timed punctuation mark for the accomplishment of locating a place of lost innocence.

My father resumed in his video, and his voice became louder, filled with pride at having achieved something momentous. "Yes, in this school as well as on these playgrounds, I learned everything I know today. Believe me, not much more have I learned since."

I recognized that slight lilt in his voice, the one he used when telling a subtle joke or sharing a witticism. It was something to smile about.

"The left side was B2, where I studied, and the right side was B2 BIS," he said. "The difference was the right side was a French-oriented school, the left side English and business."

Based on the video, combined with what I learned about the Slager family and what I knew about my father, I imagined a scene from early 1940.

"YOU WILL COME FOR KAFFEE on Sunday?" Hilde Slager asks Hilde Stern.

"Ja, natürlich." Naturally. "I bring my special cake."

"Good. We see you then."

The Slager house, at Haaksbergerstraat #94, is a familiar location by now, as the families have spent a lot of time together in the past year. Harry opens the front door, letting in a slight breeze of early spring blossoms, right before Moritz can knock.

"There you are!" He pulls Moritz inside and waves the rest of the family to follow. "Sit down, everyone. Hilde brings out the coffee in a moment."

Walter listens and tries to understand as the Slager brothers, Hugo, age twelve, and his older brother, Johnny, talk animatedly in Dutch. The adults do the same, until the conversation quiets when Harry asks, "Walter, how is your schooling?"

Walter still struggles with speaking Dutch but manages. "Ja, it is okay. I learned this week 'The Rime of the Ancient Mariner.'" He holds up the book that contains this poem and, in English, recites, "Water, water everywhere, nor any drop to drink." His voice lilts up slightly as he smirks with a wry sense of self-satisfaction, both at his ability to recite the words in yet another language, English, including the proper pronunciation of the letter "w" as he was corrected at school, and at the idea that there could be plenty of something and still no way to enjoy it.

Harry nods, smiling. "Ja, Walter, you are right. Sometimes what is all around us we still cannot have. That was very good reciting."

"Now you boys go." Harry motions to his sons. "We have something to discuss, the adults."

"You go with them, Walter," Moritz says.

In the next room, Hugo sits down on the sofa. "Walter, should we play another game of chess? Maybe I win this time!"

"Ja, that would be good." It wouldn't require thinking so hard in Dutch all the time. But Walter is sure to seat himself nearest the dining room, so he can hear some of the adult conversation.

"We need a plan," Moritz says. "I am afraid this might go badly."

"Ach," Hilde Slager quickly responds. "Harry, you need to stop talking against the German government."

An edge to his voice now, Harry responds. "Of course, but if we all stand by and don't speak out, nothing happens. I must say what is on my mind."

"I don't want you arrested. You have children. Our sons cannot be without you. Max is so young, Harry. You must be careful with those leaflets you share around."

"Ja. I know. But these are different times. You will be able to manage if I am away from here, ja?"

Uncomfortable in the loneliness of the lingering silence after her husband's rhetorical question, Hilde Slager worries about her family's future if her husband were arrested. She stands up. "Hilde, Selma, come with me. See my angel sleep before he wakes from his nap."

"She is upset with me," Harry says after they leave the room. "But I cannot stand by."

"Ja, I understand." Moritz hastily puts down his coffee. He is sorry he drank it now that his stomach starts hurting again. "We talk to people at the synagogue to see if there is an organization to do something. Or, we do it ourselves."

Walter wonders if they'll be safe in Holland. He decides to trust that his father has thought through all possibilities, in the same way that his father has taught him to play chess. With that, Walter returns his focus to the game at hand. It is much less stressful.

HAD MY FATHER EVER MENTIONED the Slager family to me? Had he shared Hugo's name with me? At the time I first pondered these questions, I couldn't remember exactly when I had learned of the fate of each Slager family member. Memory can be like that sometimes, facts combined in a way that made it impossible to parse them apart again.

I eventually learned about the Slager family of the 1930s through two items in my father's belongings.

One was a photo. Two versions of the same photo, actually—one with scalloped edges, the other with straight edges. In the identical photos, my father, around eighteen or nineteen years old at the time, had his left arm draped over a man's shoulder, the sides of their bodies touching, emanating a closeness. Walter's wool, double-breasted winter coat fell below the knee. The other man's sports jacket covered a sweater that was neatly tucked into his pants. The outfit was accented by a winter scarf. The unknown photographer's long shadow was captured in the photo. On the back of the straight-edged photo is written: "To Walter! Love from Hugo. On January 5, 1947!!!"

The other item was a letter in Dutch, signed by a man named Hugo Slager, from Amsterdam. It was dated November 1991, a few months after my father's trips to Israel and Holland.

I struggled through a rough translation, enough to understand that both men shared health concerns and sadness related to the war years. And something surprising. Hugo seemed to have included two photos. He wrote:

I am enclosing one more very special photo!!!! It is the last photo taken of both of us on January 5, 1947. The next photo in which we are together is the photo that you sent me showing us in front of the dormitory building in Julis. Isn't that marvelous, so many years between these 2 photos?!?!?!

I looked back through my father's 1991 photos again, locating one of him in green fatigues with a group of four other similarly aged adults. Fulfilling a lifelong dream, my father had made a trip to Israel. While there, he had volunteered with the Israeli army for a couple of weeks. In the photo, I could now identify one of the other men, after having seen other images of him. It was Hugo Slager.

I had been so engrossed with my own story, my journey of "bescherts," coming upon things I wasn't seeking but needed to find, that it didn't occur to me that my father had had his own such journey.

How incredible his trips to Israel and Holland must have been. Yet I was simply on the periphery back in the early nineties. I knew he was traveling, but I was focused on my own young family, my career, and completing my MBA.

As I placed the photo of my father and Hugo on the table, I grieved the lost opportunity to ask my father exactly what had happened over the course of his journey, his own trips to Holland and also Israel. How had he and Harry recognized each other, what had they talked about, and how had my father understood the "coincidence" of being placed in the same bunk, at the same time, on the same volunteer program in Israel? What had it felt like to be reunited with his long-lost cousin-by-marriage? It was moments like these where I knew that, even though the layers of my father and my stories and histories were enmeshed, I was still on my own, independent journey, just as he had been. There was so much I had no other choice but to piece together on my own.

CHAPTER 26

INVASION

INEVITABLY, IN THE PROCESS of inhabiting my father's childhood, I would bump into memories of my own. One such memory takes place in the early seventies on Long Island.

My father was preoccupied with new police cars. As I remember, the new ones had blue lights that extended fully across the top of the car. The old ones had one red flashing light. Neat, more in keeping with the times, was my silent reaction.

"Bad sign," my father had said. "That's what happened when the Nazis came. The police cars looked different."

WALTER, HIS FAMILY, and all the residents of Enschede awaken to planes flying overhead early on the morning of May 10, 1940. Before they can turn on their radios, they hear the thud of a bomb that lands less than a kilometer away.

Later that morning, Moritz scans the local paper for additional details. The headlines tell him enough. "German troops cross the Dutch border" and "Proclamation from Her Majesty the Queen." German soldiers are in the streets, rifles in hand. Schools and factories close.

"Queen Wilhelmina has issued an official proclamation." Moritz reaches for another cigarette.

"What does the queen say?" Hilde's voice quakes, and she sits down to hear the news.

Moritz reads the Dutch aloud.

After our country had observed a strict neutrality with fearful rigor all these months, and while it had no other intention than to maintain this attitude strictly and consistently, last night the German armed forces made a sudden attack on our territory without the slightest warning.

Moritz puts his hand on Walter's shoulder, a vain attempt at comfort.

This despite the solemn promise that the neutrality of our country would be respected as long as we maintained it ourselves. I hereby direct a blatant protest against this exemplary violation of good faith and the degradation of what is proper between civilized states. I and my government will do our duty even now. You do yours, everywhere and in all circumstances, each one in the place where he is set, with the utmost vigilance, and with that inner peace and surrender to which a pure conscience is capable.

"Ja, maybe Harry has it right, to speak up. But I worry about him. I will talk to him to stop handing out those leaflets now, so he doesn't get arrested," Moritz continues.

Hilde, glancing at Moritz, does not need to say what she is thinking. She worries what will happen to her own husband.

Kurt has picked up the paper to read more. "Look at these advertisements, like nothing has changed," he says, pointing to the Rottinghuis & Co. ad on page three. It shows a drawing of a woman with exceptionally long legs and high heels. He turns to page five. "Ah, here, this is important for us now. 'Air Protection. Now that the situation of possible danger from air attacks has occurred … '" Kurt scans the eighteen directives for the most useful guidance and continues reading those aloud. "As I thought. Directive 3, we need to keep lights off, inside and outside, from sunset to sunrise so no light is seen outside. We need to get black shades so we can keep our lights on and see what we eat at night." Kurt winks at Walter. The rest of the family is lost in their thoughts of making survival plans.

On May 13, Queen Wilhelmina and her family flee to safety in the United Kingdom. It takes the Wehrmacht, the unified Nazi armed forces, five days to complete their invasion of the Netherlands, after severely bombing and capturing the city of Rotterdam and parachuting in their troops. They take over Dutch cities and towns through the technical superiority of their tanks and planes and weapons. In their Nazi uniforms, the troops shout their Nazi slogans.

The Netherlands capitulates on May 15. Just like that. It is over. Holland is no longer free. Walter and his family are no longer free.

"You see that Überfallwagen, Walter?" Moritz draws in deeply on his cigarette and holds in the smoke as a small truck—a new kind of police car—drives past their home. He exhales the gray poison, nodding toward the vehicle. "You stay away from that, stay inside when you can."

Walter would learn that the men in green uniforms—the Grüne Polizei—are an arm of the Gestapo in the occupied Netherlands. They travel around in their Überfallwagen, raid trucks, arresting people, a lot of people.

Within weeks, in June, the Grüne Polizei rap on the family's front door. Moritz rushes Walter to a bedroom, then answers the door, as if he has a choice. Walter can't hear what's happening, only muffled voices and a short wail from his grandmother.

A few minutes later, Hilde comes to get Walter. "They arrested the men. The Grüne Polizei took your father and uncle."

The family would learn that Moritz and Kurt were taken to a prison in nearby Münster, Germany. Moritz is lucky. The authorities offer him a choice.

"Mr. Stern," they say to Moritz, with a tinge of cruel sarcasm. "You always wanted to emigrate. We will give you an option now. You may emigrate to Poland. Or you may emigrate to Southern France. What is your preference?"

Moritz knows what life is like in Poland, remembering the letter his family had received a few months earlier from an aunt who had been displaced from Germany to Poland. The letter had been opened by the German censors. Moritz knows they had had to write in code. He had read aloud to his family. "We are enjoying our stay here because every day we have Yom Kippur." Given that this Jewish observance involves one day of fasting, that was enough to know that people were starving to death in Poland.

"Well, then," Moritz says to the man in charge. "I will emigrate to Southern France." This area of France, in 1940, is Vichy France, and is not yet occupied by the German army.

In their Enschede home, Walter, Hilde, and Selma spend the following summer and fall eating their increasingly meager meals in relative silence, not knowing where Moritz and Kurt were taken after Münster. They try to adjust to a life of intensified food rationing and restrictions.

In the town of Enschede, a curfew from midnight to 4 a.m. goes into effect in October 1940. The Wehrmacht confiscates people's horses. The Dutch people are permitted to listen to Dutch or German radio stations only, and by January 1, 1941, a license is required to own a radio. Eventually, all radios must be turned in.

Later that month, police make an inventory of all the Jewish people of Enschede, 1,368 of whom list their names and addresses as directed. They are unaware that this list would become a convenient way for the authorities to round them up. All Jewish people in Holland over fifteen years of age are issued yellow identification cards, which they must keep with them at all times.

ON MY DINING ROOM TABLE at home in 2017, while again looking through the documents I had from my father, I had found Oma's persoons-bewijs, her Dutch identification card. I would learn that the persoonsbewijs replaced the yellow identification cards by January 1942. They were stamped in two places with the black letter J denoting Jood, Jew.

Oma's persoonsbewijs, number 00895, included a photograph of a woman who looked far older than her forty years. Her eyes appeared tired, yet her set lips and carefully arranged hair gave away her resoluteness. The name on the card read "H. S. Stern." She was not given a middle name at birth. But, I knew, in 1939, the German government identified all German Jewish people by requiring an appended middle name: "Sara" for women and "Israel" for men.

Searching Oma's persoonsbewijs for additional hints of her life from that time, my teeth clenched. I kept returning to the J markings and thought about current events here, in my country of the twenty-first century. Even here, people continue to be labeled. Why can't we all live in peace, each one of us living true to our personal identities, addressed with kindness and respect? Or at least left alone?

As I researched my family's personal history, I also expanded my scope to Enschede and Holland. In February 1941, Nazi Germany established the Amsterdam-based Dutch Joodse Raad. It was yet another a cruel measure requiring that a selected group of Jewish citizens carry out the Nazi government's orders. This included deciding which individuals were to be transported to camps, to almost certain death.

Soon after, a local Joodse Raad was established in Enschede. Sieg Menko, formerly head of Enschede's Committee for German Refugees, became head of the local Joodse Raad and reported to the central authority in Amsterdam. As a prominent businessman, Mr. Menko had many connections—Jewish and non-Jewish—in the textile industry and the community. Therefore, he succeeded in raising funds from the non-Jewish people, who still had money, to help support those going into hiding.

Isidoor van Dam, who had also been a textile factory owner, became treasurer of the Enschede Joodse Raad. Officially, they did not suggest people go into hiding. However, it was the third person in the Enschede Joodse Raad trio, Gerard Sanders, who compiled the names of Jewish people who should go into hiding. He worked closely with Dominee Leendert Overduin, a local Protestant clergy.

Dominee Overduin convinced members of his church community and others throughout the area to provide hiding places for those most at risk of being deported. He disguised himself by dressing as a chimney sweep to avoid his own arrest. Nevertheless, he would be arrested three times.

I was taken by the stories of these men who had put their lives on the line. It was because of their brave acts that so many Jewish people survived in this part of Holland. However, my father mentioned only one of those names—Dominee Leendert Overduin—in his testimony video.

In his video, my father reported that Overduin was a Protestant clergy who—and this was my father's exaggerated recollection—had hidden 35,000 Jewish people out of the 55,000 that were saved. My father seemed impressed and appreciative that the local Catholic and Protestant church communities had worked toward a common goal to hide people and to resist the occupier.

The organization Dominee Overduin had established with the help of his sisters, Maartje and Corrie, would ultimately save hundreds of Jewish people from the region by providing hiding places for them. The Overduins also provided shelter and food for as many as a thousand people in hiding, and they have been acknowledged as Righteous Among the Nations by Yad Vashem.

In November 2018, on my return visit to Enschede, I had lunch with Evertjan, the man who had connected me with the Enschede synagogue. I said, "I plan to visit the Grote Kerk after lunch to see the plaque recognizing Dominee Overduin."

"Ah, yes," Evertjan responded. "But that church is now closed to the public. You won't be able to enter."

He could see my disappointment. "But let's try," he added.

We knocked on the side door of the Great Church. One of the stagehands, who was setting up for a concert that evening, answered. He and Evertjan spoke a few words I could not understand. The stagehand let us enter.

There, in the center of the large church, I held back my tears as I viewed the plaque and thought about the good this man and his sisters had performed. I photographed the plaque for later translation of the verse from Isaiah 16:3 that was embossed on it: "Hide the outcasts, do not betray the refugees."

After the war, Dominee Overduin would assist the new set of "persecuted" people: the children left home alone when their parents—pro-German Dutch Nationalist Party members—were detained, often with no evidence. This detail, my father had never mentioned to me. I wondered if he knew.

CHAPTER 27

CABLE GUARD

I CUED UP MY FATHER'S testimony video to listen again to one of his resistance stories.

The Dutch did not like to be occupied by anyone, by Germany or anybody. Very, very traumatic experiences there.

I couldn't help noticing the way my father emphasized and drew out the "mat" sound in traumatic.

By 1941, resistance was strengthening.

Cables ran along the main road in Enschede. The German Wehrmacht relied on the cables for their communications. In July 1941, two of those cables were cut, perhaps by resisters or perhaps by young boys.

So, they would take a hatchet and chop through the telephone cable in the ground so that the Germans could not communicate with each other.

And now what did happen? The Germans did not mind that at all.

The rest of my father's testimony about the cable guard contained information that I could not corroborate, the trauma of the cable-cutting events and its repercussions conflated to create this memory for him.

The first time that happened, they arrested twelve or fourteen people that were clergy, judges, teachers, all professional people, farm and businesspeople, to the square, and machine-gunned them down in front of the people to see. Now they told them, "This is for the sabotage."

The next day they chopped through the telephone cables again.

They said, "Look, you have your head on your shoulders and we have our head on our shoulders. We don't care if we are getting killed, but we don't want you to run our life."

What I was able to confirm was that the Sicherheitspolizei had set up the kabelwacht, cable guard, in mid-July.

BEGINNING ON JULY 20, 1941, the adult male citizens of Enschede receive notification of their assigned time to stand guard over the cable wires, often throughout the night and even in the rain and the cold as the seasons encroach on winter. Walter is exempt from these duties, being fourteen years old instead of the requisite minimum age of twenty-five.

Each section is guarded by two men who are prohibited from any other activities during their watch, including talking to other guards or passersby.

A sense of camaraderie forms, and someone writes a mocking poem about the experience called "Het Kabellied," The Cable Song. The Dutch rhyme ends with the lines: "Do you hear something? Very suspicious! Then hurry there quickly, as otherwise—imagine—they'll cut it through again."

On September 13, 1941, the cables are chopped again, cutting off the ability of the German authority to communicate, if only for a short while. The cable cutters put their lives, and those of the guardsmen, on the line. They put the lives of everyone on the line.

In retaliation for this cable cutting, seventy-one innocent people from Enschede are arrested in a razzia, raid. Of those, sixty-six are Jewish, all of whom are sent to Mauthausen where they are murdered before the end of the year. Word reaches their families in Enschede a few weeks later.

These heinous acts stimulate an even stronger Dutch Resistance in the Enschede area and prompt the realization that matters are going to worsen. Those in fear for their lives due to their outspoken or public resistance go into hiding.

The kabelwacht duties are discontinued on December 23, 1941.

MY FATHER'S TELLING of the kabelwacht incidents differed from those that are documented by historians. He recollected that, after the September 1941 cable cutting:

> *... they took double the amount of prominent people and killed them on the public square. Now they told them, "This is for the sabotage."*

His excitement suddenly subsided, and he spoke more quietly.

Then the cables did not get cut anymore.

Had my father confused the announcement of the execution of a different group of men—in October 1942 in a nearby town for different sabotage acts—with a 1941 public square shooting in Enschede that did not occur? Regardless, a miscommunication or misunderstanding left an indelibly traumatic memory with my father. Another memory that he would never directly share with his own children, yet one that would impact us nonetheless.

The truth remains, however, that the story of the kabelwacht could be seen only as a traumatic one. The Jewish community was hit heavily, including our family; I would later find that among those sent to their deaths in the razzia was a distant cousin.

Still, the resistance was strengthened.

CHAPTER 28
CITIZENSHIP

I KNEW THAT GERMANY had stripped citizenship from Jewish people, yet I was shocked to find images of the physical evidence, the cards for each of my family members stating this fact.

DURING THE WEEK of October 13, 1941, the *Staatsanzeiger*, the official publication of the German Reich and Prussian State, publishes the list of Jewish people whose German citizenship has been stripped. Moritz, Hilde, and Walter are on that list.

A card for each of them documents that fact along with their altered names: Moritz *Israel* Stern, Hilde *Sara* Stern, Walter *Israel* Stern. They are officially stateless.

Along with the rest of German Jewry, they had no say in this decision. No one asked them. It doesn't matter that most of their ancestors had lived in Germany for five or ten generations. It doesn't matter that most German

Jewish people, until the 1930s, and even during the 1930s, had seen them-selves as German first, that they had heavily assimilated into German culture and life.

BY 2018, I'D BEGUN THINKING about applying for German dual citizenship. I had learned that it was my right, according to Article 116, para-graph 2, of Germany's Basic Law, given that my father's citizenship had been revoked due to his religion between the years 1933 and 1945. But I couldn't bring myself to "choose" German citizenship. The thing was, I wanted to want it. I thought of the hate-filled 2017 rally in Charlottesville, of the synagogue massacre in late 2018 in Pittsburgh. I wanted my sons and their descendants to have options, in case they were forced to flee their homeland.

As part of my research, I read a book called *A Place They Called Home: Reclaiming Citizenship*. The anthology, edited by Donna Swarthout, contained a collection of essays written by children or grandchildren of German-born Jewish people whose citizenships had been stripped from them during the war years. These stories of a "new Jewish return" to Germany resonated with me, the authors capturing so eloquently various aspects of how I felt. The ambiguity, the ambivalence, the messiness of it all.

Each story told about a home that was no longer a home, about a place in Germany that felt like it fit, felt like it was the right place to be, felt like where the author came from. It needed to be reclaimed. I almost felt that way too, having always identified more strongly with my German heritage than with my mother's Hungarian background. Yet, I could feel my father and Oma looking down on me with disappointment. *This is too far.* I could almost hear their voices.

Would I dare to try to regain my rightful German citizenship? I tried to imagine that my father and Oma would have understood the current political state in which I was living and would have valued my need to have a European Union country's citizenship, for me and especially for my descendants.

It was when reading *A Place They Called Home* that I first learned the word Heimat, homeland. A kind of spiritual home-place, where one was *supposed* to be.

Even though my father's family lived in Bocholt for only about forty years, it felt like my home. The place from which I came. Perhaps that was because my father and Oma had both been born there, and that was the place they had held in their own hearts and souls. Perhaps one can inherit the DNA of Heimat just as well as the DNA of family trauma.

Throughout the stories, I paused my reading now and then, unable to see through the tears in my eyes. *Was Germany my land? Was Bocholt my home? Was it a kind of a family spiritual Heimat that I must reclaim?*

I knew this was part of my journey, working out the answer to this essential question of my identity. I allowed my thinking to evolve. I also realized that I would be questioned by friends and people new to me about why I would pursue a German citizenship, after all that had happened. In the end, it needed to be *my* choice and only my choice. No one, at least not in this moment, could take that away from me.

CHAPTER 29

LETTERS

WE TEND TO FORGET THE VALUE and importance of letters. Before email and texts existed, people were excited to retrieve their mail and find something other than bills and advertisements and catalogues in their mailboxes. They made expensive phone calls only on special occasions like birthdays or other significant life events. But in a letter, you were allowed to write as much as you desired, to provide your reader with all manner of detail, even to draw a picture or enclose a photograph.

When I was a child, my parents encouraged me—strongly coaxed me—to write letters to relatives, especially to Oma. In retrospect, I'm glad I did, as it must have given her great pleasure to receive these ultra-short missives in her mailbox in Florida throughout the winter months. I only wish I had written her more often.

I recently came across some thin, blue airmail letters that I had written to my parents from my semester abroad in Israel in 1981. My mother had saved them. We talked by phone only twice during those six months, but I wrote to my parents many times each week.

It wasn't until 2017 that I understood what my father had saved in his own archives. I pulled out a set of yellowed, airmail-thin paper with blue-inked German script that I could not decipher, except for the location "Rivesaltes" on the top of one of the pages. There were five documents in all, some including letters to two different parties, possibly in an effort to make the most of scant and costly supplies.

Once I had the letters translated, I realized that Moritz had sent them to his family members who were already in America. It was difficult to determine exactly to whom each of Moritz's letters was written. Although some started with the name of the intended recipient, most started "Meine Liebe(n)," my dear(s). At some point, these letters had made it into Oma's hands, likely once she'd arrived in America.

In his testimony video, my father shared that he and Oma had received some letters that Moritz had sent to Enschede during the war, through a Swiss intermediary.

We had a friend in Switzerland that was the daughter of the rabbi who circumcised me in Germany. He sent a letter to her, and she sent the letter to us.

I did not find any of those letters. Nevertheless, in my white-gloved hands, I oh-so-carefully lifted the feather-light gems that were in my possession to the scanner, then replaced them in their archival sleeves.

These letters were precious connections to a dark history, to a person so closely related to me—my grandfather, whom I would never meet. I learned some things about Moritz and his life after his arrest and pieced together more about my father and Oma's life in Enschede. And how they might have experienced letter writing. I don't know what Oma wrote to Moritz about the news in Enschede during 1940 and 1941. Exactly what Moritz wrote to Oma, I also don't know. But I could piece it together pretty closely from the series of letters Moritz wrote to his family in America, the ones in my possession, in combination with historical events in Enschede and the information my father had shared in his videos.

IT IS ALREADY JANUARY 1941, and it has been months since they've heard from Moritz. Walter, now fourteen, examines the envelope that has arrived, aching to receive news from his father and uncle. Instead, the letter is from Switzerland.

"Mutti, look, you have a letter." Walter hands it to his mother, and he sits on the sofa next to his grandmother.

"Ja, this is from our friend from a long time ago. Her father performed your bris milah in Germany when you were a baby. Let's see what news she has from Switzerland."

Walter reaches for his sketch pad, waiting for his mother to read the letter aloud. Instead, he hears a deep inhale, a reverse cry.

"Ach du lieber Gott. Look, inside is a letter from your father!"

"Mutti! Read it!" Walter puts down his pad and moves to the edge of the couch, and his grandmother follows suit.

"Meine Lieben," Moritz opens.

You will surely know that since some time I am interned here in France. Thanks to God, I can tell you that my health is good and that, given the circumstances, I am satisfied, since at least we can enjoy some freedom, and I am together with many people, including very nice colleagues.

My address: Moritz Stern Ilot K. Baraque 21 Camp de Rivesaltes. It is a nice, clean camp and I think that this abode will be long-term. This camp opened to the German refugees, like me, only a few days ago.

Unfortunately, the sponsorships for dear Selma and Kurt were recently burned with the collected inventory of the American consulate in Rotterdam, which you surely must know. I wrote again to Hermann and expressed appreciation for the sponsorship and requested that he would renew this sponsorship, to send one document to the American consulate in Rotterdam and the other to the American consulate in Marseille. It is self-evident that all expenses will be completely incurred to him. I wrote about our work switch into the chemical industry, Hilde, so he knows we have practical work experience. How goes the work for you?

I hope to see you soon. Kisses, your Moritz

"Rivesaltes." Hilde remembers French geography. "That is in the South of France, in Vichy, near the Pyrenees." She moves to the table to write her reply. Walter and Selma suggest sentences to her now and then.

Meine Liebe. We are doing well enough here. My work keeps me busy still. Walter manages alright with school and the other children. He has his friends and even a girlfriend I am not supposed to know about. She is a nice girl. What is your work?

Cousin Gisele writes that they are relieved to be in America, you can imagine, after her husband's time in the concentration camp already by 1939 and then their time on the St. Louis. Gisele still writes me about that voyage, how her husband said, "I don't go back, or I throw myself in the water," he was so sick from the camp. They were fortunate to board another ship on 1 March last year, as you know. They are living in New York still. She writes that their young Hans earns 10 dollars per week, and she stays in the house.

My mother misses her sister and brothers and their children. We have letters sometimes from them. We can understand the state of their lives without the details. I hope the best for Uncle Paul, he tried so much to help us. I hope that we can do the same for my other uncles.

Kisses from all of us, your Hilde, Walter, and Selma

Hilde slips the letter into an envelope and writes the Rivesaltes address on it. She places that envelope inside a second envelope, which she addresses to their Swiss friend. Hilde adds to the second envelope a separate letter of thanks to their Swiss friend. "I go mail the letter this afternoon," she says, her voice still shaking.

A couple of weeks later, Hilde receives another letter. This one brings particular excitement.

"Mutter, Walter, come quickly, another letter and something special!"

"Meine Lieben," she begins, reading aloud.

I wrote to my brother Gustav again in America. He sent me funds, dollars, but the warm clothing didn't arrive. I was able to use the funds very well. I learned from our friend in Switzerland that my sister Mathilde's daughter in America is engaged. I wish them the best. I wrote Gustav that Walter should learn something practical at the end of his schooling after he arrives to America.

I am taking care of horses in the camp and transporting grain from one area to the mill and from the mill back to the camp so they could bake breads and so on. I hope you like this drawing from my friend in the camp. He is an artist.

Please leave three Marks for Walter. Kisses, your Moritz

"But look here, at this! You see, he is doing okay, he has a reasonably good life!" Hilde holds up a colored-pencil sketch of Moritz with a horse. Walter silently notes Moritz's gray appearance, not the healthiest look, but realistic nonetheless.

"Look at how natural an image this is," Selma adds, "with his neat hair and knotted tie. And nice colors, like with crayons or something."

"And here, he holds the horse reins." Walter points to his father's hands on the reins, near the head of the horse. Neither the horse nor Moritz looked directly at the artist, each gazing off in opposite directions almost as though they are looking out for guards. Or planning a way to freedom.

Hilde places the sketch on the table and runs her fingers tenderly over the image, down the front of the horse's long face as though she can feel its hair, then along Moritz's cheek, ear, neck, finally resting on his chest.

"Wait here a minute." Hilde walks to the drawer where she keeps the photographs the family still has. She selects a few of Moritz and lays them out on the table. Next, Hilde shares stories with Walter—where each photo was taken, for what event, something memorable about Moritz.

"This photo, here." Hilde points to a photo of a group of men, many in button-down jackets that contain the letters "PG," prisonnier de guerre, French for prisoner of war. The men wear a variety of caps. Of the eleven men in the photo, only one smiles, an odd, eerie kind of smile. The remaining men appear not particularly happy but also not particularly upset. They patiently, or impatiently, wait for the photographer to complete his task.

Hilde moves her finger across the image of Moritz. Then she marks an X above his cap with blue ink and places the photograph in Walter's hands. "This isn't the first time your father is interned in France. Also, he was a prisoner there twenty-five years ago, when he was fighting in the German army. A lot of Jewish people fought for our Heimat in the Great War. A lot of people lost their lives. Your father managed to escape from internment in France, back home to Germany."

These men in the photo, as prisoners of war in a French camp, might have been fortunate to avoid the terrors, the mangling, the deaths that pervaded that war.

Walter understands the irony and shakes his head slightly. He is deeply confused and looks back and forth at the two images—the photo of a prisoner of war who fought for his Heimat and the sketch of a gray man sent to labor by the same Heimat. "When will he return to us?" Walter wants to ask, but he doesn't.

Years later, in America, Hilde would label the back of the World War I photo, this time in pencil. "Moritz as prisoner of war in France." But for now, she retrieves her writing paper and begins.

Meine Liebe,

Thank you for the picture. It is a very natural image of you. And we will cherish it of course. Stay safe, caring for the horses. We looked at other photos of you and I told Walter the stories—your experience last time you were in France in a war fighting for your country. I cannot say more now. I cannot share the anger I feel in a letter. "Mother" might be watching. Is Kurt with you still? Mutter is longing to see him again and awaits a reunion with the family.

Kisses from all of us, your Hilde

The next letter arrives a few weeks later, this one from a new camp.

Meine sehr Lieben!

I received on 2 April your letter. Some days later, I received also all the sponsorship papers from Philadelphia. I expressed my thanks to my brothers for their part. As for myself, I am naturally doing everything possible to be able to leave Europe quickly. We will perhaps all be together with my sister, Mathilde, in New York one day soon. The time I spend on emigration is turning me into a hermit.

I changed my address, that is to say from Argelès to Récébédou. The place is located circa 9 kilometers distant from the town of Toulouse. My current address follows: Moritz Stern, Camp de Récébédou Baraque 9 Par Portet (Nort Garan). The money sent to me has unfortunately not yet arrived, so I wrote to Mrs. Warschawski in Switzerland.

Recently, I received a suitcase with garments and pieces of clothing. After changing clothes, after months I once again felt a wish for culture, because when for more than 10 months one wears one and the same suit, that is only the back and pants of the suit, so you might well think that the same is not the most elegant. Kisses, your Moritz

Hilde writes her husband devotedly, while realizing his desperate situation.

Meine Liebe,

I am glad to know you have new clothes finally. We too hope to see you home here soon or when all of us come to New York. Harry is gone from Enschede now, to the east.

I don't write you what happens in that case because of "Mother."

In the meantime, we remembered the queen's birthday on 31 August. Papers dropped from the sky with a drawing of her face. "Netherlands will rise again," it was written underneath. People made copies and sold them. Also cigarettes in red boxes rained down from the planes. You would have enjoyed that.

In June, Walter passed his exam for the Dutch Gymnasium, but now Walter no longer attends the school, it is not permitted. He is doing well for himself, he is tirelessly busy but it is not too much for him. His boss has already promoted him, also later he will be an apprentice for him.

Kisses from all of us, your Hilde

One day, another letter arrives. Walter keeps rereading the last lines:

I go to another camp now. I don't know if I am able to write anymore. Kisses, Your Moritz

It would take Walter a few months to absorb that this is the final letter.

I SOMEHOW ALWAYS KNEW that my grandfather was murdered in Auschwitz, but I cannot recall learning it for the first time.

In ninth grade, I took a Holocaust class in Hebrew High School. We watched the film *Night and Fog,* a French documentary with footage of prisoners arriving at Auschwitz.

My grandfather, I wanted to call out to my classmates. That's what happened to *my* grandfather, to *my* family. That's where *he* was murdered by the Nazis. Once again, I felt apart, different, a sense of not belonging—among my peers, who had multiple grandparents, and within my family, where the loss of my grandfather was never discussed. My grandfather felt so distant to me, back then.

It has taken me years to learn and to absorb my family's story.

When I read and reread the translations of my grandfather's letters to people in America, I wondered how much of the hope that Moritz felt, then the hopelessness, made it into the letters that he wrote to Oma and my father, the letters I had not seen. I was perplexed as to why no letters addressed to Oma survived. After all, she had old photos and documents. She had the drawing of Moritz with a horse. But no letters to her from her husband survived to be passed on to me.

The drawing will forever be indelible in my heart. The words my father spoke about it in his testimony video danced in my head.

He looked a little grayer, but it is a very natural image. And I cherish it, of course.

Now *I* had it. In *my* family album. And I cherish it. Of course.

What also has remained indelible in my heart was the story of Moritz as a prisoner in France in two World Wars. The first time, held by France as a prisoner of war for the crime of being a German solider. The enemy. It didn't matter that he was Jewish. Many Jewish people fought for their German homeland in that war.

Twenty-five years later, Moritz was a prisoner in a second World War, again in France. This time he was sent there by the German government for the crime of being Jewish. How does a people, within twenty-five years, turn from conscripting Jewish people into their army, even decorating Jewish soldiers for bravery, and memorializing Jewish war losses in cemeteries and churches and town squares, to arresting them, putting them into forced labor camps, and sending them to their deaths? Had humankind gone crazy?

Moritz struggled to obtain freedom as he was moved through various camps in the South of France—Rivesaltes, Argelès, Récébédou, and finally, Septfonds. Each letter that I have from Moritz to people in America, except the final one, included requests for affidavits and financial guarantees, and each letter shared concerns over obtaining a sponsorship and a visa. Each letter discussed money, except the final one. Each letter expressed hope. Except. The final one.

In his letters, Moritz warned his readers that the letters would be censored, and so I assumed he didn't write things exactly as they were. The final letter was written to Uncle Paul, Selma's brother, who had made it to the United States. This was the letter that most haunted me, as there were many references I could not understand. I both wanted to and didn't want to understand. It's the letter that was the most emotionally expressive.

Septfonds, 17 June 1942

Liebe Onkel Paul,

I have waited until news came that you succeeded on your journey. I heard this after a few days through my sister & brother whose addresses you know. I am happy that in spite of difficult circumstances you were successful in achieving your goal. For me it was impossible for reasons you know. I have resigned myself not to emigrate, although I have left nothing untried. Incidentally, I think that the war will be over by November or December, although what can we really say? During the entire course of the war our estimates have been 100% in error. Up to now I have gotten news from you punctually each week, and I always hear only the best. The last letter I myself received from you is from 29 March. The letters stay somewhat optimistic. Miss van Z. always comes. Hilde writes to me very devotedly.

I still want to find out Uncle Otto's address through the Geneva Red Cross. There are many ways to Poland, and also from my relatives. I previously received your letter from Casablanca. Mr. Sternberg comes here every day. You know well who I mean. My current job requires much work, but it is good for a man and the time goes by quickly. Once again all the best greetings to Julius, Gisela, the youth, and again many greetings to the other Lennebergs. Moritz

Moritz continued, possibly a few days later:

Hilde wrote the following today about Walter. Walter is doing well for himself. He is extremely busy, but it is not too much for him. His boss has already promoted him and has promised to keep him as an apprentice in the future. I inquired about Uncle Otto but unfortunately nothing can be done. I cannot get his address. I do not want to write about this to you because of Mother. Incidentally, they communicated with me from there that everything was in order in the extended family. I received your letter from Casablanca. Many thanks for the package you sent with food; send my thanks to Kurt as well. For several months I have been stable administrator. I have to look out for four horses & the work that goes with it. I earn 180 Franks per month and have the benefit of not having to live in the barracks anymore & some other comforts. I wish you, Paul, only the best, stay well and get better. With the most heartfelt greetings & hope to see you again.

Your nephew, Moritz

I have wondered, after listening to my father share about how life was relatively good in the camp for my grandfather, how often young Walter opened the album to look at the drawing of Moritz with the horse. I don't recall seeing the drawing displayed in my home. I don't recall seeing or being shown this picture. Yet, even as a child, I knew, somehow, of an unspeakable tragedy. Too painful, I presume, too much of a reminder of heartbreak and loss. I am saddened to look at the picture too. All the more reason I will show it to everyone who wants to hear about my father's story, about the pain, and more so about the good that can trickle through the unspeakable atrocities.

Do we display the things we cherish, or do we keep them hidden? I had avoided using the beautiful tea china my mother left me because it reminded me that she was gone and because I didn't want the china to break, as it was one of the few remaining physical reminders of the material possessions she enjoyed. I resolved, in that moment of understanding, to take out the tea set for three (!) and use it whenever I had the chance.

I thought about the items my parents chose to display. There were the Vincent van Gogh prints—the sunflowers and the picnickers under a draw-bridge—hanging in the dining room. There were the pieces of driftwood hanging in the living room that my father had collected from the local Long Island white-sanded beach. But there were no family photographs from the "old country" hanging on the walls or adorning the dresser tops. None in my parents' home nor in Oma's home. I couldn't begin to absorb the depth of the pain, of the effort to keep horrendous memories and terrible secrets tied tightly inside. They were strangled yet still alive. Whimpering to be set free. In quiet but ever-present anticipation of an industrious, curious, slightly obsessed daughter who would begin to uncover them.

CHAPTER 30

YELLOW STARS COME TO HOLLAND

I REMEMBER FEELING A SHOCKWAVE go through me the first time my father showed me his yellow star, the one he was required to wear in Holland. Yet, I cannot recall where I was, what my father said to me, how he held the star, or if he was even holding it at all. But he must have shown it to me. The brightness of the star glaring at me, its too-obvious gold-yellow, with the word "Jood" written in the middle, are indelibly imprinted in my mind. I remember asking if I could take it to Hebrew school, to show the other children this significant item. I sensed there was something about this request that disturbed my father. Still, I am unable to recall the interaction, to conjure that moment. At the age of about ten, I could absorb only what a child can take in about the meaning of such an item. But the unspoken horror of it hung in the air.

Until I started my research, I knew little of the history of the yellow stars. I didn't know where they were made and that each country had the word for

"Jew" in their local language printed on their stars. On April 29, 1942, the Nazi occupiers required all Jewish people of Holland to wear a yellow star on the left side of their clothing, while both inside and outside their homes. The Jewish people had to pay for this privilege. Each person over the age of six was required to purchase four stars.

Within three days, half a million stars, enough for the entire Jewish population of Holland, were manufactured and distributed. In a bitter twist of fate, all the stars for Holland were manufactured in the De Nijverheid textile factory in Enschede, which the Nazis had taken over from the van Gelderen family in 1940.

The stars were printed on bolts of bright-yellow fabric, each six-sided badge outlined in black, containing the Dutch word for Jew, Jood. A dotted line outside of the star showed where to cut so that the star could be sewn onto clothing with a small seam.

Having multiple stars was practical, it turns out, enabling wearers to avoid having to sew, rip, and sew repeatedly onto various outer garments, as using a safety pin was not permitted.

In the midst of learning this history, I would look at the star I had—the one my father had worn, and saved, and left for me to examine closely. I noticed that it was neatly lined, with a white cloth backing. The stitching was impeccable, a pride of workmanship coming through, while the dotted lines peeked through one of the sides. Was this a slight imperfection or a metaphoric attempt to escape the constraints and restrictions of cruel men?

CHAPTER 31
A TRAIN RIDE

I USED TO COMMUTE TO WORK daily from Sharon, Massachusetts, to Boston via the commuter rail. I would race to catch the 7:35 a.m. train to South Station and reverse my commute around 5:00 p.m. It's an easy twenty-eight-minute ride, some of which traverses the Neponset River Reservation area, where tranquil views of the river greet passengers who sit in comfortable high-backed red seats, perhaps inviting them to relax and appreciate nature.

These same waters swept right up to the tracks after a rainstorm or winter thaw, offering a sense of wonder and beauty. The conductor would walk through the car after each stop, "Tickets, please." I showed my ticket without thinking twice about this habitual action.

These commutes usually calmed me, providing precious time between readying my elementary-age kids for school and reaching my workplace, or after an intense day at work as I transitioned to a hectic evening back home, preparing dinner and helping with bath time and bedtime activities. On the train, I read books or thought about my day or planned an upcoming event for work. Sometimes I'd meditate.

Of course, the commuter rail often lived up to its less-than-perfect reputation for keeping to a schedule. Sometimes a train was delayed due to a breakdown, sometimes because of weather conditions. I experienced these delays more than a handful of times. Sometimes a broken-down train resulted in standing room only on a later train. Summertime overcrowding on the commuter trains was frustrating, anxiety-inducing, sweat-producing, and even enraging when it resulted in someone being late for a critical work meeting. Or fainting.

One vivid train-delay experience involved a time when our crowded and overly warm train was stopped for a while in Back Bay Station, an underground station not far from my endpoint. I felt claustrophobic, as if the platform walls were so close I could touch them, if only my window could be opened.

The more I lingered on this need for air, the more I could feel myself tense up. I tried to remind myself that my extreme anxiety would be fleeting. The train would move on and I would get out. I would walk through the station, to the street with the masses, and we would all proceed on our various routes to work. I would be fine.

Except it was more than that. Hot, overcrowded trains and being stuck in tight quarters were also the legacy of a family history to which I was getting too close—flashbacks to a past that was not mine yet something my body had inherited.

ON AUGUST 24, 1942, Moritz's time in the French labor camps comes to an end when he is transported to the closest transit camp, Drancy, just outside of Paris.

One week later, on the morning of August 31, 1942, Moritz, together with 759 other adults and 242 French children, is herded onto one last train ride by a security team that includes an officer and eight men.

Transport #26. Train 901-21. Origin: Drancy Camp, France. Destination: Auschwitz-Birkenau Extermination Camp, Poland.

Moritz quickly surveys the space as he climbs into the cattle car. These rides are not intended to provide a comfortable passage from home to work, certainly not back home again. They are, Moritz well knows, intended to provide the most efficient transportation possible for cargo that is deemed worthless, in need of destruction, annihilation.

Moritz tries to find a spot near the tiny window or at least along a wall that he can lean on. He attempts to stay close to the bucket filled with precious little water, and away from the empty bucket that would quickly overflow with urine and feces. As he visually examines the details of this car for loose boards, his tired mind searches for one last gasp of hope for a plan to survive, until the car is filled and he can no longer see the floor or the walls. The doors close on the one hundred people, each individual person-cargo standing upright, with barely enough room to move, sit, rest, faint, urinate, or defecate.

Moritz and the others are jolted slightly, with no room to fall far, at 8:55 a.m. The slow, laborious ride is underway. Many are embarrassed to use the empty bucket to relieve themselves, instead holding it in for as long as they can. But quickly, the water bucket is empty, and the latrine bucket overflows. The stench is intolerable, the heat of the packed car in the height of summer is brutal. In one car on Transport #26, some men attempt an escape. Women on board yell at them to stop. "How can you?" one cries. "Didn't you hear the orders? They'll kill everyone!" The men give up.

A day or two or maybe three later, the train stops. Some of the more able-bodied men are let out, presumably to provide needed labor about one hundred kilometers away from Auschwitz. The cattle car doors slam shut again, providing only one breath of fresh air to the cargo inside before the heat and stench again overwhelm all on board.

Later, Transport #26 slows as it passes under the sign: "Arbeit Macht Frei," Work Sets You Free. It makes its final cargo stop on September 2.

The cargo is ordered off the train and sorted. The more fit or desirable prisoners are sent to the tattooist, where they are scarred with a series of numbers marked on their arms. Twelve men and twenty-seven women from this transport are selected for slave labor. They receive the numbers 62897–62908 and 18827–18853, then are sent to their new jobs.

Those who are less fit, undesirable to perform the work required by the Nazis, undesirable for participation in the many medical or science experiments conducted at the camp, and undesirable to sexually please those in charge, are sent off in a different direction immediately after arrival. These people with families, with hopes and dreams, with so much life left to live, are to be entirely eliminated from the earth, only their ashes to remain, floating in the camp air and in the neighboring villages, the stench of their burning bodies weaving through bunks and fences and trees and homes. Only the memory of their lives would survive—if anyone remained to remember them. On September 3, Moritz enters the gas chamber, his limp body soon carried to the ovens for cremation.

Moritz would send no more letters to his family, who would not know his fate for some years. His incessant planning, initially to prosper in Germany, then simply to survive, had been terminated. His life was ended, but his memory and legacy would live on because of his plans— plans that enabled his wife and son to survive.

Ultimately, his foresight allowed the granddaughter he would never meet to be able to uncover his story and memorialize him.

A FEW TRIGGERS REMIND ME of a past not my own. Crowded, delayed train rides are one such trigger. When I see a large smokestack, even if it is the remnant of a long-defunct, once-vibrant industry in a remote part of New England, I feel ill, a pain nagging in the pit of my stomach.

The sign in the Frankfurt airport marked "showers" made me quake. Sometimes, even the wood-burning pizza ovens so common in restaurants today are a reminder of the camps. I've learned to cope, take a deep breath, and use the rational side of my brain to disconnect the current-day experience from the inherited, unspoken ones. I travel to where I need to go. I take in the scenery on a New England weekend away. I enjoy my pizza.

Still, I quietly, and often subconsciously, thank my grandfather for his efforts that saved his wife and son.

CHAPTER 32
BICYCLES TO HIDING

ONE OF MY FAVORITE JEWISH HOLIDAYS is Simchas Torah. It is a joyous holiday capping off the many autumn holidays and celebrating the cycle of the Torah. In synagogue, it is customary to end the annual reading of the five books of Moses and begin again. Traditionally, children and adults parade around the synagogue sanctuary during each of the seven circular hakafos processions, carrying the Torah scrolls and singing songs of joy.

After the processions, the Torah reader chants the final verses of the Torah, then immediately starts again: "In the beginning, God created heaven and earth … " The reading of the Torah, as in all of Jewish life, as in all of life everywhere, is a cycle. It doesn't stop, it doesn't end. It goes round and round, sometimes with abundant joy, sometimes with intense sadness and loss.

IT IS OCTOBER 2, 1942, in Enschede, the day before Simchas Torah and the end of the Sukkos holiday week. Walter, Hilde, and Selma aren't at synagogue this day of the holiday, opting instead to remain at home. They open the front door as a neighbor runs past, screaming. "Run and hide, the Germans are coming and picking up the Jews anywhere."

During this raid, the police arrest Jewish people from the synagogue and elsewhere in Enschede with no notice, despite an attempt by the Joodse Raad leadership to warn people. They had sent a telegram to other sections of the regional Joodse Raad urging them to spread the word: "Make sure backpacks and suitcases are packed." Those 114 Jewish people, who do not understand the meaning of the message or choose not to heed the warning, are rounded up during the evening of October 2, and transported to Camp Westerbork early the following morning.

Hilde acts quickly and decisively to keep her family safe. She contacts a smuggler, someone in the Resistance, who will help them. The man tells Hilde to meet him at dusk on the evening of October 3—the start of the Simchas Torah holiday—with her family, in a certain location. "I will have the bicycles ready, and we will ride to a farm where you can stay. And bring money, whatever money you have."

"Komm, Mutter." Hilde looks at her mother as they pack their bags. "We cannot bring all these things. We come back for them after."

"Ja, you are right. But I need these photos of Kurt. Until I can see him again."

"Ja, noch besser, even better. I take a few photos too, and the drawing of Moritz." And then, more slowly, to hang hope in the air, "We will see them again."

The family grabs their sparsely filled bags, packed only with clothes for a couple of days, some mementos and documents, perhaps a gem or two as insurance, and whatever money they have. Hilde checks the kitchen for suitable food and adds some stale bread and potatoes to each of their bags.

It is not quite dusk as they step out of their house, perhaps for the last time. Hilde locks the door, questioning when, or if, they will be back again, and if their furniture and dishes and linens and clothing will still be here when this is over.

The family of three, each wearing their yellow Jood star, walk down their street with a heightened sense of who might be watching.

"Turn here." Hilde chooses the less-busy side streets to avoid being seen, as they make their way to the designated meeting location. She wonders about the hiding place they are going to. Has she made the right decision? What will these people be like? Will they keep everyone safe? It is starting to get dark out when the smuggler spots them, their yellow stars giving them away. He stands next to two bicycles, each of which has a small luggage rack on the back.

He straddles one of the bicycles and says to Selma, "You hop on the back." Once Selma is seated with her bag across her shoulder, the man points to the other bicycle, then to fifteen-year-old Walter. "Now you." Walter straddles the second bicycle and holds it steady as his mother gets on the luggage rack.

The man adjusts the pedals in preparation for beginning the ride. "Hold on to the seat. Keep your feet up. And stay quiet. We don't want to draw any attention to ourselves."

Walter places his right hand over his heart, where his mother had sewn his yellow star onto his jacket. "Shouldn't we remove these?"

The three hastily remove their stars and stuff them into a pocket. Walter knows that, as Jewish people, owning a bicycle has been illegal since June. Riding one at night and being identified as a Jewish person would be a disaster. They would be arrested, perhaps shot, if they were caught. But without the stars on their jackets, riding at night with passengers on the luggage racks is nothing extraordinary.

The man begins pedaling. Walter follows into the dusk-turned-dark, out of town. They circumvent the guards that are stationed at the end of town and ride toward St. Isidorushoeve on the bumpy dirt pathways.

I DON'T REMEMBER EVER BIKING with my father. The only time I saw him get on a bicycle, he was shaky and seemed to lack confidence. Wasn't biking something you never forgot how to do? And I also don't remember Simchas Torah celebrations with my father. I recall being in synagogue as a child, parading around carrying a paper flag, following behind the Torah scrolls. But I cannot conjure my father in those images. It seemed he always had to work.

Until recently, I hadn't realized that Simchas Torah was the day in 1942 that my family had gone into hiding.

Now, my celebration of the holiday has become one of being *able* to celebrate. Even during the higher-security years, around the Kuwait war and after the Pittsburgh synagogue shooting, we were free to celebrate. Even during the COVID-19 pandemic, there were ways we could celebrate—though perhaps not in large groups with singing—knowing that things would be better the following year.

Yet, my father's last childhood Simchas Torah in 1942 was the beginning of the end for so many souls. And an altered life for our family.

CHAPTER 33
MEETING THE LANSINKS

SITTING AT MY DESK in early June 2018, I obsessed over the map, trying to locate options for where the bicycle path that connected Enschede with St. Isidorushoeve might have been. I wanted to rent bicycles and retrace this part of the path. But I couldn't bring myself to do it. Instead, I listened to my father's account again, with my eyes closed. I tried to imagine the fear, the stress, the sweat associated with his experience.

ONCE OUTSIDE OF ENSCHEDE, Walter no longer notices the chill in the October air as a waning moon barely lights their way. He pedals behind the smuggler, focusing on maintaining his balance, while his mother holds tightly to the luggage rack. For an hour and a half, they travel along the dirt roads used by the farmers until finally arriving at one of the farms.

The women hop off the backs of the bicycles. Walter and the man lay the bicycles down on the ground and walk in place to loosen their tired muscles, sore from pedaling for so long. The building where they've arrived is half house and half barn. The man guides them to the door on the family home side. As they enter, two young men in their late twenties or early thirties and their father greet the group. The "boss himself" is Jan Lansink, a widowed sixty-two-year-old farmer and father of the household. He and the two sons are not entirely prepared for their visitors' stay. The sons stare at their new responsibility, as though these strangers who appeared in their home are from outer space. It seems to Walter that they don't know what is happening, that they aren't expecting three guests. Or perhaps they are, but now the reality of their extraordinary commitment is apparent.

Walter, Hilde, and Selma are exhausted from the dark and bumpy bicycle ride. It is difficult to feel safe, to sleep soundly on the living room floor, as the gravity of their situation dawns on them more clearly. They can never be seen until the war, God willing, comes to an end, with the invaders losing. Perhaps in a few weeks or maybe months. Can they manage much longer? They will have to take it one day at a time.

The farmer is in his bed, hoping for the best. He is one of many farmers in the area who hide Jewish people and other "enemies" of the Nazis. Times are tough all over the country. His children are embarking on lives on their own farms. He needs help to work the fields, to care for the animals, churn the butter, do the housework. Life will have to continue as they already live it. Most importantly, the immediate need is to provide a proper hiding place on the farm for his new family of refugees, if any of them—the refugees as well as his own family—are to survive. He makes a plan. But tonight he must try to get enough rest to greet the challenges that will follow.

In the morning, the farmer hires a carpenter.

ON AN OVERCAST, cool June morning in 2018, Seth, Josh, David, Robin, and I arrived in our rental car at an apartment in a town not far from St. Isidorushoeve. We noticed two men standing on a second-floor balcony of the address we'd been given. They watched us approach. One man was Evertjan, the person who had located Jan and set up this meeting. The other man must have been Jan.

Jan Lansink, the grandson of the farmer who was also named Jan, was himself now a grandfather, and he lived in the apartment. Jan greeted us at the doorway, his eyebrows knit with the seriousness of this deeply emotional, even austere, occasion. Jan, along with other Lansink family members, had spent time with my father in 1991 during his return to Holland. I'd learned that they had exchanged letters and phone calls with my father. Jan knew about my brother and me, and about our respective children.

Jan and his wife, Wilma, offered us a seat at the dining room table. "You found the address okay?" Evertjan translated for Jan.

"Yes, the directions were easy," I said.

"Would you like some cake?" asked Wilma.

"That would be nice." I thanked her, though, as excited as I was, I had little appetite. Until a few weeks before our trip, I couldn't imagine I would be "reunited" with the Lansink family. My father had left me their address, but my "someday I will write to them" intention kept getting pushed aside, until I thought I'd missed my chance.

When I'd connected with Evertjan through the Enschede synagogue website, I must have provided enough of my family's history, along with the Lansink family name. Unbeknownst to me, Evertjan had taken it upon himself to call every Lansink—and there were many—in the area until he found the right one. He had only needed to make one call. Jan agreed to meet with us. To me, this was a miracle.

At their dining room table, I handed Jan and Wilma the gift bag I had prepared, sweets from Boston and something more symbolic: a round wooden box with a cover that slides open. Engraved on the cover was a tree, a symbol of life, and of our family research.

Inside it, I had placed a few Tikvat Yisrael tokens as symbols of hope and remembrance. I watched as Jan separated the yellow tissue paper that protected its contents. Jan looked up at me, his mouth opened as if to call out, but no sound emerged. His eyes filled with tears.

I didn't understand. After all, it was merely a wooden box. Not a photo of our 1940s families together, not old letters between our families—family photos and old letters would come later. Jan said some words in Dutch that I didn't understand. He stood up to retrieve something from a nearby hutch. It was a wooden box, rectangular, with a curved top into which was carved a tree. Jan opened the box and showed us the rosaries inside. It took me a few minutes to piece together this miracle inside a miracle.

In that moment, I remembered what my father had shared in his testimony video about his 1991 visit to Holland:

> I went back to Holland to meet the grandchildren [of the boss himself, Farmer Lansink]. I went to Israel first. I brought them religious artifacts, like rosaries and little things. And also, I planted trees for their parents who saved our lives. Each one got a certificate with a nice frame with their name on it and a photograph of me digging a hole and planting the tree. They loved it, of course.

The tree-inscribed box was one of the "little things" my father had given them. I hadn't known.

We sat there, Jan and Wilma on one side of the table, Robin and me across from them, with everyone else standing nearby, tears flowing freely. This wasn't sadness, yet it wasn't happiness. It was the realization that I had to be right where I was at that moment. The journey, no matter what I planned or didn't plan, had taken me where I needed to be. Perhaps I had no control over it. Perhaps my father had been leading the way the entire trip, leaving hints for us, or guiding others to do what was necessary. At some level, I like to think he needed this as much as I did.

After collecting ourselves, we shared family photos with the Lansinks, identifying respective family members for one another. "Look at this one." Jan pulled out a letter from my father, written in Dutch. It contained a photo of my father sitting on a park bench with Josh as a toddler. I looked up at Jan, eyes wide now, excited. "This is Josh!" I pointed to my now twenty-eight-year-old son standing next to me, then I snapped a photo of the letter. Jan smiled. A circle was coming closer to being completed.

I could have stayed there all day, all week, if they had let me. But Evertjan said, "We need to go, now. They are waiting for us at the farm."

Jan and Evertjan had planned a visit to the farm where Jan's father and grandfather had hidden my family. I rose, not wanting to leave this moment, yet moving my body as instructed. We got into separate cars and followed Evertjan, Jan, and Seth, who were in the lead.

"I can't contain all this emotion," I said to Josh, David, and Robin. "Meeting Jan was enough, and now we are going to see the farm where it all happened."

"I know. This is amazing. Sabah would be pleased, wouldn't he?" Josh said.

"Absolutely. I wish I could have made this trip with him all those years ago. I didn't really understand. He didn't share the details with us." No response was needed. We were learning the details now.

We exited the highway and made our way down narrow streets that likely once were the dirt roads my family had traveled. We made this trip freely in the light of day, not by bicycle, not under cover of night, not having to remove any markings that would identify us as Jewish. We parked in front of the former Lansink farmhouse and were greeted by the father of the family who currently lived there.

We entered this building that had been half barn and, after a renovation, was now fully a house. Multiple generations of the current owners' family sat in the living room on that Sunday morning, ready for our arrival.

Suddenly, it was as if I left my body. I was standing in the living room where my father and Oma and great-grandmother had spent their first night. My view of the scene, however, was from a few feet up, near the ceiling, looking at us all. At my father's children and a grandchild, together with a Lansink family member. I felt my father there, in that moment, floating next to me.

The current residents told us things, showed us photos. I cannot recall the details, only the feeling, the deepest sense of overwhelm I thought I could possibly feel. A combination of incredulity that I was in this space and deep gratitude that I had been gifted this opportunity.

I wondered what this resident family was thinking, what they had told their children about these American strangers who would be coming into their home.

After some time—it might have been three minutes or thirty, I'm not sure—someone from the house asked us a question I did not expect. "Would you like to see the attic now?"

There was a palpable space between the question and my response, not a hesitation to answer, but a shock at the offer. I stated simply, "Yes," as I continued to watch the scene unfold. In the midst of experiencing one of the deepest connections with my father's story, a moment I had yearned for though dared not hope for, I felt disconnected from myself.

I had watched my father's 1991 video of his own ascent up into the attic of his hiding. I couldn't have imagined the attic space would still be accessible. I ached to have had this experience together with my father, yet I knew he was right there with me in spirit, as he had been so frequently on this journey.

Still, this time, he wasn't smiling or finding delight in our discovery. This was a serious moment—one of unspoken trauma mixed with a deep appreciation and love for this place. I followed our host's instructions. My mind somehow told my body what to do, and I proceeded to walk toward the staircase with my family, my father's presence floating nearby.

CHAPTER 34

CLOSETS AND CAR BENCH SEATS

IN THE FORMER LANSINK HOME, at the top of the staircase, my family and I entered a room and approached a closet. A closet! I could hear and feel my father near me. Unlike my experience watching and listening to him in the testimony video proudly describe his helpfulness, now I heard him whispering to me. "I suggested to build a hanging closet in front of the secret entrance to the attic, so that whenever somebody would inspect the area, they would look through the clothing and they'd see nobody, but they could not find that little knotty pine wood door to our hiding place, the secret door inside the attic."

My father had stepped into the role of family leader by then, aiming to please as he always had, as he helped the carpenter build a secure hiding space.

Then, on that day in June, I heard a popping noise, followed by a gasp from Robin, who stood ahead of me. Then my own gasp, audible to others, or perhaps only to me. One long, collective gasp. The breath of my father's lifeline intersecting with ours. Someone had just pulled away a hidden door from inside the closet, revealing the attic space behind it.

I followed. Inside the closet. Through the hidden doorway. Into the attic. Underneath the wooden beams. One left turn, and I approached the secret inner hiding area.

The attic area ran the length of the house. The slanted roof angled steeply on our right. There was a width of about four feet down the length of the attic in which I could stand fully upright. I felt my father acknowledging this place, as the place he remembered from 1942, and from his return visit in 1991. It was as if he continued whispering the story to me: "It was a slanted roof with shingles, and they just timbered it off. The hay and the straw was on the other side—"

As we walked halfway down the length of the attic, I asked, "Do you think this is where the straw might have been?" I might have been addressing my present-day family. More likely, I was asking my father.

I heard his voice continue: "—so we could make a nice little living quarter out of it with a hot plate in, and a pail as a latrine and covered with a potato sack—"

I was struck by my father's tone, denoting a sense of almost fun, like playing house.

Evertjan pointed downward to a small opening low on the inside wall of the attic space and said, "This is where they would hide."

Again, my father's voice: "—and we would go down a few steps to our little nooook. And within a day it was all fixed."

My father pronounced "nook" like "nooook," which I found endearing. I started pronouncing it that way myself, even in my head when I'd read the word or imagined the space. The nooook was a space within the attic, under the attic floor, and above the ceiling below.

The family of three had needed to scooch down, perhaps shimmy a bit from the main attic area to get into the space where they slept each night and where they hid when inspections were imminent. Oma often used the German word rutsch for such scooching, as in "rutsch closer to me on the sofa," with the "so I can hug you" part left unspoken.

David and I bent over to look inside. "Originally, the steps down to the space went a little lower," Evertjan explained to us. "The ceiling below was raised up about a foot during the renovation."

Even if it were two feet higher, the nook area was so much more claustrophobic than I already felt in the attic space where I stood. My father hadn't mentioned that in his video. David placed his hand on my back as my tears flowed once again.

Back in 1942, while my family was in hiding, the plan appeared to be that when an inspection would occur, the inspector might enter the Lansink house and not go to the second floor. Or he might go to the second floor and not inspect the closet. Or he might enter the closet and not see the hidden door. Or he might see the hidden door and enter the attic that was above the barn area and not see the second, lower access point to the nook.

"Can you see Oma and Selma rutsching back into the hiding space?" I turned to face David, incredulous, remembering that my great-grandmother was seventy when she went into hiding.

Again, no reply was needed. David and I embraced, barely clearing the peak of the roof along the attic center. Our father hovered close to us, in front of the nook.

Someone snapped a photo of us. I was aware that no photo existed of our father, Oma, or our great-grandmother when they were standing in that same spot, while they were stretching their legs in the morning, or before hurriedly preparing to rutsch back into their nook when they heard the inspectors arrive.

Releasing each other from the embrace, we sought to confirm our understanding. "So, this area was above the cow barn?" David asked. Evertjan translated Jan's reply. "Yes, the cows were below."

I had never heard my father cry on the video he made of his return to this spot. But I couldn't stop crying now. I imagined my father being overwhelmed not only by his personal experiences here, but by the pain and sadness his children felt for him in that moment.

I continued trying to orient myself to the layout of the hiding space as I stood in the former Lansink attic. I pointed downward. "Inside that nook—that's where they created their bedroom."

Someone in our group asked, "What do you think they slept on?"

I remembered my father's testimony. "Dad said they built a bed and filled it with straw for Oma and her mother to sleep on. The nook was full of mice and fleas, but he said, 'it was a bedroom.'"

It was later that evening, as my family and I discussed our experience over dinner, that the questions kept coming. I cued up my father's video to fill in the story for all of us.

WALTER'S MOTHER and grandmother have a bed of straw. Now, Walter needs a bed. Farmer Lansink knows what to do. He goes outside to a haystack, where he has allowed a Jewish family to hide their automobile. He pulls out the two bench seats from the vehicle and carries them up to the attic. Walter helps shimmy them into the nook and notices that they are on a slant.

"Do you have some books, so I can make these level?" Walter asks his host, who obliges.

"You are okay, Walter?" Hilde asks as she climbs into her straw bed next to her mother that night. She's always had her own place to sleep, except for the fourteen years she lived with her husband. Now she shares that bed of straw with her mother.

"Ja, of course, this is a nice bed to sleep on. It is comfortable." Walter leaves unsaid that he knows whose car these seats belong to.

BACK AT MY FAMILY DINNER the evening after our visit to the hiding place, I paused the video and added my own reflection. "Dad said it was a 1938 Dodge that belonged to his girlfriend's parents. It was a poignant moment on the video when he said, 'this was all supposed to be secret.'" I remembered how the pitch of his voice raised, as though there was more to the story that was not to be shared. What memories of a long-lost girlfriend would forever remain unspoken?

And there was something else about the story—about the car bench seat—that reminded me of a clubhouse I'd had growing up.

FOR ONE SUMMER, MAYBE TWO, it was one of my favorite places to play. My clubhouse was in a small area on the right side of our two-car garage. The space was used for storage rather than for a car. I would sit on my special seat, looking at the sheer curtains that I had painted and hung over the windows, high up on the almost immovable garage doors. An old picnic table sat below the curtains, piled with things I cannot now discern. Underneath were the soon-to-be recycled newspapers and magazines my brother collected for his Cub Scout fundraiser.

Lest anyone question exactly where my clubhouse was, I painted an orange and brown double line from the garage entrance, on the side of the garage where my father parked his car.

The focal point of my clubhouse was my seat. The car bench seat that my father had removed from his station wagon, which allowed him more space to store the packed-up eggs for door-to-door delivery to his customers each day.

One afternoon, while I was in my clubhouse, on my special seat—I have no recollection of what I was doing while there—my mother called me into the house. She spoke calmly and frankly. "I don't want you to play on that bench in the garage anymore."

"Why not?"

She responded so matter-of-factly while preparing our dinner in the kitchen that I didn't understand the significance of sitting on this car bench seat. "Because I said so." She might not have used those exact words, but that was the message. She might have said, "It belongs to your father. He uses it for work, and you shouldn't play on it."

Though my mother's reason was clearly weak, I said, "Okay."

I went back outside to play, walked into the garage, and sat right down on the car bench seat.

I was ten, and my mother did not understand that I couldn't not do this. Still, I felt a little guilty.

With ambivalence, I continued to hold clubhouse meetings from my seat on that bench or hold secret conversations with my girlfriends there. Sometimes I'd watch the pile of recyclable newspapers and magazines grow under the picnic table. Although my mother's words never left me, my love for this forbidden spot kept luring me in. There was something unspoken about it. A secret my parents kept close. But since they weren't going to tell me what it was, it wasn't going to stop me from doing what I had to do: sit on a car bench seat in a quiet, dark space. Somehow it was comforting.

David didn't remember my clubhouse. Only the newspapers he'd collected nearby.

I never asked my parents about the car bench seat. If I had, perhaps my father would have described his hiding place to me face-to-face, rather than my having to learn about it via video years after his death.

AFTER AN EXHAUSTING DAY VISITING the Lansinks and the old farm, I fell asleep with a jumble of memories and emotions swirling in my mind: the trauma of living in an attic; the image of my father helping the carpenter build hiding places within hiding places to keep them safe; and, finally, the gratitude my father showed throughout the video he had left us.

A nice bed ... It was comfortable.

The family of three would spend 909 nights, and night-like days, in hiding—days and nights of some combination of gratitude and loss, calm and terror, despair and hope.

CHAPTER 35

IN HIDING

IN THE EARLY WEEKS OF 2020, the COVID-19 pandemic hit. My husband and I stocked up on three weeks' worth of food. We had all the comforts we could possibly need. I had the luxury of hunkering down, spending my days within a one-block radius of my house. I appreciated our spacious home, plush bed, running water, working electricity, and the availability of heat and air- conditioning. I was grateful for sunlight and all the greenery I had to look at or tend to. I had Internet access and email and phone and TV. I had my work. And I had my book-writing project.

And yet, I had a lot of time on my hands, time to be filled with something. Like so many, in the beginning, I baked bread and prepared wholesome and creative meals. I walked around the block, over and over again, happy to meet neighbors I'd never seen before. Thrilled to breathe in the fresh springtime air, I opened our windows wide. Then summer, and fall, and winter air. The whole time, I never lost a sense of gratitude, even as I started to feel claustrophobic about my self-imposed isolation.

I also spent a lot of time thinking about my father in hiding. As much as I wanted to get closer to feeling what he felt, it was challenging for me to imagine his daily life. How he had passed time that was so much emptier than my own, so much bleaker. So much darker. How did he know when it was time to get out of bed, given that he had no access to daylight in his nook? What was his spirit-lifting self-talk?

All I had were the words he shared in his testimony video. I watched him lift his right hand and touch the ends of his thumb and forefinger, forming an "okay" sign, as though describing the quality of service and excellence of food in a fine restaurant.

Food was brought to the room every day, oh yes!

THE FARMER HANDS Walter a plate of freshly cooked eggs. "This is enough for you?"

Walter indicates his response by touching the ends of his thumb and forefinger. "Hartelijk dank." Thank you.

The farmer nods and leaves similar plates with Hilde and Selma, along with a chunk of bread.

Walter tries to settle into a routine.

Breakfast of eggs, a midday meal of brined pork and potatoes with butter. At first, he and his mother and grandmother avoid the pork, but in a few days, they realize that to survive, they must eat the black-market item, which was stored in the attic behind the hay.

Selma, set in her traditional ways, continues to refuse the pork, never eating it. Pork is tref, not kosher, forbidden to Jewish people except, perhaps, in life-threatening situations. She eats only the boiled potatoes with butter.

Every morning, the farmer also brings fresh milk to the attic. After a few days, Walter demonstrates for his mother and grandmother the ideal way to churn the milk into butter. He places the butter churner on his bed—the car bench seat—and churns quickly, resting every minute for a few seconds. "So no one downstairs can hear the sound."

Later in the morning, the farmer retrieves the buttermilk and the butter, making both items available for the midday meal and breakfast the following morning. Walter has plenty of buttermilk to drink.

Walter, Hilde, and Selma live above the cows. A constant stench wafts upward. Fleas inhabit the straw beds, and mice scurry about the attic floor and throughout the secret hiding space. To be in the fresh air would be dangerous—the family can leave their attic to go outside only at night, when the dark will protect them. They walk along the farmhouse, trying to keep their legs strong and their lungs healthy. Five or ten minutes later, they must return to the safety of the attic.

But the farmer realizes that his refugees need sunlight, so he cuts a small hole in the roof over the attic, removes a shingle, and replaces it with a piece of glass. Sometimes, they put a little matchbox to wedge open the glass for some fresh air, hoping no one passing outside will notice.

Walter also does the ironing for six people on the farm.

IMAGINING MY FATHER'S EVERYDAY life in hiding reminded me of my own mother. During my childhood, she ironed in our sunlit kitchen while she listened to the news or the Mets game on her radio. She would spritz the wrinkled sheets, then iron them to a crisp, smooth flatness. It seemed like a meditation: spritz, iron, breathe, listen, repeat.

It was harder to visualize my father during his teenage years in a dark attic. I thought about him ironing. *Did he carefully press the linens and clothing to a crisp, wrinkle-free smoothness for his family? Did he iron the farmer's family's clothing and linens too?*

During the coronavirus pandemic, as I baked my breads and cooked any food I wanted, I was grateful to have plenty. And so, too, was my father grateful for the food he had been given. My time in pandemic isolation helped me to appreciate my father's gratitude in his exceedingly more austere isolation.

We had enough food to eat. Yes, the farmer treated us like we were king and queen.

As an adult, my father was anemic, and he died of aplastic anemia at the age of sixty-seven, possibly due to childhood malnourishment.

I live in a time and place where food of all sorts is abundant, even during a pandemic. I was not hiding in the dark, or breathing stale air, or being bitten by fleas or worse. I was not in imminent fear for my life.

Like Selma, I made the choice to eat only kosher meats and to avoid mixing milk and meat, as outlined in the Jewish laws of keeping kosher. My great-grandmother made the same choice. And, possibly because of that choice, she would not make it to America.

CHAPTER 36

RADIOS AND NEWS

AS THE COVID-19 PANDEMIC SURGED, I spent my free time reading books and keeping myself busy sewing cloth face masks for healthcare workers and for my friends and family. With so much going on in the world—hopeful vaccine trials, election results, a coup attempt in the United States—I tuned into the news daily. Though I did not equate our pandemic and political times with Nazi times, my mind went there, and I tried to gain whatever insight I could.

I also paid more attention to what I knew about my father and how he had found ways to occupy his time.

During those three years that I was in hiding, nearly three years, I did read a lot. What else could I do? I made my own chess set made of plaster of paris to kill some time.

During the war, I had nothing to do. I made brooches. I hand-painted them, which had the Dutch lion on it and national things, with a little pin glued behind it.

*During the war, I had a map on the wall tracing the movement of
the front[lines] and the Russians moving back ... the Germans, the
Stalingrad battle.*

According to my father, the BBC News, which was broadcast in various
European languages at designated times each day, kept him and the rest of
Europe updated with the real story, the truth of what was happening during
the war.

Perhaps the map was pinned or nailed on the attic wall, or maybe affixed
to the inside of the steeply sloped roof, near enough to one of the six illicit
radios that were stored in my father's corner. I had to work harder than usual
to imagine the scene. I didn't want to be in the dark, odoriferous, too-cold
attic. Yet in my mind, I *needed* to go there for a short while.

IT IS NOVEMBER 1942, one month into hiding. Walter takes a break from
his chess set creation, leaving it to dry. Donning his headphones, he tunes in
to the BBC and listens closely.

Walter had recently started his map project. He has two sets of pins—
black pins represent the German Wehrmacht and yellow pins symbolize
the Russian forces. He moves the pins around on his makeshift map, then
stands and takes a half-step back; that is all the space he has to admire his
updates. One by one, almost meditatively, he presses the pins deeper into
the wall, marking the location of troops on the battlefront. That way, the
pins will not fall out when he connects them with the strands of twine that
the farmer had offered him. The outline of the eastern war front is now in
clear view.

Walter had been following the Battle of Stalingrad since that summer,
when he was still in Enschede. Back then, everyone had been alarmed that the

German Wehrmacht was pushing toward Stalingrad, with a goal of occupying the industrial city and killing all its male residents.

Many others have also been following the military movements as best they can. The German and Russian troops are engaged in heavy warfare in the city, on land and by air. There are attacks and counterattacks. It would all be thrilling for a teenager to monitor, if it were not for the fear of what would become of his own family should the German Wehrmacht succeed in yet another invasion.

Each day, Walter listens to the news and adds pins or moves the existing pins and adjusts the twine. By November, the black pins are firmly planted in Stalingrad. Soon, the yellow-painted Russian pins surround the black pins.

"Ja, how is it now?" Hilde says, shivering. The beginning of their first winter in hiding is already cold.

"Look, they are surrounded now, no supplies can get through." Walter's voice lilts upward with a tinge of joy at the news and with pride in his map. The black pins were trapped in Stalingrad and suffered greatly, with limited access to supplies during the brutal winter.

Walter adjusts and repositions the Stalingrad battle pins until February 1943, when the yellow pins will succeed in taking back their city.

During breaks from the news and his chores, Walter works on his brooches. Most of the brooches have images of a lion, a Dutch national symbol. The farmer had provided supplies to Walter, something to keep him busy. Walter picks up one of the round, half-domed pieces of wood, which is about one-and-a-half inches in diameter, then he selects from among three painting brushes.

After applying a base coat of paint—this time he chooses white, and others will be coated in golden yellow or bright blue or red—he sets it down to dry and paints a few more similarly. Once the base coat dries, Walter paints a yellow shield-shaped background and, when that dries, he adds a detailed red lion within the shield's borders. The finishing touches are the sharp claws projecting from the beast's paws and the tongue protruding from its mouth, always a different color than the lion itself, this time blue.

Walter looks at the blue paint. Perfect, he thinks, for the Zionist brooch design he sketched out the previous day. He paints a blue base coat on another piece of wood. When that dries, he adds a white Magen David, linking the two triangles so they look as though they are intertwined, inseparable. In the middle of the star, he paints a golden-yellow rising half-sun. Along the top in Hebrew lettering, he uses the finest brush to paint "Tikvat Yisrael," hope of Israel. He leaves this special brooch to dry, admiring it with satisfaction and a sense of longing and of hope. Always hope.

One evening, as his brooches sit drying and after he dumps the latrine outdoors, Walter settles into his corner to turn on the radio. He adjusts his headphones in time for the news. The usual battle updates. But this time, a sickness overwhelms Walter as he listens intently to the BBC explaining the story of mass murders and of the crematoria in Auschwitz-Birkenau.

As the BBC shares details, Walter sweats, even in the chilly attic. He can't move. In his mind's eye, he sees his father burning in the oven, as though he is there himself. He cringes. He closes his eyes, tightens his lips. He is thankful that his mother and grandmother aren't listening. He allows the waves of shock to rush through him, vowing not to share the news with them. He must digest this for a while. Alone.

Soon enough, everyone in Holland will learn of the Nazi atrocities. Allied forces drop pamphlets from airplanes, pamphlets with photographs of Jewish people hanging, Jewish people being shot. Some are naked. The entire world comes to know of the extreme cruelty and ugliness perpetrated under Nazi rule. Few speak up.

I LEARNED THAT THE BATTLE OF STALINGRAD, the first significant Nazi defeat, had provided some hope to those in hiding, to their protectors, and to all who had prayed for freedom once again. I thought about the COVID-19 vaccine—at one point in time a vague possibility, then news of successful clinical trials, FDA approval, then shipments, and vaccines in people's arms. I could only guess how many glitches would arise and how long it would be before our country—our world—experienced herd immunity, which would mean freedom from the killer virus.

My family in hiding in Holland must have contemplated how long it would be until their own liberation and at what cost. They had to have hope— the gift given to humankind for such situations. They could not know it would be more than two long years and millions more lives lost before they would enjoy freedom. But my father seemed to always have hope.

That made me wonder if there were more brooches with the symbol of Jewish hope, hope of Israel, hope that the sun would one day rise again. More brooches like the one my father gifted to me, the one that I always kept near. I liked to think that he had given a brooch to his grandmother to lift her spirits as she worried about the welfare of her son, Kurt. Perhaps that was the brooch that I now had.

Not long after the hopeful BBC news of the Stalingrad battle outcome came the devastating revelation of mass murder, the genocide the Nazis had been carrying out. Upon hearing the news from the BBC, my father had imagined correctly. His father, and likely Uncle Kurt, *were* killed in Auschwitz. His father *was* gassed and then burned in the ovens. My father pieced all this together as a sixteen-year-old, listening to the news.

Although I have always enjoyed listening to public radio, tuning in during lunch or dinner to hear the latest news, I would emerge from a session of book research and writing to hear NPR broadcasts that confused me. Why were they talking about Nazi salutes and Nazi flags and hate-based mass shootings? Trying to digest present-day stories about neo-Nazis, white supremacists, and a rally in Charlottesville—and their related violent acts and cruel chants—was too much for me. I could as easily be trying to process the news of the 1930s and '40s.

During my pandemic isolation, I was forced to remind myself of my father's outlook, his sense of gratitude and of hope. Mindful that, although the virus could kill me, I did not live each day in hiding, in the dark, in constant fear. I mostly had control of my interactions to reduce my risks. Throughout the ordeal, I chose to linger on my father's words.

We survived.

We learned how to survive mentally, we learned how to survive physically.

CHAPTER 37

THE HEAT WAVE

IN JUNE 2018, back at my desk, I listened to my father's video story again. I vaguely remembered my father telling me about machine-gun fire coming through the floor of the attic from below, that this was how they would check for hidden people. I was shocked that I had forgotten this horrendous detail.

There was one inspection story, however, that I do recall my father telling me directly, when I was an adult. Now, I could add more details to his story based on his intense description in his testimony video.

Six times during the time we were hiding there, the inspectors came to inspect the premises. They were knocking on the walls and on the floors and on the doors to see if there was a hiding place someplace ... Only once we got caught.

IT IS SUMMERTIME 1944, and it is sweltering, especially in the attic of a farmhouse in Holland. Selma and Hilde decide to take a big risk. They need fresh air. Emerging from the safety of their nook, out of the attic space through the secret panel and clothes closet, into one bedroom, and then a little farther, into another bedroom, they take seats at an open window. The hot, but bearable, fresh air periodically blows into the room, offering relief as the women click their knitting needles together.

They talk infrequently and in hushed voices. They breathe. They knit.

Walter remains inside the attic space, closer to the hiding nook, working on one of his projects.

And then, unexpected and unannounced as always, the sound of army boots. Two sets of boots. They stomp up the stairs.

Walter quickly weighs the options and realizes that he does not have enough time to get his mother and grandmother into the attic because they are sitting two bedrooms down from the attic entrance, too far away.

Instead, Walter grabs the latrine—the pail with the potato sack—and pulls it into the hiding space. He closes the closet door and scrambles into the nook, latching the door behind him, locking it up. Remembering his experience with machine-gun fire, he positions himself down low in an area above a main-floor brick wall so that the machine-gun bullets will not hit him. He crouches, waiting.

At the bedroom window, Hilde and Selma pause their knitting. They, too, wait. A tall policeman approaches and stands in the bedroom doorway looking at the women. Behind him is a shorter man.

The tall man looks around the room and speaks Platduits, the local dialect. "Gujen dag. Bo is't vandage?" Good day, how are you today?

Hilde knows enough of the local dialect to respond. "Foi, wat is et heite vandage." It is very hot today. She is perplexed by the struggle of the shorter policeman, whose hat peeks above the tall man's shoulder, but who cannot get a full view of the bedroom.

"Nee, nee." The taller man addresses the shorter man while continuing to look at the two frightened women. "Don't look. That is the farmer's wife. She is not dressed properly. She is going to bed now. Please, don't look."

The tall man turns around. "Let's go." Waiting until the shorter man also turns around, they both descend the stairs. They leave the house.

Hilde and Selma rush to the nook and knock on the door, their sweat soaking their clothes. "Walter, let us in!"

Walter is now shaking with relief that there will be no bullets this time, and he unlatches the nook door to let them in, then locks it up again. Walter sees how pale their faces are, pale like a sheet.

"What happened?" Walter is incredulous that the men had left so quickly.

Hilde raises one finger to her pursed lips. Walter understands her message: *Don't talk.*

Soon, their farmer races up the stairs, into the closet and attic, knocks on the nook door. "It is okay now," he says. He sits with them a while and they comfort one another.

They will learn later that the tall policeman is a member of the Dutch Underground. He knows people are in hiding on the Lansink farm, which is the reason he accompanied the shorter policeman. Because of his quick thinking, the tall man prevented the shorter man from seeing the two Jewish women knitting at the window. He saved their lives.

MY FATHER CONCLUDED this story on his testimony video.

We were very cautious for the next two weeks. We did not know whether or not the other fellow would have any—

My father didn't complete his sentence. He added a pause that brought me a little closer to him, to his trauma.

But nothing happened. We were lucky.

CHAPTER 38

THE PIG
(OR WAS IT A COW?)

DURING ONE OF MY VISITS WITH JAN LANSINK, he asked, "Did your father ever tell you the story of the smuggled cow?"

"Yes," I replied. Although in my father's testimony video, the cow was a pig. "Was that in exchange for the electric butter churner they kept in the small brick building near the house?" I referred to the structure on the farm that we had been shown during our visit there. The structure had a high, peaked roof covered in red clay tiles. Inside, there were bicycles and an old machine.

Jan nodded.

And we both smiled, as my father had done while telling the story.

"**WALTER, COME,** help us lift the pig into this cart." Farmer Lansink points to the heavy carcass. Walter calls him Vader Lansink, Father Lansink, now. They plan to smuggle the slaughtered pig into town in exchange for an electric butter-churning machine for their milk room.

Once the pig is in the cart, Vader Lansink pats its hindquarters, as a kind of farewell. He looks at Walter. "So, you won't need to churn by hand any longer. It will be done with a motor and all." He nods his head once at Walter. Vader Lansink offers many supportive gestures.

Walter covers the pig with straw so no one will see the black-market item. One of the Lansink sons attaches the cart to a horse and rides into town. Close to his destination, the Lansink son is stopped by guards, who address him. "Halt! What do you have there in the cart? Come with us!" As soon as they move the straw and find the pig, they take the Lansink son to jail.

When Vader Lansink receives word of the arrest, he begins the weeklong negotiation for the release of his son. The day after his return, they slaughter another pig and put it in the cart. But this time, they place the animal inside a box, in a clever deception should the cart be searched again.

The Lansink son attaches the cart to a horse and rides into town. This time, the son delivers the pig to where it belongs. He exchanges it for the motor and the equipment for the butter-churning machine, which is put in the same box where the pig had been.

Vader Lansink shows Walter the machinery, smirking at their success. "You do not need to churn the butter by hand again." He offers Walter another short, caring nod.

IT DOESN'T MATTER whether the trade was made with a pig or a cow. I'd learned that slight discrepancies in the stories I have uncovered have little role in their essence. What mattered was that Vader Lansink took serious risks, in defiance of the local authorities, to improve the lives of his family and his refugees. And it was not lost on me that my father seemed to look up to Vader Lansink as a father figure in the absence of his own father.

CHAPTER 39

HAIRLINE SITUATIONS

I LEARNED FROM MY FATHER'S TESTIMONY video that the Lansink family hid three other Jewish people and over a dozen non-Jewish people on the farm. The non-Jewish people were there because they refused to work for the German industries or go to the war front.

> *And therefore [the non-Jewish people] had no choice but either go to a concentration camp or go hide. So our farmer, who saved our lives, Lansink, would take these people in. And there was no limit. He took another one in. He built a chicken coop with a potbelly stove for them to survive. And they were all helping him do work on the farm. They put on wooden shoes, they put on blue-jean overalls, and they were working on the land, which we couldn't do. We were not allowed to be outdoors. To be exposed.*

None of them, not even the other Jewish family, knew about my father's family. Yet somehow, my father knew about them. I imagined this was because my father lived in the same building as the Lansink family and so had daily opportunities for conversation with the Lansinks. My father shared other close-call stories, hairline situations as he called them, in his testimony video. He shared enough of the details that I didn't need to work hard to imagine the scene.

A MAN COMES TO HIDE on the farm. He no longer wants to fight in the war. He is a local boy, Henrik, a volunteer for the German SS in Russia. No longer wanting to be involved, he leaves his duties to seek safety on the Lansink farm.

One evening, the Lansink daughter rides her bicycle home in the dark, as is her routine. This time she is surprised by someone. "Halt!" a loud voice harshly cries out. "Halt! Will das Fahrrad das haben!" I want that bicycle from you.

The Lansink daughter recognizes the voice and hops off her bicycle. Lifting the front wheel and spinning it, she shines the bicycle light on the man's face. There he is, in his SS uniform. "Henrik, you are not supposed to wear that. You are supposed to be hiding."

In the farmhouse kitchen, the Lansink daughter reports the situation to her father, who makes a plan.

The next day, the police come. The tall fellow has been in the Lansink home before. He arrests Henrik, who is now wearing civilian clothing, and points his finger at him. "If you say one word of what you know, I will tell them you are a deserter from the East Front. You were SS, and I have your uniform in my possession. I can tell them and will show them who you are. And if I do, you will be shot to death right there."

Henrik is put in a cell below the Gestapo. He keeps silent and does not leave the jail until after the war.

On another day, the St. Isidorushoeve farmers and their refugees hear a plane overhead. It descends rapidly, then there is an exploding sound, as though it had been hit by gunfire.

Two uniformed American pilots eject in their parachutes before the plane crashes. They land in the Janssen farm, which neighbors the Lansink farm.

Without a word, farmer Janssen grabs a butcher knife and, as if he's been drilled on what to do, he slashes the ropes off the parachutes. The pilots have their guns on Janssen, and now also on Janssen's wife, who has come to help. One of the pilots waves his hands at Janssen with two brief horizontal crossing movements, indicating silence.

Mrs. Janssen hides the parachute in some straw as Mr. Janssen leads them to the potato cellar, where they can hide. Then, quickly, he spreads the pepper kept for this purpose, to prevent the German shepherds, sure to arrive soon, from finding them.

Having calculated the exact farm where the parachutists came down, the commander arrives by motorcycle within twenty minutes. The officer in charge steps out of the motorcycle's sidecar and struts, menacingly, toward the Janssen couple. "Where are they?" he demands. But they say nothing.

After pressing for information to no avail, the officer and his men tie the farmer and his wife to separate trees. For hours, they torture them with knives and whips. They also tie the son and daughter to other trees that face their parents. Not one Janssen utters a word.

The German shepherd sniffs out the area and cannot find a scent that would lead the officers to the American pilots.

Finally, the commander and officer leave.

IN HIS TESTIMONY VIDEO, my father recalled the day when Vader Lansink took the Janssen family to the hospital. As he spoke, my father pointed to himself, as though *"our farmer"* belonged to him, to his own family.

> *After twenty-four hours, these people all were taken to the hospital*
> *by our farmer. And we were afraid that the Germans would just—*

He abruptly ended his story there, as the interviewer interrupted with a follow-up question about the name of the family. My father shared the name, then he concluded this story with a general statement meant to mask his own pain. He smiled as he remembered.

> *No, we had quite a number of interesting anecdotes during the war.*

During another of my visits with Jan Lansink, I brought up the story. "My father mentioned the Janssen family. Did they live near your family's farm?" I sought to confirm the accuracy of my father's account.

"Ja," he said. "They live near my current home too."

As much as I wanted to talk to the Janssens, knowing how physically close I was to them, I couldn't bring myself to ask questions that would likely corroborate the intensity of my father's recollections. But how could I almost literally touch my father's experience and not pursue further questions? In the end, I just couldn't bear the idea of causing any level of anguish in the Janssen family. After all, I had chosen to explore my father's story, to dig into the trauma and feel the pain of it all. Perhaps the Janssens had experienced the trauma firsthand, or perhaps they absorbed it by way of a story or its unspoken presence in their own childhoods. *My* needs were not necessarily *their* needs, and I would not take the chance that I might amplify trauma in someone else in order to ease my own.

CHAPTER 40
THE BUTTON

MY FATHER, OMA, and my great-grandmother spent years of their lives confined to the barn-side attic on the Lansink farm. On Easter Sunday, which was also the week of Passover—two-and-a-half years after their bicycle ride to the Lansink farm—something they long yearned for happened.

The war came to an end ... April the first, All Fools Day, 1945.

WALTER, HILDE, AND SELMA freeze in place in the attic when they hear voices coming from the main floor of the house. Someone is talking with Vader Lansink. It doesn't sound like a German soldier, and they know the Allied forces have been making progress in the area. But they don't move, just in case. A few minutes later, someone runs up the stairs.

One of the Lansinks enters the attic and shares the exciting news. "You are free. We are all free. The war is over! There are some Canadian soldiers in the house. Come downstairs!"

The moment they had hoped and prayed for has finally arrived. Can it be right? Is this a trick?

Walter ventures out first. His mother and grandmother cautiously follow out of the attic and down the stairs. Selma moves slowly due to an illness. As they approach the kitchen, they hear the broken Dutch spoken by Allied soldiers, with some English interspersed. Hilde's eyes fill with tears as she smiles broadly.

The soldiers look at the thin, pale, frightened family entering the kitchen. This is a sight they would likely never forget as they look back and forth between Farmer Lansink and his refugees. One soldier reaches into his pocket. He looks at Hilde, cocks his head to the side, and pulls out a small item.

He holds out the button to Hilde with an open hand, and with a kind voice, feigning surprise, he says, "The button came off my pants. Can you sew it back on for me?"

Walter laughs and says, "It's like a mitzvoh, this soldier, like he is performing a good deed for *you*, Mutti. With the button!"

Hilde sits on a chair, shaking and giddy, as she prepares to perform her first act in freedom. Someone hands her a needle and thread, and she begins to sew, to reattach a lost button, rejoining it with its rightful garment.

As the soldier waits patiently in another room for the return of his pants, Hilde relishes every moment. There is a smile frozen on her face as she pushes the needle through the cloth and pulls it through the other side, repeating these movements she had learned to do so precisely as a child in her family's Bocholt store.

Walter's eyes are fixed on his mother's deft movements. A wide grin appears on his face as he plans his own first act of freedom.

IN THE MIDST OF MY RESEARCH, I attended a Passover seder at the home of friends in New Jersey. This ritual feast marks the beginning of the Jewish holiday and brings with it many traditions and long-revered practices, which Jewish people all over the world enact to celebrate our ancestors' liberation after years of slavery in Egypt.

Our hosts didn't verbally ask the question, but it was written on my place card, "If you could add something new to the seder plate, what would you add and why?"

I could think of nothing, because I'm a seder plate purist and don't believe in altering or adding to the ancient Rabbinic tradition. In that moment, I hoped I wouldn't be called on for a response.

Yet, one week after the seder, as I listened to my father on his testimony video tell the story of his liberation, it became obvious to me how I would have answered my hosts' prescient question.

I vowed to add a button to my seder plate the following year as a symbol of my family's freedom, a symbol more immediate in chronology than the seder plate symbols, by over one thousand years. A button to represent the bitterness and the sweetness, the gratitude and the hope, all wrapped up in one small item that signifies my family's personal journey. I purchased on eBay a World War II Canadian soldier's uniform button to sit on my seder plate.

To me, the button was also a reminder of the Lansink family. From my father's testimony video, I was surprised to learn that Jan, whose grandfather and father had hidden my family, was unaware of the extent to which his family had put themselves at risk.

In his testimony video, my father told a story about a conversation he had had with Jan, Farmer Lansink's grandson. Jan had asked, "What about my father? I asked him so often what happened during the war, and he would not talk about it. All he would answer is, 'Jan, I was doing good. You have nothing to be ashamed about. We were doing good. We were hiding some people. And saving their lives.' Walter, tell me the story of the war. What happened?"

And so, my father told him the story of how Jan's grandfather and father had hidden and protected them. He also told Jan about all the others, twenty-three people in total, including six Jewish people—my father's family and another family of three hidden elsewhere on the farm.

In the video, my father went on to describe Jan's shock. My father was delighted he was the one who shared this tremendous news with his new friend.

He didn't know! [Jan] was surprised! His father would not tell him, he was too modest ... From what was happening at the time, they would not speak much.

CHAPTER 41
BICYCLES TO FREEDOM

MY FATHER WAS EIGHTEEN years old at liberation. *Still a child,* I thought. A child who had already lived through more horror than most adults experience in a lifetime. I pieced together the details of the immediate post-liberation days based on his testimony video.

WALTER WALKS OFF THE FARM for the first time, shuddering as he passes dead horses lying on the side of the road. They had been shot. Nearby, a stack of bicycles is piled high into the sky. German people had stolen them, Walter presumes, from the Dutch people, and then discarded the bicycles here as they ran away from Allied forces.

"I need my own transportation," Walter mumbles to himself. He selects the nicest bicycle he can find, then rides it back to the farm.

"What do you have there?" Vader Lansink is quietly proud of Walter's new acquisition.

Walter smiles, also proud of himself. "Well, you gotta survive!" His voice lilts upward, like at the end of certain kinds of jokes.

Walking and cycling for the first time in two-and-a-half years is not easy. The next morning, Walter wakes up with a fever. He lies in a bed—a real bed—in one of the upstairs rooms as his mother lays cool cloths on his forehead and chest for two days until his fever is gone and his energy returns.

Upstairs, after breakfast, Hilde watches Walter as he gently places most of the wooden brooches he had hand-painted while in hiding, the ones with the Dutch emblems on them, into a bag. He responds to her unspoken questions. "I'll be back in a little while. I want to sell these in town."

He throws the bag over his shoulder and heads outside, sharing his plans with Vader Lansink, who nods.

Walter looks for his bicycle, the one he had found on Liberation Day. "My bicycle is gone, stolen." He speaks aloud to no one, to the world, as he looks around for it unsuccessfully. He walks off the farm, on a mission, his venture into entrepreneurship, into freedom.

Okay, look, I survived the war, Walter rationalizes to himself, *I can find another bicycle.*

He returns to the pile of bicycles and examines them once again, before pulling one from the pile. He sets it properly on its wheels, lifting the front one and spinning it to be sure it works and gives no friction. He does the same with the back wheel. It is in good order, he determines, perhaps even nicer than the one he had first selected. He hops on and rides into town, the breeze of freedom a thrill on his tired body.

Walter finds people in the streets sharing stories, trading wheat and brined pork and other goods, out in the open, something that had been long forbidden. Approaching a group, he pulls out a couple of his wares. "You would like to buy a brooch? Look, it has the Dutch lion I painted on it." His thin, pale body gives pause. The group understands what that means.

The people are so happy to be liberated, they give Walter some of their money, which has little value anyway. He sells two, then four more. Eventually his bag is empty. Each sale ignites delight in him.

Later, he tells his family and Vader Lansink. "I kept myself busy for a worthwhile cause."

AS I LISTENED TO THE END of this story on my father's testimony video, I pulled out my wooden brooch and held it in its protective casing, examining its details. I imagined myself finding one in a shop near St. Isidorushoeve or in a Dutch museum. Perhaps my treasured brooch would suffice.

My brooch was a nugget, a gem that, to me, held the entirety of my father's story of escape, of hiding, of survival. It was a physical item that exemplified his creativity, ingenuity, and entrepreneurial spirit. It showed his love for the land of Israel that was not yet a country. My brooch epitomized my father's resilience, his love of family, and his appreciation and gratitude for all he'd been given amid all that loss.

It was not fear that had moved my father forward in a productive and positive direction. Above all, the brooches were—and mine is—a manifestation of his unrelenting hope. The one star in my father's story that remained unshattered.

CHAPTER 42
MY MOST BELOVED KURT

MORE THAN SEVENTY YEARS after my father and his family had found freedom, translators struggled to decipher the German words in letters I had found among my father's documents. I was especially sad that the translators were unable to make out much of the letter written by a very ill Selma on freedom's doorstep in Holland. The parts that were legible brought me to tears each time I read the translation.

Selma had written, more accurately scrawled, a love letter to her son, Kurt. Perhaps she forgot that she had started one letter when she wrote the second, more complete one.

While examining my great-grandmother's letters, one short word—a name—appeared to be slightly offset, separated from the words surrounding it.

Kurt, I could make out, *Kurt!*

The phenomenon was repeated, each time with more distinction. It seemed to me that my great-grandmother thought the name of her son and the exclamation point that followed it were one and the same. Perhaps this was how the letter writing unfolded.

"HILDE, GET ME SOME PAPER. I want to write a letter." Selma speaks weakly and with some difficulty after having finished the broth that was her supper.

It is May 4, 1945. Hilde, Selma, and Walter had just listened to the news report, this time on a radio that did not have to be hidden away in the attic. The German government had agreed to surrender Holland, and a cease-fire is to go into effect the following morning. Hilde starts writing letters of her own. She is desperate to locate her husband and so many relatives in an attempt to regain a connection with the outside world. The war in Europe is coming to a close.

Hilde props up her mother against the pillows on a bed in the Lansink home. The bed is luxurious in comparison to the hay they had slept on for so many days and nights. Hilde hands her mother paper and a pen and something to lean on. "You would like some help writing?"

"Nee. I will write myself to Kurt."

Isisdorahofe, Selma writes on the top line, misspelling the name of the town where she lived in hiding—and where she would die in freedom.

Mein innigst geliebter Kurt! My most beloved Kurt!

Selma envelops her son's name in a hug of barely decipherable extra spaces.

When you receive these lines, I will be no more. How sorry I am that I cannot see you anymore I can surely tell you. Five years' hope for a reunion, and now shortly before the end it does not go anymore. What do I have of loneliness when I have all of you to think about and always to hope! Today I am worse, and it does not go farther, and I write to you.

After writing half a page, it becomes challenging for Selma to continue. The writing turns to scrawl, and her weakened grip on the pen leaves behind lighter, more thinly inked lettering.

You dear Kurt are not lost; Hilde and Moritz and Walter give you help. Go also with Seligmann [family in the United States], who will perhaps help you … You would not believe how many worries I have had. To my husband I go, now we have one and another.

The strain of the writing, the drain of sitting up, the pain of not seeing Kurt again, overwhelms Selma. She sets down the paper and pen and sleeps.

The next morning, Hilde brings her mother a cup of tea and helps her take a few sips. "Good news today," Hilde reminds her, as her joy and sadness are all mixed up inside. "Let's remember this date, May the fifth, Bevrijdingsdag. Liberation Day has arrived. The Nazis are gone from here. There is celebration everywhere here in Holland."

Hilde wonders how many more days her mother will survive so she can experience this freedom.

Selma looks at her daughter, eyes glimmering from behind the shadows of illness. "Take this ring from my finger." With great effort, she stretches her hand out to her daughter, the small emerald loose on her middle finger.

Hilde looks at her mother. "That is your engagement ring, Mutter."

"Ja, now you take it and keep it. When you look at it, you remember the good days in our Heimat."

Hilde reluctantly takes the ring, placing it on her own finger so she will not lose it.

Selma's hand reaches toward her daughter again. "I need to write to Kurt. Hand me that paper and pen." Hilde patiently complies, handing her mother another clean sheet of paper and the pen.

My most beloved Kurt! Selma begins on a new page. This time Kurt's name is higher than the words that precede it and surrounded by even more space.

> *I already wanted to write to you, but now … it does not go more … It is too bitter for me … I have asked too much, and I am sorry. When you receive this letter, I will be no more. How sorry I am that I cannot see you anymore I cannot tell you … Every hope to see you again goes away soon …*

Again, getting tired halfway through the page, her writing becomes less legible. She pauses to wipe the tears from her eyes. And when she can write again, many of the words are the same as in her previous attempt.

Selma turns over the paper and continues writing on the back, adjusting her position, now writing on a slant, almost the entirety of it indistinguishable.

Then, as an afterthought, under her signature, she writes, *For Paul and Otto many heartfelt greetings from me as well.*

The letter and pen rest on the bed as Selma again sleeps. Hilde picks up the letter, places it under the page written the day before, and folds the pages into quarters. She places them in an envelope, seals it, and leaves it on the nightstand. She will need to find Kurt, to send the letter to him, to fulfill her mother's dying wish.

May 7, 1945. Selma takes her final breath on the farm where she had been hidden and was now free, with her daughter and her grandson by her side. She is buried in a small Jewish cemetery in nearby Hengelo. After the funeral, Hilde places the letters to Kurt with her other family photos, awaiting a joyful and tearful reunion that is never to be.

Over the following months, Hilde determines what will be written on her mother's gravestone. She is not able to locate close family to assist with this duty. The plain granite stone is inscribed in Hebrew with Selma's name and the date of her death, along with her parents' names. Then in Dutch: "Here rests my dear mother Selma Herzfeld, Rest in Peace."

There is no mention of her being a beloved grandmother or wife or sister or aunt. Nor would there be a husband or sister or brother to come visit.

MY GREAT-GRANDMOTHER DIED on May 7. And exactly forty-five years later, to the day, her great-great-grandson, Josh, was born.

Though Oma barely mentioned Kurt to me, I know she had tried for years to locate him. In 1950, the city of Bocholt replied to the reparations office at the regional court in Münster, stating there was no longer a Jewish community, nor any documents of the Jewish community, in Bocholt. Oma was advised that the death certificate of Kurt Ludwig Herzfeld, who presumably died in Auschwitz, could be obtained from the Special Registry Office Arolsen, Waldeck district. But there was no death certificate. And Oma was never able to hand Kurt the letter their mother wrote.

When I began my research, aching to know more about my great-uncle Kurt, I, too, could find no death certificate. All I could locate were a couple of records on the Yad Vashem website. "Kurt Hersfeld," born in 1913, was on Transport #19, Train 901-14 from Drancy to Auschwitz-Birkenau Extermination Camp on August 14, 1942. But entries for "Kurt Herzfeld" were less committal about his arrival at Auschwitz-Birkenau.

I could only mull over the possibilities, my stomach in knots thinking about each of them. *Had he died en route, crammed into a too-tight cattle car? Or had Kurt been thrown overboard? Was he shot by guards who didn't like the way he looked at them? Or had he escaped the train only to die trying to survive the elements?*

I scoured the Internet, which Oma didn't have when she was searching. *Against all odds, had Kurt escaped and come to America, but never been able to find his family?* No matter where I looked for answers, I did not find any.

Living with the unknowing, the uncertainty, of what had happened in Uncle Kurt's final days devastated me. It had to be unbearable for his half-sister, not knowing if there was any hope of handing him the letter of love from their mother.

I returned to what I could know or reasonably surmise. I examined a photo of Selma's gravestone, likely taken in 1947, before my father and Oma left for America.

Once in America, Oma penciled a notation on the back:

Selma Herzfeld;

Oma's mother; Your grandmother;

Buried in cemetery; at Hengelo, Holland

There's a blue-penned X marked above the gravestone in the photo, announcing its location in the Hengelo cemetery. Perhaps Oma made this mark in case some later generation might want to visit—if they could determine the location of the Hengelo cemetery and identify the holder of the sleutel, Dutch for Schlüssel, key.

I needed to stand where the blue-penned X had led me.

In June 2018, my goal was realized. My great-grandmother's gravestone looked the same as it did in the 1940s photo, perhaps a little darker from the elements, with some green spots that showed its aging. The pebbles blanketing her grave were still there, white as snow, with a few gray flakes in the mix.

Evertjan was the one who had offered to take us to visit my great-grandmother's resting place. He obtained the sleutel and, in the late afternoon of our first meeting with Jan Lansink, the same day we had visited the attic and toured the Enschede synagogue, we drove to Hengelo together.

Evertjan had already scoped out the location of the grave in the cemetery, and in no time, my brother and I and our family stood in front of it, reciting the Mourner's Kaddish. We might have been the only relatives to have visited since my father in 1991, and before that, not since Oma and my father in 1947.

David walked to the gravestone and gently placed our Tikvat Yisrael marker on top. I imagined my great-grandmother looking upon us with gratitude for the visit and for acknowledging her with our marker. The image on the marker was identical to the one her grandson had so carefully and lovingly painted on wood while they were in hiding together for those 909 days and nights.

his small
ont of
to

CHAPTER 43
RETURN TO ENSCHEDE

I DISCOVERED THAT, in this region of the Netherlands, as a percentage, twice as many Jewish people in hiding would be saved as in other parts of the country, including Amsterdam.

At home, as I continued my research prior to our first trip in 2018, I was eager to absorb how my father adjusted to liberation during the months after his grandmother's death. I resumed his testimony video.

So we were liberated. We came out of all of this. And we found a nice little home in Enschede.

At that time, the farmer took a horse-drawn cart, loaded with firewood, loaded with food of all sort, loaded with clothing, and he brought it to our location and he helped. His oldest son and I, we were unloading the firewood in the backyard of our building. He did everything for us to be comfortable and survive in comfort.

I examined Oma's Dutch identification card and learned that, during the second half of 1945, three addresses were added to it. The last address, listed on December 12, 1945, was on Kortenaerstraat, one street away from the synagogue, a place to which my father continued to be drawn.

My father explained his perception of how the Dutch people had saved the synagogue.

They told the Germans, "Don't burn this building, or break it down to rubble. Keep it intact because it's a monument, and it is listed as a monument."

This building was under the protection of monuments, and the British as well as the American Air Force knew not to bomb this building. They [the Dutch] went to the Gestapo and they suggested to use the building, the synagogue, as an ammunition dump. This way they could save the building. The Germans listened to that. They also made a prison out of it.

Now when the war was over, I had to see, of course, I had to see my old synagogue again. I took video pictures of it and photographs, and this, to me, was a big deal.

When my father refers to his 1991 trip to Holland, in this section of the testimony video, he scrunches his face and shakes his head, as if to underscore that this was truly something special, like the eighth wonder of the world. Watching him, I scrunched my own face, shaking my own head. How I wished I could have visited with my father when he was there in 1991.

Instead, I imagined his 1945 rediscovery of his beloved building.

"I WILL SEE YOU FOR SUPPERTIME," Walter says to his mother as he runs out the door. He is on his way to explore postwar Enschede. His first stop is the synagogue where he had celebrated his barmitzwoh six years earlier. He walks slowly around the building, rememorizing the image: *a huge copper dome on the top and to the left and the right two smaller domes, and made of yellow stone, a gorgeous building, a square tower with a clock in it.* He smiles, thrilled to see it is still standing. *Such beautiful handiwork.*

After examining the outside details, Walter enters the building. Breathing deeply, he walks into the large, domed sanctuary. He runs his fingers along the mosaic-inlaid walls, up the steps to the bimah, around the space under the large dome. It is different, but the same. Then, something extraordinary. His eyes are drawn to a piece of fabric, a black-and-white-striped tallis. He picks it up, opens it, and folds it carefully, recognizing it as his own. The tallis, now held tightly in its owner's fist, is transported home.

"Mutti, look what I found!" Walter calls as he runs. By the time he flings open the house door, he is panting.

"What is it, Walter? Are you okay?"

"Ja, ja. I found my barmitzwoh tallis. My barmitzwoh tallis. Look!"

"The synagogue, you can go inside?"

"Ja, they saved it. The Dutch people saved it, even with all the buildings around here bombed out." Then, under his breath he says, "This is a miracle."

I DO NOT KNOW EXACTLY where in the synagogue building the tallis had lain, waiting for my father to find it. The tone in my father's voice in the video upon telling this story made clear, though, that this was a moment of joy in a world of rebuilding.

My father kept his special black-and-white-striped tallis until his death, and it is one of the few items my brother took with him after we cleaned out my father's Florida condo. David still has it.

BEFORE JOSH AND I RETURNED for our second trip to Germany and Holland in November 2018, I wrote to Evertjan. He assured me they would hold Shabbos services when we planned to visit, whichever week we would be there. It was set, then, that we would complete the dream that my father could not on his 1991 trip. We would pray in my father's beloved synagogue on Shabbos of Thanksgiving weekend 2018, at the end of our weeklong second trip.

As Josh and I prepared to leave our Airbnb flat, I called him into the bedroom where I had slept that night. "Come here, I want to show you my view."

We looked out the window together, to a perfect view of the synagogue, seemingly there just so I could take the requisite photo from the perfect angle.

I was acutely aware that Josh was not comfortable attending services in this synagogue where we would not be permitted to sit together. As we crossed the street, I asked him, "How are you feeling about going here?"

"It's not something I want to do, but I love you and I know how important this is to you."

"Thank you. I love you too," I said with an overflowing heart.

Evertjan greeted us warmly. A few men and even fewer women trickled in, all pleased to meet the guests from America. They all seemed to know about us. We took our seats in the small sanctuary, the room that had once served as my father's Hebrew-school classroom. Josh sat near the windows on the men's side. I sat with a clear view of him through the circular-patterned wooden latticework mechitzah, the partition that separated the women and the men.

I followed the familiar service easily, using the Hebrew side of the Hebrew and Dutch prayer book. Periodically I checked what the Dutch word was for a Hebrew word. *How did they write God's name? What was the Dutch translation of Judaism's central prayer, the Shema?* And, later in the services, I looked at how the "prayer for our country" differed in the Netherlands from the American version I was used to.

At the start of the Torah service, each man picked up a tallis. I was stunned to see Josh following suit as each of the men donned his own. Josh knew the blessing and the proper way to place it across his shoulders. That didn't surprise me. What brought me to tears for the first time that morning was seeing Josh, the mirror image of my father at about the same age, wrapped in the same style black-and-white-striped tallis as the other men wore, the same style as my father himself wore when he became a barmitzwoh. I felt my father watching over us then, with both longing and joy. He felt closer to me at that moment than at any other point on my trips.

Our friend Irene, the synagogue fundraiser, was there too. She approached me. "What is your Hebrew name? The cantor would like to say a misheberach in your honor."

The misheberach was a special blessing that included the recitation of my and my father's Hebrew names. Irene passed along the name I told her: "Raphaella Raizel bas Alexander haKohain." The cantor called it out during the misheberach. They were kind and thoughtful to honor me, and I was privileged to have my name recited together with my father's in his sacred and beloved space.

But that didn't prepare me for what happened next. Josh appeared at the table on which the open Torah scroll lay. It was directly in front of me, visible through the latticework screen. Josh was calm, though I knew he was totally out of his comfort zone. He decided to accept his own honor of being called to the Torah as a way of respecting me. Josh followed the protocol: he used his tallis to kiss the open Torah scroll in the spot that would be read next, then he recited the prayer over the Torah reading.

I felt my father there, silent but watching. The woman seated next to me smiled and nodded.

CHAPTER 44

CAN LIFE "NORMALIZE" IN ENSCHEDE?

IN ENSCHEDE, my father and Oma continued experiencing loss and its traumatic impact as they attempted to determine their new path into an uncertain future.

My father didn't share the details with me, nor did he reveal them in his videos. I didn't know much about the remainder of his and his mother's life in Enschede, though they lived there until August 1947. It was a difficult time in the early postwar years. Food remained rationed, and many in the community weren't certain how to react to the survivors. The photos and documents I gathered helped me fill in the blanks. My father and Oma must have been struggling to find or create some semblance of normalcy in their lives.

THE LATE SPRING WARMTH of 1945 brings hope.

"Mutti, I got the job. I start tomorrow." Walter is excited as he returns home from meeting his new employer.

"Ja, that is good. Where? What will you be doing?"

"At Firma Bührmann, on the Usselerweg. It's only a five-minute bicycle ride." He explains his role as an assisting central-heating fitter and plumber, then continues. "I need to find overalls for work. Everyone wears overalls. And I must bring my lunch to work every day."

Hilde smiles, thinking how pleased Moritz would have been with Walter's steps toward learning something practical. "You will learn good skills you can use in America one day."

"No, Mutti. I don't want to go to America. I know our family is there. But you know I am a Zionist. This brooch I painted, the one I kept—" Walter opens the box that shelters his brooch, the one painted blue with the white Magen David and a sun rising in the middle. "I always had hope about the land of Israel. I want us to emigrate there."

But Hilde needs to live with relatives once more. Her sister-in-law, Mathilde, invited them to live in her neighborhood in New York City. A few other relatives, those fortunate enough to have left Germany by 1939, are already in America. There is no word yet about Hilde's husband or her brother, or other aunts, uncles, and cousins who were not able to leave Germany in time.

Like her son, Hilde is a Zionist, but her sadness consumes her. It will be hard making a life in a new place, with new people, with more struggles. She keeps this to herself. For now.

Hilde checks regularly with the Red Cross and other groups that provide information about survivors in displaced persons' camps and elsewhere. Will she find her husband's or brother's names? Or the names of other dear ones?

This is her new normal.

On January 20, 1946, Hilde writes a letter to the Central Registration

Office for Jews in Amsterdam, requesting information about Moritz and the others. One day in May 1946, a letter arrives from the Office, addressed to her. She sits down at the table and steadies her shaking hands, opening the letter with hope that mixes uneasily with fear, and begins reading the Dutch.

In anwoord op Uw schrijven d.d. 20.1.46

In response to your letter dated January 20, 1946, we give you the following copy of the answer which we received from Paris:

Then, indented under this introduction, in French:

... We regret to let you know that:

STERN Moritz, born 11 April 1891 in Meudt,

Was deported on 31 August 1942 from Drancy in the direction of Auschwitz.

To this day, his name is not on the lists of liberated that we possess.

As for the other people, we do not find a trace of them despite all the research we have done ...

She fights back tears, straightens herself in her seat, and pushes out her lower lip. She will continue checking the lists, writing letters. Perhaps some relative in New York knows something. Perhaps someone in her mother's German hometown has returned home. Perhaps someone she loves is still alive.

Hilde finds comfort where she can. One comfort in her life is Vader Lansink and his family. The Lansinks hold several celebratory life events postwar—weddings, births—and there are photos commemorating them.

Vader Lansink and Hilde visit each other. One afternoon they stand in front of a pine tree, near bicycles that are propped up along the trees. Vader Lansink places his arm around Hilde's waist and looks at her as she looks directly at the camera that captures the moment. Both smile broadly.

During another visit, this one on the farm, Hilde holds a baby with both her arms as Vader Lansink places his arm protectively around her. They both look at the camera as another photo is taken.

On another day, January 5, 1947, Walter visits with his cousin, Hugo Slager, who survived the war by living with "foster" parents. Both young men are fatherless now and they discuss their plans. Late that afternoon, they pose for a photo. Walter drapes his left arm over Hugo's shoulder, the sides of their bodies touching, emanating a closeness. Walter's wool double-breasted winter coat falls below the knee. Hugo's sports jacket covers a sweater that is neatly tucked into his pants and topped by a winter scarf. The unknown photographer's long shadow is captured in the photo.

A few months later, in April 1947, another letter arrives to Kortenaerstraat. It is from the Red Cross in The Hague. Hilde is convinced that Moritz and Kurt would have made their way back to Enschede by now, if they were alive, if they had been liberated. She sits down and opens the letter slowly, not wanting to read its contents, but needing to know for certain. She begins reading the Dutch.

De ondergetekende verklaart hierbij ...

The undersigned declares herewith that upon information received in a letter dated 28 March 1947 from the "European Service of Research of Jews who were deported or disappeared," 8 Avenue de Verzy, Paris, to the Bureau that

Moritz STERN, born 11 April 1891 at Meudt

on 31 August 1942 was deported from Drancy (France) to Auschwitz.

Since then, no further information has been received about the sought individual;

Furthermore, that generally, individuals transported to Auschwitz were immediately gassed upon arrival and subsequently cremated;

It can be established that Moritz Stern died on or about 3 September 1942 on arrival at Auschwitz as the result of gas.

Hilde sits, alone, staring into the unknown future when her son opens the door, returning from a day at work in his dirtied overalls. "Mutti, what is it?"

She hands him the Red Cross letter. Walter slumps in a chair. "So, it is definite then. What about Uncle Kurt?"

"I heard nothing. But I tell you this, we cannot go to the land of Israel. There will be war there, I feel it. I am so afraid to lose you too. Please. We go to America. Together."

This isn't the first time Walter had heard this argument from his mother. But now, he must go along with her wishes. "Ja, Mutti."

Walter's Zionist dreams are gone, up in a poof of a few words in a letter from someone he doesn't even know. He will find other ways to support the land for which he yearns. He will go to America with his mother and make a new life there.

On May 20 they purchase passage on a ship, due to leave the port of Le Havre, France, on August 14.

Walter tells Bührmann of his plans and, on August 7, receives a reference letter in English that he reads aloud to his mother, proud of his work history.

By this we elucidate that WALTER ALEXANDER STERN born at Bocholt on 10 November 1926 since V-day 1945 up to 24 July 1947 was in the employ of our installation and mounting industry as an intending central-heating fitter and plumber.

During this period, he performed the various proceedings charged by us for our full contentedness. He is an honest and reliable person.

His discharge is given on his own request.

Firma J. Bührmann / Enschede / Centrale Verwarmin

"That is good," Hilde says. "You can continue your studies in America. Just like your father wished."

They silently continue packing their belongings in the wooden crates they had gathered. Hilde looks at each photo, letter, and document, deciding which ones will accompany her into her new life. She holds out a photo of her mother's grave. "I won't be able to visit you again," she whispers, and she places it next to her mother's letter to Kurt, which she still hopes will one day find its way to him. Next, she runs her fingers over the six photos of Vader Lansink that she will take with her. She will probably never see him again. Writing letters will have to suffice.

Walter folds his letter of reference and places it with his pile of memories that include the Tikvat Yisrael brooch and the scallop-edged photo of him with Hugo Slager.

"What will you do about the Bocholt property?" Walter asks his mother at supper that night. They have found out that downtown Bocholt lay in ruins after the Allied bombing of March 1945. Their former property is amid the rubble.

On May 28, 1947, Ernst Weber applied to unblock the property, so that he could rebuild it. Permission was granted on June 27, "provided that there are no claims registered against them. Inquiries into these cases show that there is no suggestion that sales were made under duress."

On August 12, 1947, a document is typewritten:

The widow Moritz Stern, born Hilde Stern, Enschede (Holland) Kortenaerstr. 61 claims the former right of joint-proprietor of the House Bocholt, Geburtsstr. 35 and requests a registering of a non-negotiability notice. The present owner is the Merchant Ernst Weber, Bocholt.

This information is given in respect of the notice dated 27 June 1947 regarding the unblocking of the above-named house.

Hilde tells her son that she has asked someone to assist her with requesting a "non-negotiability notice," then she finishes packing her things.

The following morning, Walter seals up the crates in time for his girlfriend and her family to arrive for a farewell gathering.

"Here, this is for you." Walter hands his girlfriend a small box. She smiles and opens it, finding inside a photo of Walter. The perfect size for her locket.

"Thank you," she says. "I will always cherish this and our time together. Here, I have some photos for you." She hands him a couple of herself.

"I will also cherish these." Walter is somewhat numb from the overwhelm of leaving.

"Come, gather around the box, and I will take a photo of you all together," the girlfriend's sister says. The group gathers in a circle on the stone patio outside the Kortenaerstraat house.

The girlfriend and Hilde stand in the back of the group with their arms around each other, the others in a circle with one woman, unsmiling, who sits on the crate.

The photographer motions with one hand. "Make like you are just now painting your name, Walter." He moves the paintbrush toward the wide side of the crate and places it on the last letter of the name that is already painted black: "STERN."

"Ja, good." The seated woman stands and walks toward the photographer. "Now let me take a photo. You were shaking the camera. Everyone, sit on the crate!"

The new photographer positions the camera sideways to get a wider shot, capturing the labeled crate and the packaging paper that litters the stone patio.

The girlfriend stands behind the crate, as there is no room left for her to sit. Walter stands on the other side of the crate, placing one hand on his hip. He is satisfied that the labeling was clearly printed: "STERN. NEW YORK. RIVERSIDE DRIVE. 834."

He looks, unsmiling, toward the camera, and he ponders what his new life will bring.

Walter will keep the two photos. The Dutch word "verschrikkelijk," terrible, is written on the back side of the blurry one.

The beginning of the long journey to America has finally arrived. The girlfriend, Hilde Slager, and other friends accompany Hilde and Walter to the train station. They get on the train and make their way to Le Havre, France, where they board the SS *Marine Falcon* on August 14, 1947.

Each ship passenger is asked upon embarking: "Your country?"

"We have none," responds Hilde.

"Stateless." The worker logs the word in the ship manifest.

On August 23, as the SS *Marine Falcon* enters the calmer harbor, the passengers find some relief from the sea sickness that plagued their crossing. Walter takes a photo of this new world.

Then, Hilde points toward the same New York skyline. "Look, there she is. Lady Liberty awaits us." As she weeps for her losses, she wavers between feeling hope for the future and fear of the unknown path that lies ahead.

PART III
RETURN HOME

GEBURTSSTRASSE #35, BOCHOLT, GERMANY
IRENE STERN FRIELICH: JUNE 27, 2019

I PAUSED TO TAKE IN the shiny brass plates, in place of the glittering glass shards that lay in the spot eighty-one years earlier. I would be forever captivated by the names inscribed: Selma and Kurt. Hilde, Moritz, and Walter …

It was more of an unknown lifelong inevitability to resolve something … The souls of all five individuals memorialized in this spot must have felt a similar intensity as they watched with us and over us, crying their own tears of pain and sadness, with longing and gratitude—and I would like to believe hope for the future.

"All people come from the same source and return to the same source. We must all learn to love and be loved unconditionally."

—Elisabeth Kübler-Ross, *The Wheel of Life: A Memoir of Living and Dying*

CHAPTER 45

BEING GERMAN

BEFORE I MADE THE THREE illuminating trips that entwined with my father's life in Europe, the words "I am going to Germany" were difficult for me to speak, though I have always identified as German.

Without effort I could say, "I am a wife, mother, business owner, friend, flutist." And yes, "I am German." And for as long as I can remember, I have dreamed of visiting my German ancestral hometowns so I could smell the air, feel the same stone walls, see the same gravestones that my ancestors saw.

I imagined it—as I am known to do—yet I never thought I would be able to turn that dream into a reality. Before I started my journey, my family's story and my ancestry seemed unknowable. But my efforts, my obsession, paid off. I did make my dream a reality. I never thought I would visit the country where so many of my relatives were murdered. I never imagined I could step foot in the country my father swore he would never go back to, a land that had seemed so far away, so forbidden to me. But then I did stand with my feet, my entire body, and part of my soul, in the same places my own father had stood when he was a child, with his traumatized feet, body, and his soul.

One night in June 2018, after finalizing plans for our first trip—with a heavy sense of guilt—I had a dream. A vivid dream. I saw Oma, from the neck up, her face firm and proud and loving all at once. I told Oma my plans to see her birthplace, and those of her mother and father. I told her I would visit the place she had fled. In the dream, she didn't respond. Oma was not pleased I was going to Germany. Yet at the same time she was allowing it by her silence. This was exactly Oma. She must hold to her obstinate vow, even if she understood the need for the next generation—for me—to return. And perhaps to reconcile with it.

It was a fleeting dream, the only one I remember having had of Oma in the thirty years since her passing. It told me all I needed to know.

I was heading in the right direction.

I was going to Germany.

CHAPTER 46

MEUDT

ON THE SECOND DAY of my second trip in November 2018, in my ancestral hometown of Meudt, I heard a haunting, ancient melody. El Malei Rachamim—God, full of compassion—a prayer for the souls of the dead. I had heard this prayer chanted at funerals and on special days of remembrance for the dead throughout the year. It caught me by surprise, in the small and well-maintained Jewish cemetery in Meudt where I was standing, to hear it chanted by a man from the United States, surrounded by six torches lit to remember the six million Jewish people who perished in the Holocaust.

The chanter stood at a podium facing the attending townspeople and seventy descendants of the Jewish people of Meudt. Many of us had traveled from around the world to be together on this occasion. We all listened intently. As the afternoon sun moved behind the nearby homes, the winds picked up, and we shivered in the cold.

Even though I had visited Meudt five months earlier, I felt compelled to return for this National Day of Mourning, comprised of a series of ceremonies commemorating the victims of the Holocaust and of the two World Wars.

e for this event, which I had only recently learned about. Meudt, hallenging name to pronounce. I went through all sorts of variations til I heard it in German—Moyt. The vowel combination *eu* sounds like *oy* as in the word for new, *neu*, pronounced noy. The soft, rolling hills in the tiny and pastoral town of Meudt, an hour west of Frankfurt and not far from the Rhine River, captured my heart.

I don't remember hearing my family talk about Meudt when I was growing up. I'm not sure my father realized that his father was born there, as evidenced by the worn slip of yellow legal-sized lined paper on which he had roughly sketched out part of his family tree, each name clearly written in uppercase black or red lettering and in a rectangle of the same color. The red-inked names, I would come to realize, were victims of the Holocaust. Harry Slager and Max Slager from Enschede were among those names listed in red. *Did my father, as I did, ache to get closer to his family history, to remember those lost and those who survived?* Next to the names of Moritz and his siblings, my father wrote: "All born in Montabaur, Germany." My father might not have known that Moritz had moved to this town next to Meudt with the family not long after Moritz and his two full siblings were born.

Our earliest known relative in this family line, not in my father's sketch, was Jakob Moyses, who lived in Meudt in the 1700s. He was my fifth-great-grandfather. His daughter, Eva Jakob, married Haium Isaak, a butcher and cattle dealer. They had four children. Their progeny, in the 1800s, assumed last names as one step toward asserting their status as equal citizens. Each of the children took on a different last name: Löwenstein, Heilberg, Lahrheim, and Stern. Most of the Jewish descendants of this town, thus, are my cousins, most of whom I had never heard of, and none of whom I had met.

Before the ceremony started, Stefan Assman, a Meudt resident who had meticulously documented the Jewish history of the town, led us to what is believed to be Eva's gravestone, the oldest in the only German cemetery we were able to enter without the Schlüssel, the key. Eva's is a small, worn stone with only Hebrew writing and a wide streak of light-green moss draping itself from the bottom to near the top of the stone. The first two words are clearly legible: "Chava bas … " Chava, a likely Hebrew name for Eva, daughter of … and, a couple of words later, what looks like Yakov, Jakob.

I studied Eva's gravestone, running my eyes over its surface imperfections and then to the Hebrew writing. I felt a deep sense of gratitude to Eva for creating this family, my family, and appreciation that her gravestone and this cemetery have to some extent survived the ravages of the war and time. I caressed the stone, imagining that her soul sensed us there, some two hundred years after her death.

In the middle of the cemetery, we found one of the tallest gravestones, higher than my tad-over-five-foot height, with the name Isaak Stern engraved in German under Hebrew writing. Isaak, my great-great-grandfather, was Eva's grandson. Isaak's polished gravestone looked almost new. I wondered how it had weathered so well since the 1860s.

At the top of Isaak's stone, as well as many others in this cemetery, were engraved two outstretched hands, thumbs almost touching, the symbol of the Kohain, a member of the Jewish priestly tribe. Isaak was a businessman, perhaps a trader, who married Sarah Kahn, who was from a nearby town. They had ten children, one of whom was my great-grandfather, Alexander.

Missing in the cemetery was a gravestone for Johanetta, Isaak's mother. It was odd not to find it, mainly because Stefan had shown us her house, still standing, still the same structure, he had told us. And not five minutes' walk from the cemetery. *Had her gravestone been destroyed? Did it wear out? Was it somewhere else?* Stefan also showed us the house, one block from Johanetta's, where Alexander and Fanny, my great-grandparents, had lived before they moved to Montabaur.

Generations of my family lived in this quaint town of Meudt, at least five generations, in peace, until—

My distant cousin's moving recitation of El Malei Rachamim brought me back to the present. Here we were, eighty years after the extinction of Jewish people from this town, welcomed back by the community to pay respects to our ancestors and offer a remembrance to those who are gone, who were taken in the Holocaust and war. A cousin turned to console me, but I could not be comforted in that moment.

The Meudt mayor, Egid Zeis, spoke in German. I followed along in the English translation provided by Stefan Assman. The words were so powerful, so timeless, and so very timely:

"I welcome all of you to the commemoration of the National Day of Mourning this [2018]. Of the descendants of our Jewish families, I very heartily welcome especially Bert Woudstra who, at the age of eighty-six years, is the oldest participant at the commemoration this year. Annually, the local community of Meudt commemorates the National Day of Mourning to remember all the soldiers killed in action and the missing people and also the victims of terror and violence.

Every three years, we here at our Jewish cemetery in Meudt commemorate this day together with you, the descendants of our Jewish families."

Our Jewish families. I'd heard this before. Our guide, Stefan, had used that same phrase when he introduced us to Meudt during our June trip. I found it unusual, a sort of term of endearment for the Jewish people of Meudt, "*our* Jews" rather than "*the* Jews."

Mayor Zeis continued in the German version of the following:

"This regular remembrance traces back to the initiative of Ludwig Falkenstein, August Hanz from Dahlen, and our former mayor Rudi Bendel from Meudt.

It was Ludwig Falkenstein who, directly after World War II, came back to his home country, Germany, and who essentially made it possible that conciliation and emotional recall between the people here in Meudt and the former Jewish community could happen here locally."

Conciliation, reconciliation. How could this be?!

"This is also shown by the monument that was erected on this site in October 1964, and that remains, of the deportation of the twenty-five Jewish citizens of Meudt.

It definitely was a matter of the heart for Ludwig Falkenstein, who had survived several concentration camps, to come back to his home village, Meudt, and to make reconciliation after all the misery he had to bear his suffering."

Ludwig, a survivor, had the courage to reconcile. His fellow Meudters were willing reconcilers. Could I, a child of a survivor, unlock my fortress door to allow conciliation or reconciliation?

"Every three years the community celebrates this matter of the heart and so renews the promise and the willingness of the people of that time who have trodden this difficult path after World War II. We see this as a mission and a legacy to pass the events of the history on to the following generation as a reminder of all the misery and horror that happened during the Nazi period in Germany and in Europe."

Reconciliation, preferable when possible.

"In these days, we also remember the destruction of our synagogue eighty years ago."

Remembering, necessary, always.

Stefan had brought us to the site of the synagogue, where a memorial stone had been erected in November 1988, on the fiftieth anniversary of the destruction of this structure and its sacred contents. Before its demise, it had existed for over one hundred years. Mayor Zeis continued:

"Jewish life had a long tradition in Meudt. Jews lived in Meudt for more than three hundred years. Out of only some persons at the beginning, a rather large Jewish community developed in the course of time, which at least since 1835 had its own synagogue. In 1905, 105 Jews were living in Meudt. This corresponded to a high ratio of more than thirteen percent of the total population of Meudt. This surely may be regarded as a clear symbol of their integration into the community of Meudt and that they felt good here.

This changed when Hitler came to power in 1933. Some of the Jews of Meudt could flee to foreign countries or could emigrate and so could escape deportation. Twenty-five persons did not succeed in this. They perished in the Holocaust.

Last week on November ninth, many people of Meudt and of neighboring communities here had our commemoration to remember all these events. Afterward, they visited, next to this cemetery, the war monument for the fallen troops in World War I to recall the horror of World War I, which ended one hundred years ago.

Among others, the memorial plaque on the war monument also contains the names of young Jewish men of Meudt who lost their lives [fighting] in World War I for their country and their people like all the other fallen troops.

If you look at the memorial plaque on the war monument, you see the close intertwining of the Jews in our village. The Jewish names are inscribed among the names of the other young men of Meudt. This coexistence was finally destroyed in 1938.

And exactly because of this reason, it is so important for our community to celebrate this day of mourning and of remembrance together with you, dear families Falkenstein, Heilberg, Lahrheim, Löwenstein, and Stern.

We also set an example, however only a little example, against right-wing populists who, in the meantime, are represented in all state parliaments and in the German Bundestag and who try to split our society with their paroles and gestures."

Mayor Zeis closed his speech at the cemetery with words that shocked me, in that he captured my own concerns so powerfully, and he did so in a public setting, in Germany, right where I was standing!

"Right-wing populists are very popular not only in Germany but also in almost all countries in Europe and also in the United States and in Brazil. Everywhere, someone tries to pigeonhole the population and to intimidate or to inflict hate campaigns on groups of real democrats.

Still, we have honest politicians and responsible human beings who counteract these efforts. The French state president Macron is one of them. He has said it in his speech in the presence of invited guests in Paris on the commemoration of the end of World War I. He warned of the 'demons of the past' which include fascination with isolation and national egoism, among other things. From his point of view, Europe is jeopardizing what has been achieved.

Ladies and Gentlemen! Attending this ceremony, we set an example. I ask all of you to sustain your efforts to raise your voice against aggression and expressions of hatred so that meetings like today at this place are conducive to reconciliation and are possible."

As the local band played and others spoke, I felt comforted by the mayor's message. A sense of empowerment washed over me. Someone, a mayor, in Germany could say the words that I needed so desperately to hear. If it were possible to say these words in Germany, there was hope in the world.

On our walk back to the Gangolfushalle, the town hall where the community had hosted us all day, I said to Josh, "There are almost as many descendants of the Jews of Meudt here today as there were at the population's height in 1885."

"They said this was the largest Kristallnacht memorial they've ever had," Josh said. "It's amazing that most of these people are our cousins!"

In 1871, the Jewish population of Meudt was seventy individuals—the size of our 2018 gathering and 10 percent of the town's population at the time. In 1933, the Jewish population had fallen to forty-five souls, and in 1939 there were twenty-three, all of whom were transported to Theresienstadt in 1942. There were twenty-five Meudter Jewish people known to have been murdered in the Holocaust, and their names are engraved on a memorial in the cemetery.

Today there is no Jewish community in Meudt.

Yet, simply knowing that Eva's descendants do live on is some comfort to me. I hope to return when perhaps the turnout will top 113, the highest population of Jewish people ever recorded living in the town. Perhaps my cousins and I will share stories about how we coped during a pandemic that shook the world or discuss the impact of the 2020 US elections that brought a sliver of hope to the world. Perhaps Meudt's mayor would have a more positive outlook to share with us next time.

At the Gangolfushalle, we completed our visit over Kaffee und Kuchen. We had spent much of the day meeting one another, our cousins, the requisite questions being: "Which family line are you from?" and "Where do you live?" I met cousins from the United States, Canada, Switzerland, England, Brazil, and Israel. And I met my oldest cousin in attendance, Bert, and his wife, Els.

"Where do you live?" I asked Bert.

"In Enschede, Holland," he answered, as if I had never heard of the small city.

"What?!" My face brightened, and I leaned in. "On which street?" A ludicrous question, as I knew the names of only six streets, but the words had escaped before I could retrieve them.

"I live on Kortenaerstraat."

"That's the street my father lived on." My shock met Bert's raised eyebrows. "It was the only house he lived in that we couldn't locate when we visited in June. Josh and I will be in Enschede again at the end of this week."

"You will both come for tea on Friday?" Bert and Els's invitation overwhelmed me.

"We would love to!"

As it turned out, Bert and Els lived one block from the last address where my father and Oma had lived before coming to America in 1947. There was no longer a building in its place, but Els knew where the address was, and after our tea, directed us to the parking lot up the street.

Josh and I found the spot. We stood within the footprint of my father's and Oma's last home in Europe.

Were we standing in the kitchen? A bedroom? The living area? The patio where my father, unsmilingly, had labeled his wooden crates for the trip across the Atlantic Ocean?

Was my father here with us now, yearning for the postwar life he had had to leave behind?

CHAPTER 47

HEALING HEARTS: CAN THERE BE RECONCILIATION?

A COUPLE OF DAYS AFTER the Meudt activities, Josh and I went to Bocholt to have a highly anticipated meeting with Markus Weber.

Our first visit to Bocholt had left me saddened, dissatisfied, detached, and longing for connection. At least we had our relationship with Monika, the teacher we'd met at the local Gymnasium, one of the few places in town where the people had greeted us openly and warmly the previous June. I was holding on to the idea that, if we did return, we might be able to make a better connection and be welcomed by the town officials.

My renewed attempts to find the right people in Bocholt proved fruitful. This time, town officials invited us to a small reception in our honor on the first night we were back in Bocholt, in the restaurant of our hotel. But we had other business to attend to before the reception—Josh and I were meeting privately with Markus Weber for late-afternoon coffee.

The sun was already low in the sky when we arrived at the Weber store that Wednesday afternoon. Being a few minutes early, I once again climbed the staircase, moving slowly, purposefully, with a sense of presence, toward the imagined dining room windows. I looked out across the street, pretending I could see what had once been my family's neighbors, warm neighbors, in an industrious and growing town of ninety years earlier, when my father was a baby.

I knew my way through the clothing racks this time and maneuvered through the sacred space, where one must hold one's voice at a respectful level, speak respectful words, acknowledge the memories that were lurking on the floor, in the corners, and back down the stairs. The memories that weren't mine also accompanied me and surrounded me with a sense of disdain for the meeting I was about to have. Yet, the soul of this space knew the meeting was inevitable and accepted my plan. It wanted reconciliation as much as I did.

"We will go to the Brückencafe. It's close by, okay?" Markus suggested once we found each other.

It felt like my fantasy of sitting together in the Röster coffee shop, behind Markus's store, had broken in half, as if one of the mugs I had purchased there on our last visit had fallen to the floor. I wanted to sit in that space, with Markus this time, and tell him the story of Röster and Stern. More than that, I wanted a conversation with Markus, something life changing. But I hadn't understood that yet.

We walked the short distance to the Brückencafe and sat in a comfortable corner at a wooden table—gemütlich, I remembered my mother calling it, the feeling of being tucked away, cozy. In the down-to-earth space, we placed our drink orders.

I provided some context for Markus. "We came back again so soon so we could attend a Kristallnacht ceremony in one of my ancestral hometowns, Meudt. Of course, I had to return to Bocholt. This time, the town invited us for dinner."

I explained that our visit in June had been to see my ancestral hometowns and to retrace the path my family had taken during their escape from their home on Kristallnacht in 1938, my father's twelfth birthday, to the temporary safety of Holland.

Markus nodded his head, seemingly interested.

"For each survivor," I continued, "there had to be multiple people who helped—people who showed courage, compassion, and kindness. On our June trip, we visited the places where people had helped my family."

Our drinks arrived—cappuccinos for Josh and me, with a spice cookie on the side, and espresso for Markus. We thanked the server.

My pounding heart reminded me that there wasn't much time. I mustered my rehearsed line. "You told me you were interested in photos of what your place looked like in the 1920s. I have them here. Would you like to see some of them?"

"That would be nice," he said.

I handed Markus the photos I had curated from my father's collection, three black-and-white images of my family's 1927 store on the top.

Markus pulled out his cell phone and turned on the flashlight. "It's dark in here. I want to get a better look at the details in this photo."

I struggled to calm myself, to allow the moments that strung together to evolve. To sit silently for a while. The cappuccino machine in the background released its steam.

"Look at that. There was a sidewalk with a curb, and cars must have driven on the street in front of the store." Markus observed the details. He was more interested in the photos than I'd expected he would be. I didn't know until later that he was an amateur photographer. Like Uncle Kurt had been. Like my father had been.

I hadn't asked Markus to look at the other photos that were underneath the top three that showed what his store once looked like. But as he did, I revealed a sliver of my father's story.

"That was the first time my father, as a baby, was taken for a walk on the Geburtsstrasse."

Next was the photo of my father with his parents in the backyard. I pointed to the boy. "That was my father. He was twelve when they escaped to Holland." I watched for hints of Markus's feelings about all this. "Mr. Röster was the first of the eighteen individuals who helped save my family."

As darkness fell outside, the low café lights gave away the glistening in Markus's eyes. He looked at photos and patiently, intently, listened to selections of my family's escape and survival story.

I hadn't yet known how Markus's family had come to acquire what had been my family's property, and I'd been clear with myself, well before planning this meeting, that I would do my best to avoid creating any discomfort for Markus. It was his store now, and his home was in the space above it. Whatever the circumstances had been, I had no interest in anything but connection with this man, and our shared ancestral space.

I explained to Markus the mystery of my family's furniture. Although I knew, from my father's testimony video, that the furniture had made it to Enschede, I hadn't uncovered yet how that came to be. I secretly hoped for the highly unlikely scenario that it was the Weber family who had moved it. It was equally unlikely that, had they done so, Markus would even know that piece of lore.

Markus seemed perplexed. "No, I don't know how they would have gotten their furniture. Sometimes things like that happened. I spoke with my cousin after we met in June. There are no photos. No family stories from my grandfather."

I didn't ask, I wouldn't ask, *What did your grandparents do during the war?*

Nevertheless, Markus shared a small part of his own family's story. "My grandfather was injured in the East."

I was not sure which grandfather he was talking about.

"He was hospitalized for months. I have some letters he wrote home but haven't been able to look at them. It is too difficult."

Markus shook his head slightly. "What a senseless war it was." He went on to voice his concerns about the dangers of the AfD, Alternative für Deutschland, a right-wing political party in present-day Germany, and extreme rightist movements throughout Europe and the United States. He was concerned, and was adamant, about how important it is that we never forget the atrocities of World War II.

We both teared up. This was not a meeting of discord. It was a start of reconciliation, though I didn't have that word for how I felt in that moment.

I fidgeted with my cookie. Markus hadn't yet come to terms with his own family's suffering either. This surprised me. I was beginning to understand that the other side—the "enemy" in my mind—might also have inherited trauma. Non-Jewish German people had also suffered greatly during the war. This realization splintered my reality and opened a perspective that would give momentum to my healing. I'd never been permitted to think that way. We, my family, the Jewish people—*we* were the victims!

We continued to share family stories as we sipped our warm drinks in the scant hour we had together.

"Oh, one more thing, Markus," I said, before we parted.

"Yes?"

"Did you participate in the school's exchange program in Canton?"

"No, I didn't. But my older brother did. I've visited Canton many times, even last year. I know the Red Line train to get to Boston. I love Boston."

We stood and hugged each other, promising to connect again either in Bocholt or Boston, perhaps in Canton. I sat back down in my gemütlich corner, with Josh, not yet ready to leave. I fidgeted further with the cookie on my saucer, took a breath, and adjusted my scarf.

I could barely absorb knowing that Markus had been in Canton, a couple of miles from my home, a year earlier. It was conceivable that he had visited Canton decades earlier too, when my father was still alive and visiting me in Sharon. I fantasized, because why not, that my father had shopped in the same local grocery store on an early summer afternoon in the 1990s, during a visit with me and my newborn, Josh.

MY FATHER WALKS DOWN the produce aisle at Shaw's Supermarket, passing a young Markus. They nod at each other, a simple politeness, as they reach for the same bag of cherries. They each take one to taste before committing to an inevitable purchase. Then they smile faintly at each other, with the unspoken knowledge that the cherries, at their peak in Germany this month, would be perfect.

I EXITED THE VISION and came back to the Brückencafe, sitting across from Josh. I'm deeply appreciative that he sat in this space with me, while realizing that our experiences had to be vastly different. Later, Josh told me that he felt anticipation, hoping to hear about our family's artwork being found in the basement. He sensed kindness from Markus, who was making himself vulnerable by sharing a little of his family's story; he felt connection with another human being sharing coffee in a coffee shop.

Our family story, as all family stories, is a compilation of filtering understood facts through a cheesecloth of emotions. Some facts made it through in their original form. Some forever remain behind—the detritus, the bad stuff that our family's storytellers don't wish to pass along, that aren't nourishing, though they might have flavored our experience.

There is no way for me to know the complete and objective facts of my father's experience, or those of Markus's grandfather, because they are no longer with us. Was that important? Was the essence of the experience, what's left of sitting with someone, sipping a warm drink, and looking over old photos—the kindness, the caring, the mutual interest—enough? Or are the facts and experiences that are at that moment moving, or not, through that cheesecloth, what matters? What, in the end, will inform the next generation's story of ours?

I moved my arms into the sleeves of my silvery winter coat, stood, and zipped it. It was as though consciousness were reentering my body after its reawakening, with an expanded understanding of the world. We walked out the door. Me, a transformed daughter of a Holocaust survivor. And, Josh, the third-generation witness to the transformation.

It wouldn't be until my June 2019 trip to the Münster archives that I located the documents that would prove one of my fantasies to be true. The contract between my family and Markus's had required that the furniture be sent to Gendringen as a condition of the sale.

CHAPTER 48

THE BOCHOLT RECEPTION

AFTER MEETING WITH MARKUS in November 2018, Josh and I headed back to the hotel to freshen up and prepare ourselves for the town's reception—another event that I wasn't yet aware would further alter my perception of the world I knew.

As we walked toward our hotel on this cold, late-fall evening, the warm, welcoming glow of the lights flowed from the shops through their plate-glass windows and into the peaceful street.

"Josh, I feel so grateful that we met with Markus. And that we went to the ceremony in Meudt." My voice broke, and my eyes filled. "If either one of those things was all we did this week, dayeinu." It would have been enough.

I proceeded to sing the refrain from what's arguably the most popular Passover song, "Dayeinu"—over Josh's delighted and delightful laughter—singing it down the street from my family's former home, in a town where there is no longer a Jewish community.

Back in our hotel, I looked in the mirror to reapply my makeup, brush my hair, and adjust my scarf yet again before our meeting with Laura. She was my Bocholt city contact, and she'd made all the arrangements for that evening. The deputy mayor would join us.

"I'm glad they have a vegetarian option on their menu." Josh had scoped out the food situation when we'd checked in.

"Me too." We were always nervous about food options in a country known for its Wurst and other meats. I noticed that Josh was neatly stacking the euros he had removed from his pocket, by value, on our hotel room's desk blotter.

"Josh, what are you doing?"

"Organizing the coins, there are so many."

"Wow. That's exactly what my father did each night after making his deliveries. He stacked up the coins, just like that, then filled the paper coin holders to keep them together."

"Okay." The significance of the moment seemed unimportant to Josh. To me, though, it was another sign that my father was nearby.

Minutes later, we proceeded to the hotel lobby. When our elevator door opened, Josh exclaimed, "Ah! Monika is here too!"

Monika was the history teacher from the Bocholt St. Georg Gymnasium who had toured us around her school the previous June, the one whom we'd met through a synchronicity of events. An "old" cemetery around the corner from the school, a 1931 photograph of my father in front of the school, Josh's urging me to go inside. All of it had led us to meeting Monika.

I HAD MET MONIKA AGAIN in October in Canton, near my home, a few months after our initial June meeting. She was in Massachusetts accompanying a group of students on a Canton-Bocholt exchange program. We met in a coffee shop along with Elsa Nikolovius, the program's founder. Elsa had grown up in eastern Germany during the war years.

A few days later, Monika came to my home in Sharon so she could lend me a book of Elsa's. It was a five-hundred-page green-covered book, *Buch der Erinnerung: Juden in Bocholt 1937–1945,* by Josef Niebur, with Hermann Oechtering. I had been seeking this book of remembrance of the Jewish people in Bocholt, but with no luck.

The book was a moving tribute to the Jewish Bocholters who had perished before their time. The book included testimonials from survivors and biographies of up to three pages of each of the 178 Jewish Holocaust victims who had been born in Bocholt or lived there in 1938. I imagined that Monika sensed the depth of my gratitude for this book as I showed her the pages that described the lives of my relatives: Moritz Stern, and Eduard and Kurt Herzfeld.

She pointed out the newspaper article included in the pages about Eduard and translated it for me. "It must have been a very nice shop and home after the renovation, to have such an article written about it," she said.

I shared something with her about the emotional difficulty of my traveling to Germany, a trip my father would not have made.

"What do you think your father would say to you right now, if he were sitting here?" Monika pointed at the empty seat next to me.

I looked at the chair, indeed wishing my father were sitting next to me.

"I think he would be pleased that I've seen his home and learned his story."

His story, though, is bigger than me. It is a universal story of those who are tormented, victimized, and oppressed, of those who have to fight and struggle simply to survive. It is a universal story of how hate can decimate communities, populations, ways of life.

BACK IN THE BOCHOLT HOTEL LOBBY in November 2018, Monika was smiling, perhaps as delighted as I was at our reunion. We hugged. It was so clear to me that we were supposed to have met. Somehow, Monika had become a critical link between my family's traumatic past and my own future, of finding the healing I hadn't realized I was seeking.

My Bocholt city contact, Laura, introduced herself to Josh and me. She introduced us to Hanni Kammler, the deputy mayor, whose welcoming smile and spoken German reminded me of Aunt Mathilde.

Laura also introduced us Josef Niebur, the author and researcher. Next to Josef was his associate, Hermann Oechtering. It was they who had documented the history of the Jewish people of Bocholt in the book that Monika had handed me the previous month.

After introductions, the seven of us were seated at a table in the hotel's restaurant. Hanni Kammler officially welcomed us in German with words about the town's history and the importance of our visit. Laura provided us with the English translation:

"As the deputy mayor, I would like to welcome you heartily this evening on behalf of the Council and administration—and especially personally—in Bocholt. It is a special moment for me to introduce the city of Bocholt, like it is in our days, to you as the direct descendants of the families Stern and Herzfeld …

"It is our generation which has the duty to pass the memory of the incidents which happened during World War II to the next generation. We have to do everything to prevent the future from repeating such outrages which were done during the Holocaust.

"I would like to tell you something about the history of the city Bocholt. The city of Bocholt was founded at around 800 (after Christ). In 1222, Bocholt received the town ordinances and privileges. Since then, the beech tree is the official emblem and used as the city's logo. The name Bocholt derives originally from Bucholt, which means beech tree.

"During the last days of the Second World War, eighty-four percent of the city of Bocholt was destroyed.

"There is a saying that every citizen of Bocholt is born with a bicycle. For the people in Bocholt, a life without a bicycle cannot be imagined.

"Bocholt wants to be an attractive, clean, and contemplative green city, where it is worth living. You can also say, Bocholt is the smallest of the big cities and the biggest village at the same time.

"Hopefully, I was able to give you a short insight into my hometown, which was your family's hometown many years ago."

I kept smiling, but my head was swirling. So many words were triggers for me.

Most of the city, including my family's former home and business, at the time owned by the Webers, had been destroyed by the Allies at the end of the war.

Of course all Bocholters have bicycles. How else could they smuggle money across the nearby Dutch border if necessary?

My father should have been able to live out his life here, in this "clean and contemplative green city, where it is worth living." He would have liked it. If only—

This wasn't the first time I experienced a Tohuwabohu, hullabaloo, of emotions. I appreciated the reception, and yet I shouldn't have had to be there in this manner. And I wished my father had been willing to return when he was alive, together with me, not simply watching me from another place.

The deputy mayor handed me the town's guestbook and asked me to sign it, as all their "guests" do. I wondered who their other guests were as I wrote:

It is so moving for me to return to the town where my father and grand-mother were both born and lived with their families. Thank you for a very warm and generous reception. My family and I look forward to visiting again soon! Vielen dank, Irene and my son Josh

After the reception, we walked toward our room in a cloud of exhaustion and exhilaration. "Josh, did you notice that everyone ate the same vegetarian three-course option that we were planning to order? And I just realized that no one even talked about placing an order."

"I know! I was so surprised. They really thought about us. Did they know we were vegetarian?"

I couldn't remember if they had asked me or if they had made the assumption that I kept kosher. No matter, they were perfect hosts, going above and beyond our expectations.

"It was weird that a town would welcome guests like that," Josh said. "I didn't feel unwanted or like an outsider that would be kicked out of this place but welcomed back into the community our relatives were forced out of."

Josh doesn't carry the same baggage I do. For that I am exceedingly grateful.

CHAPTER 49

TESTIMONY

THE MORNING FOLLOWING the reception, Josh and I arrived for our planned visit to Josef Niebur's apartment. Hermann, Monika, and Laura were there as well. I thanked them again for a wonderful evening the night before as I took a seat next to Josef at the long table. I hadn't realized Josef's interest in hearing Oma's story from me. "Tell me about your grandmother," Josef said. "What was it like for her?"

Hermann, or perhaps it was Laura or Monika, translated for us.

I began with some background. "My father, Walter Stern, gave his testimony in a video. From that video, I learned the story."

Then I shared parts of the story. "On Kristallnacht, my family was asleep, and at midnight they heard a lot of noise. November tenth was my father's twelfth birthday. My grandfather, Moritz, took everyone to the attic, still in their pajamas … Mr. Röster hid them overnight … police report in Gendringen … letter to Selma … six months later, somehow my family's furniture arrived in Gendringen. I would like to find out who sent this furniture."

Josh and I appreciated Josef's deep knowledge about the Jewish history of Bocholt. Laura continued asking questions, translating, and I continued too, attempting to add missing information from the entries I'd read in the green book.

Somewhere in the middle of sharing my story, it hit me. I was giving testimony. I felt I was telling Oma's story on her behalf, with her hovering nearby, prompting me.

Oma had never shared any of the story with me. It was the research and discovery I'd done that had helped me uncover the details. It was painful and, for me, necessary. Was this part of the healing process, something I had to do to mitigate the trauma I had inherited?

I'm not sure. But it felt like I was continuing down the path that had been laid out for me, a path that revealed itself only a few steps at a time rather than its entire trail map. I was journeying through something I needed to move through, not knowing what, if anything, lay at its terminus. For now, this travel through time and space was feeding my soul. Some of the soul food was bitter and made me wince in pain. At other times it was sour and oddly enjoyable. Few parts were truly sweet. A few parts made me want more, notably the special relationships I was building along the way. The sweetness of those relationships, I hoped, would endure for a long, long time.

During this meeting in Josef's home, Laura discussed the Stolpersteine, which were to be laid in memory of my grandfather and Uncle Kurt sometime the following year. Stolpersteine, or stumbling stones, are four-by-four-inch brass plates inscribed with the names of people who have passed, set into stone. "An anonymous donor has offered to cover the cost of creating and laying your family's Stolpersteine." Laura informed us.

I felt my chest warming, a sensation I wasn't expecting. Why would someone do that? My intense curiosity, incessant questioning, could not be quelled.

"We don't know who the donor is," Laura continued. "For some people, it is important to remember the past and set memorials. So, they pay for the stones."

I wanted to thank the anonymous donor, to let them know that I would always hold them in my heart, even if I didn't know who they were. Somehow, we—the donor and the Stern-Herzfeld family—had become intermingled in a cross-generational, cross-time-and-place story. Each of us cannot exist without the foundation of those that came before. Or even those who might come after.

I needed to let the donor know how much it meant to me that Bocholters—and the donor in particular—were taking it upon themselves to remember the evil and to take the steps needed to prevent such hatred and intolerance from returning.

But I could not know who the donor was. I could only surmise. And I could not thank them. At least not directly.

I inquired about including my great-grandmother, Selma, among the memorial stones, given that she had died, I believe, because of having to remain in hiding those long years. "No," Laura explained, "these stones are only for people who were killed in the Holocaust." Selma wasn't killed, at least not directly. I let it go, pleased that Moritz and Kurt would finally have memorial stones somewhere, anywhere, let alone in front of their rightful home.

We left Bocholt knowing we would return within the year to lay Stolpersteine for Moritz and Kurt. I looked forward to seeing my new friends again.

CHAPTER 50

PREPARING FOR
MY THIRD VISIT TO
BOCHOLT, WITH
MY FATHER

AT THE END OF OUR SECOND TRIP to Germany, in November 2018, on the plane ride home, I turned to Josh. "I have to write a book. Too many amazing things have happened this week. My father's story needs to be told. My story needs to be told."

My son, my father's look-alike, probably already knew what I would do before I put it into words. I started writing my father's story, filling in the empty spaces with facts that I learned from my research, which I undertook with more clarity, more purpose. More drive. I *had* to do this.

Interspersed with my research and writing, my own story continued to reveal itself.

It was February 7, 2019, around 8:00 a.m., when I took a seat at my work desk, as I do each morning, to check my email before having coffee. On this morning, the work emails were overshadowed by one from Laura.

We were able to find a date for laying the Stolpersteine. The public laying of the Stolpersteine will be done on Thursday, 27 June 2019 at 10 o'clock (am) at Geburtsstrasse 35. The mayor will attend the laying, and students from different schools in Bocholt will be there as well.

I was shaking now, excited to confirm that my dream to memorialize my grandfather and great-uncle was to be fulfilled. I imagined the Stolpersteine inserted in place of cobblestones in front of their former home, as I continued reading.

The Stolpersteine will be laid for the following ancestors of your families: Kurt Herzfeld, Moritz Stern ...

As expected, I noted with relief and gratitude, my head buzzing with what I had accomplished.

Selma Herzfeld ...

My great-grandmother, who died weeks after she was liberated, who would never come to know of the death of her son, Kurt, nor of her son-in-law, Moritz, would be memorialized as well.

My heart opened, eyes widened. I continued reading. My throat opened, too, and let out a soft "oh." The kind of sound you make when you are surprised by something that seemed so right, so obvious.

Laura's email continued.

... Hilde Stern-May; Walter Stern. As you can see, there will be also Stolpersteine for your ancestors who survived the Holocaust.

This, then, is what was farther down the trail, unseen and unknown to me months earlier, what I had been journeying toward while not realizing where my path would lead me.

I wrote back that day to express my surprise and gratitude. I would come to learn that, now, Stolpersteine are laid not only for those murdered in the Holocaust but for those who survived yet were displaced. I could not have imagined Oma's and my father's names memorialized in the street near where they each were born.

In a way, this was a gift on top of a gift. I couldn't have asked for more.

Yet, I was moved to ask for more. There was something else I needed to do. I resumed my email.

I want to offer something, though I'm not sure if this is of interest.

My mind was whirling. Why would they be interested in my offer? But what harm could it do to ask?

I've started making presentations about my family's survival story— how they left Bocholt, crossed the border to the Netherlands, who along the way helped them, including the family that hid them in their attic. And what happened at liberation. Would you be interested in that, perhaps the evening before or after the Stolpersteine are laid? Of course, we'd need someone to help translate into German. If this is of interest, we can talk more about the logistics.

Even if they said yes, the logistics posed a challenge. My multimedia presentation would require projection for photos and videos as well as an audio system to play the recordings of my father. After all, it was his story and he needed to tell it, with my help. Yet something continued to propel me toward whatever it was that I had to do. I wasn't making decisions about what to offer, what to write. It simply flowed.

Laura's response a few days later once again caught me by surprise. I read it in my parked car, while sipping from a particularly large cup of cappuccino. It was still steaming hot, so I placed the coffee in the cup holder. Tears flowed.

Thank you for your message and your offer. We would love to organize an event where you have the chance to present your family's survival story in Bocholt ... we will sort things out and I will forward you our ideas about the setting and the place in which your presentation can be held.

I tried to pull myself together as I drove toward the highway for an appointment, all of this swirling in my head. I considered what I would need to leave out of the presentation, what required more explanation, how I could have my father's English words in his own voice incorporated into the presentation for a German-speaking crowd, and whether Laura would locate a venue with projection and audio.

The swirling intensified as I considered who, exactly, would be there, with the implied question of their ancestry. And the explicit question of whether I would be simply a curiosity to them, or whether my father's story would offer an important lesson. Or both.

And even, perhaps especially, I tried to understand what drove me so persistently to do this.

"The truth is," Elizabeth Rosner wrote in *Survivor Café*, "I am more afraid of forgetting my parents' stories than I am of forgetting my own."

Her truth resonated with me. And, I added another layer to it. I needed to *discover* my family's stories that had never been told to me. I needed to *know* what happened. I needed to *share* those stories so others would know of the pain *and* of the path to survival.

The drive to my work meeting was short, and I was forced to let go of these musings for the time being. It would all work itself out, I reminded myself. This would be as it should be. This plan to present in the town where it all began would happen. It would have a profound impact on everyone present, I decided. I didn't yet appreciate the impact it would have on me.

CHAPTER 51

STOLPERSTEINE: HOLOCAUST MEMORIAL "STUMBLING STONES"

THE DATE HAD FINALLY ARRIVED. June 27, 2019.

Having heard the traditional El Malei Rachamim prayer in Meudt seven months earlier, when it had moved me to uncontrollable sobbing, I knew I needed to hear it again in a place even closer to my heart.

This time, I stood in front of the Bocholt home where my father was born, in the exact location where the store windows lay shattered on Kristallnacht in 1938, on my father's twelfth birthday. This time, I was accompanied by Seth and Josh; David and Robin and their daughter, son-in-law, and one of their sons; and four of our friends. I had asked David to chant the prayer for the Stolpersteine laying ceremony. I stood in the scorching heat, the timeless melody drifting through the crowd, enshrouding us—this time emanating from my brother's own depths. This melody, which our father, our grandparents, and our great-grandparents would have heard, now echoed across the generations.

I, and the others around me, wilted, struggled to remain upright in the unprecedented heatwave Germany was experiencing during our visit. It was so hot that there were warnings against driving on the Autobahn, which was in danger of buckling in the intense heat. I needed water, a breeze, something to cool me down.

Bocholt's mayor, Peter Nebelo, had started off the ceremony, sharing the Stern-Herzfeld story of November 10, 1938. "At that time, just like in the entire German Reich, also many of Bocholt's citizens looked away. Some of them made common cause with the Nazis; some suffered in the face of what was being done to the people; very few protested."

As other town officials had done in my travels so far, this mayor acknowledged what the town's collective ancestors had done. Those I spoke with didn't minimize the crimes of the past generations, they didn't ignore the horrific acts, they didn't sweep it all under the rug. They, as the mayor did, said the words aloud. "We are filled above all with shame and sadness today, still, when we think of the inhumane murder machinery that the Nazis installed and implemented with almost bureaucratic meticulousness and facing practically no resistance also here in Bocholt.

"Dear Stern Frielich Family! I am delighted that you are with us today as we unveil together these memorials to members of your family. Eight of you came to Bocholt for the occasion. It makes clear how important the memories of your loved ones are to you, who have been forced down their respective terrible roads from here.

"The stones in front of the houses bring to life the memory of the people who once lived here."

The mayor explained that forty-four stones were laid in 2007 and 2008. Our family's stones, in 2019, brought the number in Bocholt to forty-nine.

"Each of these stones reminds us of the individual fate of a person who was torn out of our urban society.

"Here and now, we want to work against oblivion and remember the people who were violently attacked in the most brutal manner in this place, in this street, in this very spot. I would now like to end this commemoration with a quote by the former Federal President Roman Herzog. He said on 27 January 1996, when he declared the day the National Day of Remembrance of the Victims of National Socialism, 'The memory must not end; it must admonish also future generations to be vigilant. Therefore, it is important to now find a form of remembering that will work in the future.'"

Some of Monika's students spoke next. They had visited Auschwitz a few months prior and wished to share their thoughts. In yet another example of the efforts among German people to acknowledge their part, and to remember what happened, Holocaust education is an integral component of the high school history curriculum. *Is it enough?* I wondered, recalling that Monika had participated in a special program at Yad Vashem, learning how to teach Holocaust studies from the perspective of the victims rather than that of the perpetrators.

Charlotte Boland, one of Monika's students, shared this during the ceremony: "My most important point was and still is that the Holocaust must not be forgotten and never be denied.

"[When I visited] Auschwitz, I realized that all these facts that I had learned through schoolbooks were nothing compared to the real impressions that I got standing in front of the gate. That horrible place really did overpower me. Especially the well-known inscription above the entrance: 'Arbeit Macht Frei,' [Work Sets You Free], truly had a different impact seeing it with my own eyes. But I still couldn't imagine the huge number of victims that were deceitfully greeted by these sarcastic words ...

"My own moment of understanding was the last day in Oświęcim [the Polish name for the town]. We were all standing around an old train wagon which had been used to transport the first victims to Auschwitz. At that moment, I realized that these people did not have the choice to go back to their hotels—like we had.

"I still am not able to tell you about how it must have felt to be forced to live and to die in such a camp, but even though I might not be able to find the right words to express what I have seen, I want to share as much as possible with as many people as possible today. That is my goal and my responsibility."

Another student, Elisa Berger, shared her thoughts.

" … After returning to Bocholt and seeing my family again, I immediately tried to explain everything I saw, felt, and thought during my journey. I felt responsible to let them know about my experiences and to share my new knowledge about the Holocaust. That's why I pressured myself not to forget anything important and not to leave anything unsaid …

"As a young person I now know how important it is to learn about history and to not forget about all these millions of people who were just like you and me."

And Luca Bölte shared.

" … I will never forget this trip, and I see myself and every other student of our group as ambassadors who will make sure that the terrible crimes under Hitler's power will not fall into oblivion. In addition, tolerance, peace, and equality must be spread throughout the world because crimes that took place under Hitler's power must never be repeated … "

A fleeting moment of sadness wafted through me as the students spoke, sadness that I had not yet had the courage to visit Auschwitz. Yet, I also felt I'd taken on a burden, inherited a burden, simply being the child of a survivor. It's a burden unlike that of other Jewish people whose families had reached safety well before the Holocaust.

After the speeches, the mayor and I unveiled the Stolpersteine. I paused to take in the shiny brass plates, in place of the glittering glass shards that had lain in the spot eighty-one years earlier. I would be forever captivated by the names inscribed: Selma and Kurt. Hilde, Moritz, and Walter.

I extended my hand to the mayor, and we made eye contact. No sentences were exchanged then, nor before, nor after.

I moved aside, the heat still enveloping me, and watched as government officials paid their respects. One by one, they stood in front of the stones for a few moments, then placed a single white rose next to my family's names. Feeling the presence of my family who were being remembered, I wondered what they thought about the crowd attending this service, perhaps more people than had attended the funerals of my father or Oma.

Before the ceremony began, I had looked around at the crowd. There were the officials, Josef Niebur, Monika and her students, the owner of the store and his family and neighbors. There were people from the Jewish community of nearby Dinxperlo, Netherlands, and new friends associated with the National Onderduikmuseum, Museum of Hiding, in Aalten, the Dutch town to which my grandfather had smuggled his money. Even a distant cousin whom I had only recently met spent the entire day with us, taking time off her job in Düsseldorf. Dear friends of mine had traveled from Israel and from New Jersey to share in the experience. Most importantly, three of my father's five grandchildren witnessed this day.

Then my eyes fixed on someone unexpected. "Jan is here!" I blurted to my family as I rushed toward my soul cousin. "I didn't think you could make it." Jan Lansink and his wife, Wilma, stood before me, five white roses in hand.

"I wanted to surprise you." Jan said, his face somber, as though this were a moment he would not have missed. He stood near me during the ceremony.

My brother's chant concluded with a request for God to grant peace to the souls who have perished, then we sang Esa Einai, from Psalm 121. Someone had distributed copies of the sheet I prepared, and some of the seventy or more attending the ceremony, including my family members, joined in.

We sang first in Hebrew, then English. "I lift up my eyes to the hills, from where does my help come? My help comes from the Lord, who made heaven and earth." And finally, we sang it in German. I had located a German translation of the verses and, feeling that it had to be included, printed it along with the English and Hebrew. I needed to reach across the chasm that had been intractably widened some eighty years earlier, to integrate the power of the moment in all three languages. We concluded with the words "Meine Hilfe kommt vom Herrn, der Himmel und Erde gemacht hat."

That was the moment that Jan grabbed me by the hand and guided me toward the freshly unveiled gleaming brass-topped stones. He didn't just guide me, as I felt propelled forward with no other option in that moment. It was more of an unknown lifelong inevitability to resolve something, for both of us to resolve something, that needed closure. Jan, to honor his friend, Walter. And me, to remember the same man—my father—and his family.

We looked down at the stones and at the white roses placed by the town's government officials. Jan's wife, Wilma, and David, flanked Jan and me. Reading the names on the stones, we remembered those we never knew, and we honored those we did know and love—my father and Oma, whose stones were inscribed with "versteckt gelebt befreit" or hidden, lived, freed, rather than "ermordet," murdered.

We sobbed together, Jan and I, for all to see. Jan rested his full bouquet of five white roses next to my family's names. I could not yet see the intensity of the emotion in his face, as that would come when I viewed the photographs and video afterward. My own intensity was there as well. That moment, I told myself, was the fourth most meaningful moment of my life, after my marriage and the births of my two children.

I would soon learn that Jan felt almost exactly the same emotion.

The souls of all five individuals memorialized in this spot must have felt a similar intensity as they watched with us and over us, crying their own tears of pain and sadness, with longing and gratitude—and I would like to believe hope for the future.

CHAPTER 52

THE STERN-HERZFELD BOCHOLT WALKING TOUR

THAT JUNE 2019 MORNING, after the Stolpersteine laying, I became a tour guide. I considered myself uniquely qualified to take my family, old friends, and some new ones, on the inaugural Stern-Herzfeld Bocholt walking tour. I had mapped out an efficient route and equipped myself with pertinent images from the 1920s and '30s, printed on three-hole-punched paper and held together with a purple book ring.

We found the late morning even more unbearable under the heat of the high sun, the edges of the scorching day surrounding us. We persisted nonetheless. After all, this was our only opportunity with this group of people to walk the streets my father's family had once walked. We would cope with the heat.

Our first stop, of course, was the Röster coffee shop. It was a necessary stop for respite in 2019, and necessary for remembering the refuge given to my family in 1938. Our tour group gave the Röster shop a bit of business that morning, as a few at a time entered, and others viewed the back of the Weber building. I pointed out the height of the roof, the height from which my family had climbed down the tall ladder in the middle of the night. Josh and his cousins found the location where we imagined my family's cherry tree once thrived. They planted more cherry pits.

We proceeded to the site of the former synagogue to step within the dark stone outline of what had once been its footprint. I explained the significance of the memorial where the Torah ark once stood, where the replica of the shattered Ten Commandments tablets now marks this once sacred spot. We paid our respects at the memorial stone that lists some of the Jewish Bocholters who had been murdered during the Holocaust.

"See the candle and stones?" I pointed to the remnants of the most recent Kristallnacht remembrance, some eight months earlier. "They haven't been removed."

In small groups, we entered the insurance company building to view the bulletin board that described the onetime synagogue, and where Uncle Kurt's photograph of the synagogue's interior hung, uncited. Our usually talkative group was silent for a while.

We paused for lunch, provided by the city, in a function room at the back of our hotel. That day, we were in the midst of commemorating my father's places, his pains, and his losses. Yet, as we sat down to eat, the events from the previous evening whirred in the space.

The night before, Josh had reminded us about the wonders of life, about love. Our family and friends had been sitting at a table in the hotel's restaurant when I got everyone's attention for Josh's announcement. I signaled the barkeep to prepare the glasses of champagne. Josh and his partner, Adam, via video, announced their engagement. Someone in our group spontaneously started singing a Hebrew song of congratulations, and we all joined in. Except for me. I couldn't sing through the tears. I was happy for Josh and Adam. I was even more moved to hear this song, which had probably not been sung in this town for decades, much less in this building, next to where the synagogue had once been. I was mindful that, in the Nazi years, simply being gay relegated a man to persecution, arrest, and often transport to a concentration camp, where thousands of gay men had perished. Although it took decades of effort in my own country, a man could now marry another man. Love is love. The pain of the past can be transformed, or mitigated, by the hope of the future. Josh, at that moment, was the bridge between the two.

I had wanted to share my reflections on the amazing events from the night before. But we had a tour to do that day. So, after our lunch, we moved on to the old Wasserturm and the location of the "old" Jewish cemetery. One of my new German friends translated the plaque on the tall brick structure for our tour group. "It was used from 1822 until 1940, and in those 118 years, 304 persons were buried here, and in 1940 the Jewish community was forced to give this place back to Bocholt. The people who were buried here were brought to the new cemetery, 133 were brought to the new cemetery."

"What happened to all the other people?" someone asked, as if on script.

"They are here, I think," someone from the group said hesitantly. I extended my hands downward to the hallowed grounds that were covered over by asphalt and a school building.

Josh walked to the place where, one year earlier, he had embedded our Tikvat Yisrael token in a flower bed next to the school building. He moved some dirt and pointed out the token that lay there, still restless, inanimate yet perhaps aware of our presence.

I explained. "We placed this token here, under a flower, to mark the spot we feel my great-grandfather Solly was—is—buried."

Around the corner, we stopped across the street from the St. Georg Gymnasium. One person in our group noticed that this was the location of the photograph I had provided them. The one of my five-year-old father standing in front of the school. It was a small delight in a sea of sadness and complexity.

Our tour ended at the town museum, where we viewed the video showing the devastation in the center of Bocholt at the end of the war, the ruins that resulted from the final Allied bombings in 1945. And, of course, we visited the original tablet fragments of the Bocholt synagogue's Ten Commandments, black and shiny, above a book titled *Mein Kampf*, with the eyes of the book's author glaring upward from the cover to the remnants of the tablets. Or maybe directly at us, I still can't be quite certain.

CHAPTER 53

OUR VOICES, TOGETHER ACROSS TIME

AFTER A SHORT BREAK, it was time for my presentation. My father's story. Our layered journeys composed as a seamless tribute.

At home, I had prepared for this event even more intensively than I do for a work presentation. I wrote and rewrote the stories I chose to share, the words that *I* wanted to say, and which audio clips of *my father's* words to include, as well as the feelings I wished to convey.

That day in Bocholt, I would need to read from my script, because audience members would be following along in the German version I provided. Even so, and even with hours of practicing my delivery of the Stern-Herzfeld family story, dozens of times in the privacy and quiet of my home office, I could not once get through it without crying.

I expected to be exhausted by the end of this intense twenty-four-hour period. With the heat, and so little sleep the night before, plus the full swing of emotions I'd experienced throughout the day, I would need to rely on my adrenaline to see me through.

Laura greeted me in the media center, herself tired. "This is Thomas," she said. "He's set up all the technology you requested."

"Thank you so much, Thomas. Let's get connected." I started attaching various cables I'd brought with me. Projector, check. Audio, check. The audience would be able to see the images and hear my father. That took two minutes of the allotted thirty for setup, and to say that I was relieved would be an understatement. Of course, they had everything set up perfectly. This was the media center. My computer would work fine.

And so, in the Bocholt library media center, formerly the train depot where Aunt Mathilde had awaited her train back to Frankfurt early on the morning after Kristallnacht, I co-delivered the presentation along with selected audio clips of my father.

There were photos—of then and now—to illustrate the places and events my father and I described. I looked up from my script periodically to view the audience's reactions. They were attentive. Some followed along in the German translation, and others understood my and my father's English. Many wiped away their tears.

I closed with words I'd added, had translated, and inserted just before I had caught my plane to Europe. A few days before my trip, there was an antisemitic event in Germany, one that continued the increased concern about the far right's actions and rhetoric.

Now more than ever, since this story took place, we must stand up and speak up and speak out against statements of intolerance and acts of hate. Let's not allow ourselves to be passive nor to be complicit.

I encourage all of us to demonstrate our own acts of courage, compassion, and kindness. We can talk to someone who we think is different than us. We can show genuine interest in one another. We can reconcile with those whom history has separated. We can make it happen.

In this spirit, let us together honor the memory of the many individuals who helped my father and grandmother survive and who made it possible for me and my family to be here today to share this story with you.

Somehow, I managed to get through the presentation in Bocholt without crying. I answered questions from the audience and then mingled with them.

Hanni Kammler, the deputy mayor we had met on our prior trip, thanked me. Katrin, from the Röster coffee shop, whom I had met on all three visits, was happy to have the German translation and learn the complete story. Cousin Bert, who sat in the front with his wife, Els, supportively nodding his head from time to time, smiled and congratulated me on the presentation. One woman asked if I would do a reading from my yet-to-be-written book, when it was completed, in the Röster coffee shop.

I had brought my father, his voice, back to the place he had vowed never to return. I felt that now, finally, he would fully appreciate my need to bring him back to his hometown. *I'd* had to do this.

On my final morning in Bocholt, I needed to pay one last visit to the Röster coffee shop, have one more cup of their cappuccino, and say goodbye to Katrin.

Katrin greeted me with a newspaper. "I already saw your brother this morning, but I saved this for you." She opened to the article about our prior day in Bocholt, the stone laying, the presentation.

"Danke schön." I smiled broadly as I sat down to decipher the German words on the page, awaiting my coffee.

"Ah, hello." A woman approached me and sat down with me. "I was at your presentation last night. It was very moving, an important story. Thank you for sharing it with us. Maybe you will come back again to share your family's story with more people."

My eyes glistened as I considered—prayed—that the impact of this work I had needed to do for myself might also motivate and inspire others.

CHAPTER 54
Maybe One Day

IN JANUARY 2020, after months of searching and then emailing with the local German consulate, I finally received confirmation that I was likely eligible to regain my ancestral citizenship, which had been lost as a result of Nazi persecution. Article 116 of the German constitution says so.

The application, in German of course, also must be completed in German. This would take time.

I joined some Jewish-German Facebook groups to embrace what I'd missed, not being attached to that community since my father died. It seemed that everybody in these groups was searching for someone or something. Perhaps a lost relative, also long gone. Or a distant cousin that they had just found out about, who might help anchor them in their ancestral roots. Perhaps a photo of a building that was once a family member's home or a school or a store or a synagogue.

In the end, many of us children of Holocaust survivors are seeking that which we have lost and cannot possibly regain. The best we can do is to reconstruct memories and histories and pass those along to generations to come, so that the stories and elements of stories, as we've come to understand them, are remembered.

I learned in these groups that it could take up to two years for the German government to process my citizenship paperwork. With Brexit looming at the time and with the issues and concerns in my own country, the volume of applications had dramatically increased.

Yes, this would take time.

I would proceed with my application for citizenship. Maybe one day.

POSTSCRIPT
AUTUMN 2023

OUR STORIES ARE INTERTWINED—my father's and mine—on a physical level and also with unseen spiritual guidance that helped me know I was on the right path. How else to explain the many signs that pointed our way, the conversations and experiences we had that were never sought or planned? The way one experience led to the next, revealing the truth that we are all interconnected and don't know this unless we truly pay attention?

As I put the final touches on this book, I reflected on the enormously emotional and powerful few years that brought me to this point. I started with not knowing where Bocholt was, and soon found myself retracing the footsteps of my father and his family through escape and survival. I met descendants of people who had played a role in my family's journey, and I made many new relationships along the way. Each location, each meeting, offered me a key to the next experience. My life is immensely richer for having the courage to use these keys as I traveled through this physical and spiritual journey.

"Yes, of course I'd be happy to share my father's story with your group," I have found myself saying over and over again since my trips. I present the story of my father's escape and survival, much of it using his own voice from his testimony video. I focus on those who demonstrated courage, compassion, and kindness to help my father survive, and how I uncovered these stories and found the locations where they happened.

I have come closer to touching my father's life. I encountered afterimages of his grandparents and great-grandparents. I visited their homes, their synagogues, and their cemeteries. I learned what I could about their lives. I laid the stumbling stones in honor of my family, the stones which I had dreamed about laying.

Even with all these accomplishments, I am still left with an emptiness I cannot fill. I need my father. I want to be able to sit and hear his stories directly from him. I yearn to ask the tough questions and hear how he felt and what he experienced. I must learn about Uncle Kurt and Moritz and Selma and "Vader" Lansink in ways I could not discover from my research. My father has been gone for over twenty-five years. I still miss him terribly. We never had the opportunity to gain the closure we both needed but might not have known we needed.

Sharing my family's story both saddens and nourishes me, helps me to process my inherited family trauma. It gratifies me when I touch a nerve that motivates others to pursue their own family stories. But sadly, each time I present, the message is too fresh, too pertinent.

In the news every month, every week, I read the stories. Arson of a Black church, shooting at a synagogue, beating of a Sikh who was mistaken for a Muslim, a white supremacist rally filled with hate rhetoric, police violence against yet another Black person, voter suppression, ignored assaults against women. By the minute, there are smaller, quieter acts of discrimination, intolerance, and violence that continue to build the diseased culture of a country, a world. It is so painfully obvious that this behavior is deeply embedded in our society.

I am sometimes asked at my presentations, "How could you step foot in Germany, after what they did to your family, to our people?" The truth is that I am struck by the work Germany and the German people have done to "own" their past and commit to a culture of "remember" and "never again."

The people of Germany have erected memorials to victims of the Nazi regime, and they have removed statues celebrating those who had directed hateful acts. In Germany, it is illegal to display Nazi symbols. Holocaust history is taught in every high school. Individuals express "shame" at the acts of violence their ancestors, or their ancestors' neighbors, perpetrated or allowed to happen. In Germany, they name the issue, they talk about it, they struggle with it, they learn from it. They rebuilt a society that expressly values human life. Although life in Germany might be complex and imperfect, many German citizens acknowledge the ongoing struggle.

I have come to understand, through my own journey, through my own curiosity, conversations, and convictions, how much the German government and so many of its citizens are actively doing to bring about a just, tolerant, and respectful society. They took in refugees from Turkey and Syria and Ukraine, even when it was controversial to do so, as a demonstration of their humanity and values. It was a complicated decision and problems persist. In Germany there are populists, neo-Nazis, and other right-wing extremists, some violent, some attacking Jewish people and Jewish establishments. That is terrifying, and it infuriates me. Yet, in my own country, the one that has stood for life, liberty, and the pursuit of happiness since its inception, and as a basis for its existence, there are populists, neo-Nazis, and other right-wing extremists. Some are violent, some attack Jewish people and Jewish establishments. To me, that is even more terrifying.

In many German towns, the governments and residents make a point of "remembering" the Jewish people who are no longer there. Although I deeply appreciate the work German people are doing to remember, I am also profoundly sad that they are only able to "remember" a group of people, a member of which they might never have met. And when they do meet me, I sometimes feel like the curiosity, the rare Jewish person that might pass through from time to time, the one whose ancestors were slaughtered. I stand alone and lonely in my ancestral hometowns that are devoid of Jewish community. The only remnants of Jewish life are as though in a museum, remembered with memorials, photographs, and stories. I carry this incongruity, this unrealness that is very real in this current version of myself. It is complicated.

I started out on this journey seeking to touch, smell, hear, to somehow experience the echoes of my father's early life the best I could, based on his testimony video and my research. I've come away with a sense of intrigue, courage, and a deep sadness. I have engaged with suffering so that I could begin the healing process for myself and perhaps for my family. I've come away inspired by the many acts of kindness performed in the most challenging of circumstances. I gather my own courage, compassion, and, I hope, kindness, to help make our world a better place.

From the depths of my sadness and sense of loss, however, something else rises up. There is hope. A rising yellow-orange half-sun on the horizon, embraced by the loving links of a star. The *stars*, the Sterne, the Sterns, that were once shattered, are held together in a legacy of protection and hope from both within my family and from the communities surrounding us. There is hope. Always hope.

I can now prepare a limited repertoire of German-inspired baked goods—Schwarzwälder Kirschtorte and even my own take on a Zwetschgenkuchen. I can now text my new German friends and relish in their happy news and empathize in their challenging times. I can now walk past my own cherry tree—a double-blossom cherry tree, no less!—and marvel at the synchronicity of life and the paths I've chosen on my journey. And I wonder about the hidden treasures that still await my discovery.

I can now speak aloud enough German words to have a basic conversation, words that used to tense my shoulders and furrow my brows. "Tschuuss," I happily called to a new German friend as we parted ways. "Tsch-uss," they replied. Bye-bye! "Auf Wiedersehen." 'Til we meet again.

Irene Stern Frielich

ACKNOWLEDGMENTS

I HAVE THE DEEPEST APPRECIATION to the Universe for laying out this journey before me. For helping me to see so many pieces of the puzzle and find ways to fit those pieces together. For showing me the wonder in the world, if only I pay attention.

I must express my most profound gratitude to the eighteen individuals who I know of, and the many more who remain unknown to me, who demonstrated courage, compassion, and kindness to save my family. Most notably, deepest gratitude to the Lansinks who hid my family for two-and-a-half years, under constant threat of being found out. And I must thank the many people of Germany and the Netherlands of today who met me along my journey, unaware of the impact their actions would have on me.

I thank my many early readers, editors, and supporters who offered sage and kind guidance, including Susie Rosenwasser, Sheree Galpert, my Grub Street teachers and fellow workshoppers, and my family. A special thank you to my editors and cheerleaders, Lynne Griffin and Debbie Sosin, who expertly and caringly guided me through preparations of my manuscript. Deep appreciation to Cheryl Jaclin Isaac, Victoria Wolf, and Richard Wolf, whose editing, design, and coaching, respectively, helped me bring my book over the finish line.

I wish to thank the numerous people and organizations whose research and support provided me with historical context, documentation, information, and translations. Those include the Bocholt and Münster archives, Yad Vashem, the United States Holocaust Memorial Museum, Josef Niebur and Hermann Oechtering, Sonja Rexwinkel, Eric Heijink, John Breukelaar, and Josh Grayson. With gratitude to the staff and volunteers at the Synagogue of Enschede; the Aalten Onderduik Museum; and the towns of Bocholt, Meudt, and Plettenberg for so graciously welcoming my family and me. I thank those who have worked tirelessly to document the vibrancy of prewar Jewish life and the stories of Jewish individuals throughout Germany, including in my ancestral hometowns. And I thank so many more individuals and organizations who are diligent in their efforts to keep the memories of those who were murdered and displaced during the Holocaust alive.

To my husband, Seth, for following me on this journey and supporting my need to write this memoir, for reviewing the manuscript many times, and for offering thoughtful advice along the way. To my son, Josh, for participating in the journey, enlightening me with his own perspective as a third-generation Holocaust survivor and opening the many doors that appeared on our path. To my son Jonah, for his keen observation skills that helped me to see things I hadn't noticed before, and for offering his support and interest as he waited patiently for this book. All the love in the world to my family.

ABOUT THE AUTHOR

IRENE STERN FRIELICH grew up on Long Island, NY, the daughter of Margie Stern, and Walter Stern, a German Holocaust survivor. As is often the case in survivor families, the Holocaust was rarely discussed in her home, where buried emotions and unspoken truths left a gap in her life and her consciousness.

In 1993, Irene's father recorded an eighty-minute-long video testimony of his Holocaust survival story. He died in 1994. Irene viewed the video once at the time, then stored it away. She planned to watch it again "someday" and went on to immerse herself in her career and raising a family.

In 2016, as disturbing fascist echoes resounded more prominently in American politics and around the world, Irene felt an increasing urgency to learn the truth about her father's Holocaust experience. Her "someday" finally arrived. Irene dug out her father's testimony video from a pile of VHS cassettes in a storage box and had it converted to a digital format. She painstakingly transcribed the video word for word—an emotional and enlightening journey into her father's buried history of survival, loss, and hope, but which left a myriad of facts still unknown, unspoken.

In 2018 and 2019, Irene took three trips to Europe with her husband, Seth, and their older son, Josh. Together, they physically retraced the Stern-Herzfeld family's escape route on Kristallnacht from Nazi Germany to temporary safety in the Netherlands and even visited the attic on the Dutch farm where her father, grandmother, and great-grandmother were hidden for two and a half years. Irene continued to conduct extensive research at home and during each trip abroad. She compiled volumes of archival documents, collected letters and mementos, met individuals whose relatives had known her family in the 1930s and '40s, and connected with strangers in current-day Germany who are committed to keeping the stories alive—and who soon became friends. Shattered Stars, Healing Hearts is the culmination of Irene's years-long quest to unravel her father's—and her own—story.

Irene is the owner of EnVision Performance Solutions, an award-winning instructional design consulting firm. She and her husband, Seth, live in Sharon, Massachusetts. They treasure moments with their grown sons, Jonah and Josh, and Josh's partner Addie. Irene enjoys playing flute in her local concert band; kayaking, biking, and snowshoeing; and is an avid cook and home entertainer.

Irene speaks internationally about her family's story. Articles about the family have been published in German and Dutch media. She is deeply grateful to the eighteen courageous individuals who helped her family survive the Holocaust. She carries their legacy forward through this book and through her acclaimed multimedia presentations. www.shatteredstars.org